Hunting the Wren

Hunting the Wren

Transformation of Bird to Symbol

ELIZABETH ATWOOD LAWRENCE

A Study in
Human-Animal Relationships

THE UNIVERSITY OF TENNESSEE PRESS / KNOXVILLE

Frontispiece: Wren at nest with young and ivy leaves.
Drawing by Scott Hecker.
Chapter-opening illustrations by Scott Hecker.

Library of Congress Cataloging-in-Publication Data

Lawrence, Elizabeth Atwood, 1929–
    Hunting the wren: transformation of bird to symbol: a study in
    human-animal relationships / Elizabeth Atwood Lawrence.–1st ed.
        p.   cm.
    Includes index.
    ISBN 0-87049-960-2 (cloth : alk. paper)
1. Birds–Symbolic aspects. 2. Wrens–Social aspects. 3. Wrens–Folklore. 4. Animal
sacrifice–Great Britain. 5. Animal sacrifice–Europe. 6. Rites and ceremonies–Great
Britain. 7. Rites and ceremonies–Europe. 8. Human-animal relationships. 9. Nature–
Effect of human beings on. 10. Human ecology. 11. Philosophy of nature.   I. Title.
GR735.L356 1997
398'.3698833'0941–dc20   CIP   96-25191

For Bob, Mark, Priscilla, Elizabeth, Jane, and Patrick,
With love

And to the birds,
For their beauty and song

CONTENTS

ILLUSTRATIONS

PREFACE

T HIS STUDY BEGAN with a tantalizing question: Why in certain
areas of Britain and Europe would the little brown wren, a familiar
and beloved song bird, be hunted and killed on a certain day or season
of the year? In recent times answers to this riddle have sprung out of
the experience and consciousness of people in various societies, and
those answers have been added to the lore of the wren ceremony, layer
upon layer, as rationalizations of an ancient ritual whose origins have
been obscured by time and changing ideologies. Like an archaeologist
digging into the earth's strata to uncover clues, one must delve below
the layers of these superimposed explanations in the attempt to get to
the bedrock of original meaning. Because of the passage of eons and the
lack of written records, there is much that can never be precisely determined, and, above all, the origin and development of various features
of the wren ceremony cannot be dated.

This book is a symbolic study, not a historical one. It is not a work
in folklore theory, although I cite material from that discipline in order
to provide a picture that includes all aspects of people's notions and
beliefs about the wren. Rather, my study is undertaken as a contribution to the newly expanding and increasingly important interdisciplinary field of human-animal interactions. Drawing from my background
in biology and my training as a cultural anthropologist, I deal with the
human relationship to nature and, specifically, with certain societies'
interactions with one species of bird, *Troglodytes troglodytes.* By eluci-
dating the ways in which that bird is perceived, a great deal can be
learned about how people symbolize animals and the ways in which
their symbolic views affect the treatment of those animals. This is a
determinative process in today's world. Human destructiveness toward

nature has reached tragic proportions, with a consequent decrease in numbers, and even extirpation, of many wild species. The domain of the wild is being virtually eliminated as the sphere of the tame—the domesticated realm—inexorably expands and encroaches upon it. Most human actions toward other creatures are motivated not by knowledge of the animal alone but also by symbolic perceptions.

This is not to imply that the details of the wren hunt have immediate application to remedies for the ecological crisis. But when we go from the particular to the general, much is revealed about a mechanism that is crucial to human-animal relationships. By unearthing the complex cognitive process by which a certain biological being becomes transformed into a symbol, great strides are made toward a fundamental knowledge of how humankind forms a perceptual image of an animal. It is urgent, if we are ever to establish harmonious relationships with other forms of life on the planet, to understand how the beliefs of a particular culture, in combination with observations about the natural history of an animal, result in a symbolic entity that elicits emotional and intellectual responses that influence society's treatment of that animal and may ultimately determine the fate of the species.

Most studies of human-animal interactions focus on the ways in which humans perceive animals rather than on exploring the dimension of the role of the animal itself in the relationship and determining how the participation of the two are intertwined. But in order to completely comprehend an animal's symbolic status, it is necessary to give full scope to identifying what qualities that animal possesses or is believed to possess, according to the world view and attitudes of a particular society or culture, that account for it being perceived in certain ways. In the case of the wren, many unusual traits and striking behavioral repertoires have arrested people's attention, stimulated their imagination, and piqued their curiosity to a remarkable degree. The resulting cognitive process has created a symbolic aura of extraordinary depth and richness.

Symbols are "a means of integrating the conscious and unconscious, the rational and the intuitive" (Cooper 1992, 12). They conceal, even as they reveal, embedded meanings that are expressed in no other way. A deeper knowledge of the symbolic lore that surrounds animals is an important key to understanding the human predicament as we become more and more urbanized and alienated from the rest of nature and are not only increasingly engulfed by materialism but also engaged in actual hostility toward the whole concept of the kind of truth expressed in legend, tale, and ritual.

No case of animal symbolism I have ever encountered seems so vivid, so complex and tenacious, and so fascinating as that of the wren. The tiny creature has been known for centuries as the "king of all birds" and "Jenny Wren"—a prime subject for celebration by admiring naturalists and romantic poets as well as for near-adoration from country dwellers throughout its range. The bird's peculiar attributes, in conjunction with people's reactions to those attributes, transformed the wren into the object of the strange and elaborate ritual that is the subject of this study—the wren hunt.

Chapter 1 deals with animal symbolism in general. The wren as a living creature and a discussion of some of the important tales and legends that have grown up around the bird are discussed in chapter 2. Prohibitions against killing the wren and the pairing of wren and robin are also covered. Details of the wren hunt ceremony and wren songs are described in chapter 3. Chapter 4 is devoted to the various meanings ascribed to the wren hunt, with the superimposed, "thin," or more recently evolved explanations followed by descriptions of the probable roots of the wren hunt, the deep-level meanings that have been ascribed to it, and some analyses of certain elements of the ritual. The final chapter examines the phenomenon of the conversion of the biological species into a profoundly symbolic entity and concludes with a discussion of the wren hunt in perspective, relating the ceremony to important contemporary issues in human-animal relationships and current attitudes toward the living environment.

In examining and describing the wren hunt and the various meanings that have been attributed to it, I have quoted from a wide variety of sources that either addressed the subject of the ritual or provided a particular insight about a topic related to the ritual. I am not implying that any or all of the data cited are "right" or historically accurate, only that they contribute to the enduring symbolic image of the wren and add to the store of surmises about the meaning of the wren hunt. The work of figures such as James Frazer and Géza Roheim is discredited by some contemporary scholars for various reasons (see, e.g., Dundes 1991b, 113). However, I am not advocating or asking the reader to embrace the methodology, theories, or alleged universalist, "depth psychology," or "myth-ritual" claims of such thinkers. Rather, I refer, where appropriate, to relevant information or insights worthy of reflection. Frazer, for example, gathered a body of data about the wren hunt that is valuable for the present study because it contains details not available elsewhere. But by citing this information I am not making use of or endorsing Frazer's beliefs or his broad theoretical framework. Also, the contributions of certain writers considered "amateurs" or "popular" sources by academicians are included because those authors observed or thought about the wren hunt or an issue associated with it in insightful and relevant ways. Most importantly, their perceptions, which are often fascinating and provocative, have contributed to the bird's symbolic image and have become inextricably interwoven with wren hunt lore.

Frazer and Roheim, unlike their later counterparts, are among the relatively small number of writers who addressed the subject of the wren hunt in any detail. Thus their observations became part of the lore relating to the wren. They are not cited as having ascertained some sort of "truth," but as contributors to the accumulated corpus of material about the wren ceremony. It is in their capacity as compilers, not as theorists, that I quote their observations. Reference to folklore works for the store of information about human attitudes toward animals that they provide by no means entails acceptance of any outdated theoretical views held by the gatherers of those data. Both Frazer and Roheim provided interesting material about the wren hunt, and to omit their roles in piecing together the fragments of existing knowledge about the ritual would detract from the value and completeness of my study, which brings together in one volume information from scattered and diverse provenances to create a compendium of wren lore.

Although I cite some conflicting, controversial, and seemingly "far-fetched" interpretations that will undoubtedly draw skepticism, these references often illuminate certain facets of the wren ritual and elicit an awareness of the vast diversity and complexity of the ceremony and the intricacy of thought it has evoked. Including these sources is part of the task of chronicling the wren's story in its entirety and viewing the ritual from every perspective. Because my purpose is to demonstrate the ways in which living beings become transformed into symbols, I am not so much concerned with an evaluation of the purported "validity" of each recorded perception of the wren and the wren hunt as with the far more pertinent fact that a particular person, on observing the wren (or even just hearing about it) and noting its real or imagined characteristics, proceeded to construct a symbolic entity (or "signifier") out of it.

The attribution of symbolism to specific objects or creatures is seldom simple or limited to one interpretation, as demonstrated by the multiplicity of meanings that have been assigned to the wren. These meanings can be and often are contradictory. As will become clear, the wren can symbolize at various times and in different contexts contrasting qualities, even those that are diametrically opposed. No one meaning is correct or most apt, because the wren possesses such a vast potential for signification that it has been transformed into a composite symbol whose many facets reflect a multiplicity of attributions. I am not drawing a specific conclusion about the meaning of the wren hunt to the exclusion of other explanations; rather, I am investigating the ways in which a living bird became a powerful symbol. It is the very multiplicity and variety of attributed meanings that are central to elucidating that transformative process. Thus in its role as a symbolic figure, the wren is often ambiguous—that is, susceptible to multiple interpretations that express different human perceptions and modes of thought. As noted by Angus Gillespie and Jay Mechling in their study of American wild animals as symbols, people "use the ambiguities of certain wild animals to reflect upon the ambiguities and uncertainties" of their experience (1987, 3).

The attribution of multiple and diverse meanings to the wren is illustrative of the force and richness of the tiny bird's inherent thought-provoking power and symbolic potential. By exploring all aspects of the extraordinary multivalent symbolism possessed by the wren, considering every piece of recorded evidence, and following the many alternative avenues of thought regarding the bird, we gain knowledge of the ways in which human beings derive meaning from a biological creature in conjunction with their perceptions of that creature. This broad approach, which takes into account various cognitive images of the wren as they have become intermingled with that bird's own form and behavior, contributes a vital new dimension to the analysis of human relationships with other animals. This will ultimately help to make those relationships more clearly understood and, perhaps, less destructive.

Anthropologist Clifford Geertz suggests that cultural analysis involves "guessing at meanings, assessing the guesses, and drawing conclusions from the better guesses, not discovering the Continent of Meaning and mapping out its bodiless landscape" (1973, 20). He likens the social scientist's interpretive process to that of the "clinical inference" used in making a medical diagnosis from symptoms presented by a patient: "In the study of culture the signifiers are not symptoms or clusters of symptoms, but symbolic acts or clusters of symbolic acts, and the aim is not therapy but the analysis of social discourse. But the way in which theory is used—to ferret out the unapparent import of things—is the same" (1973, 26). In documenting and analyzing the many meanings of the wren, a dizzying array of analogues to "symptoms" are presented, and each contributes an interlocking piece to the fascinating puzzle embodied in the wren-hunt ritual.

An inclusive range of evidence, such as that presented here about the wren, must be gathered in order to understand the whole constellation of the symbolic uses of a particular animal. And an interdisciplinary perspective is essential in order to fully explore the relationship between humans and animals as a dialectic between culture and nature. Realization of these requirements has resulted in an escalating desire among some natural scientists to collaborate with social scientists and humanists in order to move toward an understanding of the cultural and symbolic dimensions of human-animal interactions to complement their own empirical knowledge. I experienced this melding of scholarly disciplines when I participated in a 1992 conference on "The Biophilia Hypothesis: Empirical and Theoretical Investigations" organized by Professors Stephen R. Kellert and Edward O. Wilson. At that seminar, a group of scholars from the fields of biology, physiology, human ecology, psychology, psychiatry, philosophy, geography, veterinary medicine, wildlife conservation, environmental studies, and anthropology met in order to share information and perspectives about biophilia— a possibly inherent human tendency to affiliate with other life forms that could potentially illuminate and expand our knowledge of the human relationship with nature. The spirit of cooperation, interest in one another's disciplinary approach, and willingness to eliminate conventional boundaries that have so often isolated scholars within the narrow confines of their own spheres was not only intellectually stimulating but also promising: in the future, combining disciplines may help elucidate and ameliorate the present troubled relationship between humankind and nature.

People who are concerned about the fate of nonhuman life on earth, and particularly workers and scholars whose lives and careers are centered on animals, now realize that in these difficult times understanding animals biologically and ethologically is only the first step. It is not sufficient in itself to ensure the animals' well-being and continued survival. One must also learn how human beings perceive and symbolize living creatures, because those processes ultimately have a vital impact on the destiny of nonhumans who must live in today's humanized, industrialized, manipulated, and artificial world. In exploring the

transformation of bird into symbol, I will show that a dialogical process occurs. That is, the symbolic meanings that animals attain do not
result from mere projections that people place on them, as has so often
been taken for granted in past studies of animal symbolism in which
the input of the animal itself has been ignored or minimized. Rather,
those meanings result from a complex interaction, or set of interactions,
between the traits of the animal and those human symbolic attributions
that originate from observations and/or perceptions about the creature.
Exploring this process is absolutely necessary to understanding the influence of human use of cognitive images involving animals, and can
have vital implications for the whole problem of finding ways in which
to deepen and expand current knowledge about the treatment of animals in society.

ACKNOWLEDGMENTS

I WANT TO EXPRESS special appreciation to Leslie Quilliam for his invaluable help during fieldwork on the Isle of Man. I also thank Jane Killey for generously sharing her experience and knowledge of the present-day Manx hunt-the-wren ceremony and for her photographs of the event. I thank the library staff at the Manx Heritage Library for their help in research. The librarians at Tufts University School of Veterinary Medicine were very helpful in obtaining books and articles for me, and I am grateful for their efforts. My thanks go to Mark Lynch for information about the painting *Rest on the Hunt,* to Boria Sax for his translation skills and for providing an article on early wren lore, and especially to Jay Mechling for his suggestions.

I am grateful to Scott Hecker and Betsey MacDonald, who provided the art work for this book. My thanks go to Brian Paterson for permission to use his photograph of the card depicting the robin and the wren, to the Manx National Heritage for the photograph of the Manx wren boys, and to the Museum of Welsh Life for the photograph of the wren house. I am grateful to Patrick Armstrong, who generously allowed me to use photographs and other material from books written by his father, Edward A. Armstrong, an astute scholar of wren lore whose data were very valuable to me in writing this book. And I appreciate the courtesy of Adrian Rigby in permitting the use of his painting *Young Bird in Winter Landscape.* My thanks go to the Royal Society for the Protection of Birds for permission to reproduce the postcard featuring the robin and the wren, and to John and Nancy Langstaff of Revels, Inc., for permission to use the "Traditional Wren Carol" from their *Songbook.* I am grateful for the use of the illustration "The Kindly Robin" from the John Grossman Collection of Antique Images.

Denzyl Feigelson graciously granted permission for me to quote lyrics from "A Love Song." I want to thank Stanford University Press for permission to quote from Henry Van Dyke's poem, and Robert Hale Limited for permission to quote lines from Norman Iles's *Restoration of Cock Robin* and "The Seven Joys of Jenny" from Iles's *Who Really Killed Cock Robin*. I appreciate the kindness of the Bloodaxe Press for allowing me to quote from Brendan Kennelly's poem "The Wren-Boys." The poem "Wren and Man," from *Sequences* by Siegfried Sassoon, copyright 1957 by Viking Press, is quoted with the permission of Viking Penguin, a division of Penguin Books USA Inc.

Priscilla Lawrence helped gather material about the wren, was the first to read the manuscript, and gave enthusiastic encouragement. Mark Lawrence lent his fine editing skills and located library sources pertinent to the wren. I want to express my heartfelt appreciation to them as well as to Bob Lawrence, who assisted with fieldwork and supported this project in countless ways.

ONE

ANIMAL SYMBOLISM

Nature speaks in symbols and in signs.
—John Greenleaf Whittier

THE USE OF ANIMAL SYMBOLISM in cognitive and expressive behavior is probably as old as human consciousness. People's earliest artistic and ritualistic representations were created in the likeness of various living creatures who inhabited the same environment. And throughout history into the present the propensity for metaphoric expression finds its greatest fulfillment through reference to the animal kingdom. No other realm affords such vivid expression of symbolic concepts. Indeed, it is remarkable to contemplate the paucity of other categories for ideational frames of reference, so preeminent, widespread, and enduring is the habit of symbolizing in terms of animals (see Lawrence 1993). Calling attention to the extraordinarily expressive role of animals in human cognition, the famous dictum of Claude Lévi-Strauss, that animals are "good to think" as well as good to eat (1963, 89), holds true not only for preindustrial cultures but also for the most complex societies, and not only for the past, but for the present.

Whenever a human being confronts a living creature, whether in actuality or by reflection, the "real life" animal is accompanied by an inseparable image of that animal's essence that is made up of, or influenced by, preexisting individual, cultural, or societal conditioning. Thus "nature," as represented by the actual biological and behavioral traits of a particular animal, becomes transformed into a cultural construct that may or may not reflect the empirical reality concerning that animal but generally involves much embellishment. Moreover, underlying the process of symbolizing a species is a great flexibility that characterizes the categorization of animals. That even natural history is shaped to suit certain purposes is illustrated by the contemporary example of the capybara, a huge South American rodent. Observing the

1

creatures' aquatic habits, the sixteenth-century church officials who accompanied the conquistadors into the new lands classified them as fish. Today, though science has long known capybaras are mammals, "for religious and dietary purposes" they retain the status as fish. Their delicious flesh may be eaten in good conscience by Catholics during Lent. A profitable industry has been developed in Venezuela, where capybaras are rounded up and slaughtered in February for consumption during the forty days of the pre-Easter ban on meat-eating ("Fur, Fins and Fasts" 1992, 93).

Eminent scientist Edward O. Wilson has put forth the theory that human beings demonstrate a quality called "biophilia," defined as "the innate tendency to focus on life and lifelike processes," and he asserts that people "learn to distinguish life from the inanimate and move toward it like moths to a porch light." He argues that "to explore and affiliate with life is a deep and complicated process in mental development." According to Wilson, "Human beings live—literally live, if life is equated with the mind—by symbols, particularly words, because the brain is constructed to process information almost exclusively in their terms." Humankind is "the poetic species," and "the symbols of art, music, and language freight power well beyond their outward and literal meanings" (1984, 1, 74). Thus it is because "life of any kind is infinitely more interesting than almost any conceivable variety of inanimate matter" (Wilson 1984, 84) that people inevitably turn to the animal kingdom for symbolic expression.

The power of human affinity with animals is manifest not only in direct interactions between people and animals but also through the process of using animals to symbolize many aspects of life. Indeed, for a large share of the population in the modern industrialized world, relationships with animals as they are symbolically perceived have to a great extent replaced interactions with their living counterparts as once experienced by our ancestors. Moreover, it is increasingly the case that commonly held beliefs about a particular animal, rather than personal experience, generally determine the character of interactions with its species. Interpretation of an animal's behavior in metaphoric terms can result in the creature being classified in various ways, such as "good" or "evil," with effects upon its preservation or eventual extinction. The symbolizing process can enhance positive affiliation, resulting in the animal's survival, or it can cause alienation of that animal from the human sphere, with consequent persecution and/or destruction.

In everyday thought and conversation, animals appear as repositories of shared concepts and values. Societal forces give power to animals' symbolic roles, providing a lens through which preconceived ideology determines the collective view of the species. Symbolic attributes of a particular animal, however, can vary according to the cultural context and even within it. It is important to recognize that animal symbols may be "multivalent, complex, antinomic, used simultaneously to capture and display many different images and meanings at many different levels." Scholars who have "a strong belief that a symbol has only a single, true meaning often fail to perceive the ways in which symbols are used simultaneously to express and intertwine many different levels of experience and understanding" (Walens 1986, 291, 296). In employing animals as vehicles of thought, the human mind chooses certain characteristics of the species and ignores others. The way in which people emphasize some traits of an animal to the exclusion of others often reveals much about the ethos of the society from which the beliefs spring. Symbolizing with animals is not simply a process carried out by rational thought that views a creature holistically; rather, it involves deeper levels of consciousness as well as external stimuli. Natural history observations may be a starting point, but they are strongly molded by cultural constructs and by the needs of human beings to relate to the rest of creation through metaphor. Signifying by means of animals emanates from mental experience similar to that expressed in art, poetry, and religion, whose languages are also symbolic. Humankind is not the wholly rational, materialist being as is sometimes assumed, and symbolizing through animals originates from deep-level cognition, as do myths and folklore, expressing truth that is often more real than observable "fact." This is the domain where animals communicate with humanity in terms of a universal understanding that is more profound than words. It is represented by the realm of perception that P. L. Travers calls "what the bee knows . . . a time-honored wisdom from a timeless source" (1989, 304).

Animal symbolism represents a mental link to the age-old search for "man's place in nature." Through such symbolizing, there is a kind of merging—animals take on human qualities and humans take on animal qualities. Antithetically, the process of symbolizing with animals also makes use of and preserves the separateness that exists between people and animals. Cognitively, we balance the alternatives in the question that determines virtually all human-animal interactions: Are the other life forms like us or different? Though they seem closely related to people, animals are viewed as the quintessential "other."

Through contrast, they become a means of identifying what character-istics make us human and of weighing those qualities according to an imposed system of values. In a chaotic world, human beings seek their identity through reference to the alternate kingdom of the animals.

Lévi-Strauss has noted that the "central problem of anthropol-ogy" is "the passage from nature to culture" (1963, 99). Through ani-mal symbolism, key issues in the nature-to-culture transformation are explored and given concrete expression. As Wilson phrases this idea in *Biophilia,* animals are "agents of nature translated into the symbols of culture" (1984, 97). Using animal symbolism enables us to confront the beast, relate to it, and while remaining human, "take on beasthood" and "see our former selves as strange, from the outside" (Willis 1974, 66). Thus we are able to measure and evaluate ourselves, probing the enigma of what it means to be human.

The frequency with which animal symbolism is found through-out the world and has occurred over the centuries is testament to the profound significance of this phenomenon. It is intricately interwoven into the human condition because we are evolutionarily and physically, as well as aesthetically, spiritually, psychologically, and emotionally, tied to our animal kin. Even though the old ways of perceiving the uni-verse have become obliterated in their literal manifestations by the de-struction of gods and spirits and the impact of science and technology, the concepts of animism and totemism still fill the world with animals to which we are mentally and spiritually linked.

One of the most urgent issues in the present era of ecological cri-sis is the hostile relationship that so often exists between humankind and animals, with the consequent destruction of many of our fellow creatures. Analysis of the ways in which symbolic attributes become attached to animals can help explain why in some circumstances people cherish and protect animals while in others they devalue and/or destroy certain creatures. This kind of inquiry also has implications for eluci-dating the issue of animals' intrinsic value versus their worth as mea-sured by human exploitation, and has important bearing on the concept of reciprocal relationships as they should exist between people and other species. Thus understanding the symbolization of animals as it involves the synthesis of alternative modes of thought with scientific "fact" can play a vital role in contributing to the establishment of more harmonious relationships with all life on earth.

The way in which an animal is symbolized exerts far-reaching ef-fects upon people's behavior toward that species. Bats, for example, hang upside down during the daytime with their wings folded around them so as to resemble witches' capes. They ambiguously appear to be both bird and mouse, are active only at night, and possess an uncanny ability to hunt in the dark. Bats' flight is erratic, and they avoid human contact. They are generally black in color, may have a fearsome expression, and one type actually feeds on blood. For these reasons, bats have been generally viewed in Western culture as demonic beings, denizens of the underworld, and they are associated with evil spirits. Accordingly, bats have been maligned and persecuted in areas where these perceptions have prevailed.

A certain dung-beetle, the scarab, on the other hand, because of spiritual concepts suggested to the ancient Egyptians by its behavior, took on deep-seated religious significance. The insect's sacred status is traceable to the fact that it lays its eggs in a pellet of manure that will later nourish the developing larvae, rolling the material into a ball that is then buried in the sand. Noting that when the eggs hatch new generations of beetles emerge alive out of the earth, the Egyptians believed that the creature had the power to come back to life after death, and thus it became a symbol of resurrection. The ball containing eggs held between the scarab's mandibles was viewed as representing the sun, the great creative power of the universe, and therefore symbolized the sun-god. The beetle pushing a ball of dung before it was likened to the deity who daily rolled the ball of the sun across the sky. This imagery was reinforced by the observation that the sharp projections on the beetle's head extend outward like the rays of the sun. Because of the insect's symbolic meaning, the heart of a deceased person was sometimes replaced by a scarab before burial. Beetles were often placed in the mummy or tomb with the dead, or their likeness was depicted on the sarcophagus to ensure eternal life. Symbolizing warmth, light, and perpetual renewal, scarabs were widely used as charms, amulets, ornaments, royal emblems and seals, medals, and gifts, and appeared in many forms of decorative and religious art (Ward 1902, 3–4; Clausen 1962, 65–66; Lurker 1991, 104–5). Today, jewelry items made from stones carved to resemble scarabs are still popular good luck talismans.

There is a tendency for interchange of identity between people and animals because of perceived fundamental similarities and the desire either to emulate them or to differ from them according to advantages or disadvantages that may result. Cree Indians, observing the behavior of wolves and wolverines, give these animals symbolic roles in traditional stories that focus on the contrast between the two species and derive moral lessons for human society. The conduct of wolves, who live in organized packs and are viewed as sociable and hospitable, is culturally acceptable, while the behavior of wolverines, who are generally seen alone and are perceived as greedy and ungrateful, is unacceptable. The wolverine, as a solitary animal, became symbolic of egocentric individualism, in direct opposition to the cooperative, interactive nature of the wolf, which represents traits that are exemplified and valued by Cree society. Thus the Cree use differences between animal species as a "metalanguage to represent differences between Crees and other Indians and perhaps between Crees and Euro-Canadians" (Brightman 1993, 44, 48). Another analogy that was drawn from animal behavior and incorporated into human tradition is illustrated by the Cherokee Indian taboo on the meat of the ruffed grouse for pregnant women. Because this bird hatches a large brood but loses most of the young before maturity, fear of incurring similar danger to the human offspring motivates the prohibition. Under strict interpretation of the injunction, grouse flesh is forbidden to all women until they are past the age of child bearing (Mooney 1982, 285).

From ancient times, certain traditions have dictated that "those who wish to take unto themselves the spirits of prophetic animals swallow the most effective parts of them." Thus by consuming certain portions of its carcass, a person could absorb that bird's particular power. For example, "the hearts of eagles bring courage, the flesh of crows and owls imparts wisdom, and the flesh of keen-sighted hawks may lend visual acuity" (Johnson 1988, 9). I suggest that the medicinal value attributed to the wren in the seventeenth century represents a similar case of applying a specific characteristic of an animal to a human use that symbolically derives from that characteristic. When "salted and eaten raw," consumed after being "roasted whole," or "burnt in a pot close covered" and "the ashes of one whole bird taken at once," it was believed that the wren "perfectly cures the stone of kidneys or bladder" (Swann 1968, 263). This therapy, which at first seems so strange, becomes explicable, I believe, when one of the wren's most salient traits is considered. The bird is especially noteworthy for being able to squeeze through small openings and pass into narrow passages—precisely the capacities that are needed for the extrusion of bladder or kidney stones through the human urethra.

These are but a few of the innumerable examples, ranging from simple to complex, that demonstrate the ways in which human beings observe the habits and appearance of animals and selectively transform them into symbols of certain qualities or concepts that their behaviors and/or bodies suggest. Because the buffalo supplied meat and other necessities of life and "contained all these things within himself," the Sioux considered the animal "a natural symbol of the universe, the totality of all manifested forms." Because it has twenty-eight ribs, the Sioux related the buffalo to the moon, with its cycle of the same number of days. Because it returned every year, renewed like the moon, the buffalo became symbolic of rebirth following death (Brown 1967, 6 n., 80).

People in the modern industrialized world still draw metaphors from the animal kingdom. In the late nineteenth century, for example, a dispute called "The Great English Sparrow War . . . shook the American ornithological world." In the early 1850s, English sparrows were imported to major eastern cities. They adapted so successfully to the new environment and became so numerous that "by the mid-1870s they began to be perceived as a menace to the American ecosystem." A vigorous debate as to their destructiveness or harmlessness followed. The dispute may be metaphorically linked to the controversy regarding the post–Civil War immigration to the United States of millions of Europeans and Asians. Opponents of the English sparrows drew their imagery from the anti-immigrant sentiment of the day. Hatred stemmed from moral qualities attributed to the birds. They were foreign immigrants, nuisances who attacked native American birds, and their character as demonstrated by lack of cleanliness, immoral sexual habits, and production of excess noise, was alleged to be disreputable. Popular belief held that the sparrows menaced the native avian community just as foreigners threatened American society, and thus many believed the birds should be eliminated as a foreign enemy (Fine and Christoforides 1991, 375, 381).

Contemporary people continue to conceptualize in terms of animals. In the 1987 hit movie *Moonstruck,* a baker who lost his hand in an accident had been deserted by his fiancée because he was maimed. In explaining to the man, who was full of self-pity, that he was fortunate that his injury enabled him to escape a life with someone who did not love him, his insightful friend used animal imagery, comparing him to a wolf caught in a trap who chews off its own foot in order to save its life. When the recipient of the 1993 Courage Award from the American Cancer Society was honored at a party, a singing telegram was delivered to him by a person wearing "a lion costume to symbolize courage." A lion-shaped cake inscribed "You Gotta Have Courage" was baked for the occasion (Gomon 1993, 14). I have found that many people still follow the custom of eating pork on New Year's Day. Behind this tradition is the rationale that the "hog roots forward"—making it an appropriate symbol for looking toward the future on the first day of the New Year. On that day it is considered bad luck to eat chicken—the animal that "scratches backward" to the past (Hubbell 1993, 83). When Emily Dickinson is described as "plain and small like the wren" (Luce 1991, 67), the phrase is remarkably expressive in several dimensions. Comparison to the bird encapsulates her small stature, demure behavior, humility, and solitary nature and reclusiveness. The metaphor expands to include the simple yet profound, and ultimately far-reaching, poetic voice that could not remain concealed from the world in spite of the wrenlike retiring and unostentatious character of the singer.

In some cases, people have not only symbolized an animal by combining its observed traits with various perceptions but also have wondered about and sought to explain the ways in which those traits relate to the animal's history and evolution—that is, how were the creature's salient characteristics acquired? For the modern Western scientific world, Darwinism addresses this question and proposes the process of natural selection. But over time, people in other areas and of different cultures have responded to it with elaborate tales of explanation. Generally, a member of the species experiences an adventure or carries out a certain deed—good or bad—that results in changes in that individual animal's form or behavior. Automatically (in a kind of analogue to Lamarckianism), these alterations are passed on to all members of the animal's kind for ever after. (Rudyard Kipling's *Just So Stories* features this phenomenon.)

Traditional explanatory stories range from how the bluebird got its blue color to how the deer lost its gall and how the rattlesnake learned to bite. Such explanations often employ the principle of binary opposition: for example, an originally plain animal, such as a leopard or tiger, becomes spotted or striped, a large creature is made small, or a mute animal acquires a voice. The interesting way in which one salient quality gives rise to its absolute opposite is demonstrated by the case of the jet black raven. The Roman poet Ovid wrote:

> The raven once was white, in fact, so much so,
> Not snowy doves nor swans, were ever whiter,
> Nor even the geese. . . .
> He talked too much, and that was his undoing.
> Once white, and now white's opposite, the talker
> Brought this upon himself by too much talking.
> (1983, 45)

People living in the raven's range, such as American Northwest Coast natives and Eskimos, have explained that creature's black plumage through traditional stories about the painting of the bird: the formerly white raven was made black for various reasons by being rubbed with charcoal or other black substances.

These explanations seem to link empirical science with cognitive projections—bridging zoology and symbolic thought. Through different mechanisms each takes into account various interactions between an animal and its environment in arriving at answers to questions regarding the molding of species that are of considerable concern to human-animal relationships. As will become evident, some of the lore relating to the wren attempts to explain such features as the bird's extremely short tail, its feather pattern, its low flight, and its ground-dwelling habits, as well as its characteristic self-confidence, feisty spirit, and spunk, which seem incongruous with the creature's minuscule size.

Birds are among the most vivid and widely employed animal symbols, for they have many unique characteristics that stir the human imagination, generally invoking wonder and admiration. They are superb navigators, finding their way over long distances, even in fog or at night. They are builders par excellence, constructing complex nests and bowers—tasks that require skill and appear to involve conscious intent and prior planning. Some species engage in spectacular courtship rites with elaborate displays and dances. Birds demonstrate faithfulness in incubating their eggs, and show nurture, and even altruism, toward their young. Their unusual capacity for flight sets birds apart. As creatures who have mastered the air, they often represent communication between land and sky, are viewed as souls of the dead who bridge earth and heaven, or are believed to be gods from above who communicate with mortals below, as the Holy Ghost is embodied in the white dove. The unsolved mysteries of their seasonal migrations and other unique abilities give birds powers not possessed by humankind. Often beautiful in form and color, they elicit deep aesthetic appreciation. It is easy to see birds as spiritual creatures, embodying humankind's highest aspirations and most delicate sensibilities. These attributions are partly traceable to the feathers with which birds are endowed—a unique avian characteristic that makes flight possible. Thus feathers add an important dimension to the mystique of bird symbolism. As objects that are light and airy yet long-lasting, they endure after the bird's death and therefore often stand for the cycle of the continuity of life, and in some contexts can represent human contact with the divine. Moreover, during a bird's life, its feathers can be regrown after loss due to injury or sickness, and following the end-of-summer molt each year new feathers are produced, suggesting rebirth. This connotation of regeneration attributed to bird feathers is expressed by the fifth-century B.C. Greek playwright, Aristophanes: "In winter every wingèd creature molts, / And then renews his feathered coat in spring" (Hadas 1988, 234). As will become evident, wren feathers represent talismans laden with important meanings that are related to some people's concepts associated with the bird, and these delicate objects plucked from the dead wren's body play a prominent role in certain traditional elements of the ritual and ceremony surrounding the tiny creature.

Natural history frequently becomes closely interwoven with supernatural attributions. Although the crossbill, for example, uses its strange twisted beak—whose upper and lower tips cross each other—for extracting seeds from pinecones, its image as the bird who bent its mandibles while trying to pull out the nails from Christ's body on the cross is a timeless rendering of compassion shared by the animal world. The crossbill's red plumage, said to have been acquired by becoming stained with the blood of Jesus, confirms the bird's action. The European goldfinch, too, has been closely associated with the passion of Christ, especially in Renaissance art. Allegedly this bird tried to aid the suffering Savior by removing a thorn from the crown of thorns that was piercing his brow. Not only the red feathers on the goldfinch's face, suggesting blood, but also the bird's habits, led to its symbolic attribution. Members of this brightly colored species feed on thistle seeds and are frequently observed in association with that plant whose sharp spines resemble thorns. Through the perception of birds as undertaking miraculous acts of mercy, nature is perceived as sympathetic to, and in unity with, both human and godly concerns, expressing the connection between all life and its relationship with the divine.

Avian songs are unique in pleasing the human ear, imparting joy, stimulating the imagination, and often inspiring the most lyrical poetry whose symbolism reaches far beyond the actual sounds. The nightingale, whose song is its most salient characteristic, was transformed by its eloquent voice alone into one of the most powerful symbols in English romantic poetry. John Keats, in his great ode to that bird whose nocturnal notes he interpreted as sublime, created for all time the highly charged image embodied by this "light-winged Dryad of the trees" who "in full-throated ease" pours forth its "soul abroad / In such an ecstasy" (Forman 1896, 269–71). For the poet, the nightingale's voice articulates the most profound of human concerns, encapsulating not only the pain of earthly existence but also the happiness of ultimate triumph over sorrow embodied by this "immortal bird." In Keats's analogy comparing the fate of man with this ethereal creature that is immune from the kind of suffering borne by humans the nightingale became a symbolic bridge between sadness and joy, between death and life.

It is not surprising that a species of wren (the one known simply as the wren, or in America, winter wren) became deeply involved in symbolism and ritual. More than almost any common bird this curious elfin creature seems to project itself into human affairs, at times demonstrating remarkable curiosity and friendliness. As ornithologist Elliott Coues described this avian family, "Wrens are among the relatively few birds who seem to take a genuine and sympathetic interest in men. The bird watcher is likely to find them stalking him for a change" (1962, 112). Having lived in intimate contact with two species—the house wren, which closely resembles the wren, and the Carolina wren, a larger form—I have experienced firsthand the traits that make this family especially endearing. Rather than taking flight from people like many other birds, these wrens seem to welcome the human presence. They often tantalize the expectant viewer, however, by remaining concealed even while loudly announcing their whereabouts with song.

Although ornithologists are quick to point out that birds' utterances are not intended for human ears, if any birds appear to sing just for us it is those of the wren family. Long after all other birds have fallen silent, I have heard the canyon wren begin its beautiful cadence of notes tripping down the scale as I approached it deep in an Arizona canyon in late summer, as though performed especially for me. And the Carolina wren, a year-round resident in my home area, sings sporadically throughout all seasons, and often gives forth with song as soon as I go outside and approach it. Recently, I heard it singing loudly, undaunted by a January snowstorm. And on a dark, foggy, midwinter day, just as I wrote the last line of the final chapter of this book, a Carolina wren came to a tree near my window, gave its loud call twice, and flew away. Each spring, within an hour of my hanging fuchsia plants on a porch close to the back door, Carolina wrens begin building their nest in one of them. The birds continue to raise successive broods there throughout the summer, undisturbed by my family's comings and goings, though much more visible to and trusting toward those who walk quietly. If a cat approaches, the parents make sounds that I have learned to recognize as distress calls and that cease as soon as the cat is safely confined. (The appearance of a dog elicits no such response.)

The house wren also nests nearby, readily accepting the "wren house" I provide. Its song, constantly repeated throughout the day, has the same bubbling quality as that of the wren, but is briefer, simpler, less rich and intense. As with the wren, it is easy to understand the attribution of otherworldly qualities to this closely related bird, who shares the propensity for mystical insights and magical behavior. Although it ordinarily does not sing after sundown, one house wren nesting near my home suddenly burst into song at 10:30 P.M. on a certain spring night—at the exact moment when my beloved dog died.

Birds are strongly associated with the seasonal changes that were so vital a part of life for most of humankind's existence. Renewal of the warmth of the sun and the fertility of earth were necessary for human comfort, prosperity, and survival itself. Even in today's mechanized world, people still long passionately for the return of certain migratory species as heralds of spring. The return of swallows is a widespread sign of joy and hope for the earth's renewal. In many areas of America, seeing the first robin is the traditional happy portent, whereas in Britain and Europe the cuckoo is the eagerly sought harbinger of spring. The close association between the verdant seasons and that strange bird indeed led to the British phenomenon of the legendary "pent cuckoo"—according to which attempts were made to prevent the bird from departing each autumn in the belief that perpetual summer could be ensured by keeping the cuckoo present all year: "No winter could interfere with the warmth and brightness so long as the note of the cuckoo could be heard" (Field 1913, 185). In people's minds, "the cuckoo *was* the spring" (Brown 1936, 46)—not just the season's token, but its embodiment.

The wren is also intimately associated with seasonal change, though in a far different and more complicated way than other birds. As demonstrated by the case of the wren, human-animal relationships can be complex and fraught with ambiguity and may reflect conflicting emotions, beliefs, motivations, and actions. The strange contradiction between love and admiration for the tiny brown bird and the concurrent custom of persecuting it at a certain season of the year constitutes an intriguing and tantalizing enigma that demands inquiry and analysis. As the subject of a many-layered and extremely deep symbolism with wide-ranging implications and formerly the object of a complex ceremony and ritual killing, the wren possesses a unique fascination. Probably few creatures have evoked, with the same force and clarity, such profound cognitive reaction, or have demonstrated such great power and intricacy of detail in symbolic attributions (and unique events that arise from those attributions) as the small, plain bird known as the wren.

TWO

THE WREN

Nature is to be found in her entirety
nowhere more than in her smallest creatures.
—Pliny the Elder

Endowed with extraordinarily rich symbolism in Western culture, the familiar wren, whose scientific designation is *Troglodytes
troglodytes,* is a beloved bird almost everywhere it occurs. Though generally admired and protected throughout its range in Europe, Britain,
and Ireland, this bird, up through the early decades of the twentieth
century, has been ruthlessly hunted and killed in an annual ceremony
known as the wren hunt. So prevalent and tenacious is this custom that,
even though wrens are no longer actually put to death, vestiges of the
ancient seasonal tradition persist.

CHARACTERISTICS: FORM, BEHAVIOR, AND SONG

The benignly regarded creature that was so commonly persecuted once
a year, usually on St. Stephen's Day, 26 December, is a tiny, plump-ap-
pearing, russet-brown songbird with dark brown barring, paler under-
parts, and a faint light line over the eye. The sexes are similar in
appearance. The wren has broad, rounded wings and is noteworthy for
its very short, often "cocked" tail (held upward at a sharp angle to its
body). Since the bird is the only one of its genus occurring in Europe,
Britain, and Ireland, where it is a year-round resident, it is known in
those areas simply as the wren. In North America, however, the name
winter wren distinguishes this species from eight other wrens. This
designation reflects the fact that some members of the hardy species
spend the winter not only in mideastern and southern states, but also
in northern United States and Canada (Choate 1973, 85; Terres 1980,
1047). The bird is seen during the winter in temperate areas long after
its close relative, the house wren, has migrated south.

The American name also refers to the characteristic that, unlike most other birds within its range, wherever it is found the wren often continues to sing during the winter. Known as a "perennial songster," the wren ceases singing for only a brief period during the autumn molt. The song is soon resumed, and, as described in Britain by one ornithologist, when the "trees are almost divested of their leafy covering, and the cold western winds bring down the frost-bitten leaves in showers, he still sings on. . . . In winter, undaunted by the shrieking blasts and ice-covered branches, his song is heard, clear as the morning star, and sweet as the summer solstice" (Dixon 1895, 238). English naturalist Thomas Bewick observes that throughout his country the wren "braves our severest winters, which it contributes to enliven by its sprightly note. During that season it approaches near the dwellings of man, and takes shelter in the roofs of houses and barns, in hay-stacks, and holes in the walls: it continues its song till late in the evening, and not infrequently during a fall of snow" (1809, 235–36). In North America, the Aleutian Islands form of the wren has been observed singing "his thrilling soulful song" even while "buffeted by the gales that sweep down from snow-capped mountains, or drenched by frequent rain and snow squalls," demonstrating a "brave and cheerful heart under his tiny coat of thick plumage" (Collins 1960, 178).

The volume and richness of the wren's song belie its small size (three and a half to four inches). "Its singing style places it near the pinnacle of avian singing behavior" (Kroodsma 1980, 364). The song is "very charming," much "fuller, louder and more powerful than one would expect from so tiny a bird" (Byron n.d., 49). W. H. Davies's poem highlights the incongruity between the singer and the sound emanating from "Jenny Wren":

> The smallest bird in England. When
> I heard that little bird at first,
> Methought her frame would surely burst
> With earnest song.

The wren's "sudden storm of song" made the poet fear "she would break her heart and die" (1992, 89).

As a leading ornithologist has described the species, "It owes most of its charm and much of its claim to fame to its wonderful voice," its "tinkling, rippling song" being "a marvelous performance for such a tiny bird. . . . Its variety is entrancing; the full rich song fairly bursts

Wrens remain active and continue to sing during the cold and snow of winter. Courtesy of Adrian Rigby.

upon the ear with a tinge of nature's wildness; and again, at close range we hear the soft whisper song, a subdued rendering of the same trills and cadences; we cannot place the singer, the music seems to come from everywhere, but we stand amazed and thrilled" (Collins 1960, 177). American bird artist John James Audubon wrote that the wren "has a song that excels that of any other bird of its size with which I am acquainted. It is truly musical, full of cadence, energetic and melodious. Its very length is surprising. Dull indeed must be the ear that thrills not on hearing it. The song . . . acts so powerfully on the mind as to inspire a feeling of wonder and delight. At such times it has usually impressed me with a sense of the goodness of the Almighty Creator, who has rendered every spot of earth in some way of use to the welfare of his creatures" (Ford 1957, 238).

A lyrical account by Robert Lynd reveals that

Amid the dreariness of dell and thornbush, the song of the wren hidden in the wet branches of the thornbush seems all the more triumphant. It is a song brilliant as a rainbow in a wet sky—brilliant as a dance of rainbows. There is a shameless optimism in it that clothes the bare hedges with something better than leaves. There is no other resident bird so incapable of melancholy. . . . The wren never sings except to say that it is the best of all possible worlds. His must have been the voice that first sounded immediately after God saw that it was all very good. The wren is the incarnate Amen of creation. . . . He raises his song with an exaggerated boastfulness. "The wren, the wren, the king of all birds," an old country rhyme begins. He certainly swells into a king in his song. If Noah had put his cock wren out on the roof of the Ark, the flood would no longer have seemed a barren waste, but would have scintillated for him as the thing his imagination had desired.

(1938, 171–72)

Naturalist W. H. Hudson also appreciated the beauty and volume of the wren's song, and wrote of his experience in a London park, where "fifty or sixty boats full of noisy rowers were on the water and the walks were thronged with loudly talking and laughing people, their numberless feet tramping on the gravel paths producing a sound like that of a steam roller." Hudson remembered that his companion "exclaimed impatiently that it was impossible to hear a bird-note in so much noise, . . . [when] a wren, quite fifty yards away, somewhere on the island opposite to us, burst out singing, and his bright lyric ran forth loud and clear and perfect above all that noise of the holiday crowd" (1898, 320–21).

Hudson points out that the wren's song is "his greatest charm. It is unlike that of any other British melodist—a loud, bright lyric, the fine, clear, high-pitched notes and trills issuing in a continuous rapid stream from beginning to end. Although rapid, and ending somewhat abruptly, it is a beautiful and finished performance. . . . When near it sounds very loud: one is surprised to hear so loud a song from so small a creature" (1921, 103). Interestingly, it is a tropical species of wren with a voice so mysterious, ethereal, and bell-like that it is called the "organ bird" that was the inspiration for the voice of Rima, the birdlike woman in Hudson's hauntingly beautiful romance of the South American rain forest, *Green Mansions*. Although Hudson never encountered that lyrical bird himself, descriptions of the rapture and delight its song evoked in those naturalists and travelers who had heard its enchanting flutelike notes enabled him to recreate it vividly as the spiritual embodiment of nature expressed through the lovely but elusive Rima (Armstrong 1955, 82–83). Hudson wrote that her "exquisite bird-melody" was "wonderfully pure and expressive" and "infinitely sweet and tender." Its "greatest charm was its resemblance to the human

voice—a voice purified and brightened to something almost angelic"
(1989, 37–38).

The song of the familiar wren that Hudson knew in England is
often described in terms almost as glowing as its exotic counterpart: its
"wild melody" demonstrating the "power controlled by that tiny
throstle" and "its capacity for brilliant execution" with "sweet and
impassioned tones, and the suggestive joyousness of its rapid trills."
When "once heard, the song is not soon forgotten; it is so wild and
sweet a lay, and is flung upon the woodland quiet with such energy,
such hilarious abandon, that it commands attention" and ranks "among
the best of our sylvan melodies" (Chamberlain 1896, 1:271). John K.
Terres calls it a "fine silver thread of music" (1980, 1047), and Janet
Lembke writes of its "agile coloratura" (1992, 51). Naturalist John
Burroughs describes the song as a "wild, sweet, rhythmical cadence
that holds you entranced" (Chapman 1899, 244). In his monograph on
birdsong, Aretas Saunders describes the wren's voice as "most delightful. The quality is clear, sweet, musical, and high-pitched, like the notes
of a piccolo" (1951, 114). The great English poet William Wordsworth
was deeply moved by a

> . . . single wren
> Which one day sang so sweetly in the nave
> Of the old church that, though from recent showers
> The earth was comfortless, . . .
> . . . yet still
> So sweetly mid the gloom the invisible bird
> Sang to itself that there I could have made
> My dwelling place, and lived forever there,
> To hear such music.
>   (George 1904, 134)

Charles Hartshorne's detailed analysis of birdsongs reveals that the
wren's "fast and complex" utterances are noteworthy for containing
"the longest definitely reiterated pattern" of any species he studied
(1992, 127–28). Factual data on the wren's unique musical stamina is
expressed poetically by Hudson, who noted that "the bird is indefati-
gable and with his mysterious talk in the leaves would tire the sun himself and send him down the sky: for not until the sun has set and the
wood has grown dark does the singing cease" (1919, 43).

In his volume on bird music, A. L. Turnbull notes that "for so
small a bird the Wren has a remarkably loud song which it pours forth

The length, forcefulness, and volume of the wren's song are a striking contrast to the bird's small size. Courtesy of Patrick Armstrong for the Estate of Edward A. Armstrong.

with the assurance of a much larger one. There is a defiant touch about the tiny singer's shrill lyric." This "bold projection is undoubtedly indicative of courage and character." The "exuberance of the Wren is astonishing. Not only is the tempo of each burst of song terrific, but the songs are repeated at very short intervals till you would almost expect to see the little bird explode." The pace of the song "is so whirling that the Wren seems almost intoxicated with its own speed and can hardly get the notes out quickly enough." The "breathless quavers of this unpunctuated trill seem almost to choke the palpitating bird" (1943, 55). Henry David Thoreau wrote that "the steady and uninterrupted" quality of the wren's voice reminded him of "a fine corkscrew stream issuing with incessant lisping tinkle from a cork, flowing rapidly." He found the song so continuous that "at length you only noticed when it ceased" (Allen 1993, 411).

The wren utters "a staccato burst of bell-like notes," racing "up and down and all over the scale with breathtaking virtuosity. . . . One would never expect that such a small, drab bird could have such a big and colorful voice" (Kanze 1995, 52–53). An ancient Greek source used the epithet "trumpeter" to describe the "wren's amazingly loud and vigorous song" (Dunbar 1995, 383).

Song of the wren translated into music. Courtesy of Patrick Armstrong
for the Estate of Edward A. Armstrong.

Vocalizations are indeed very loud: wrens may be heard at six
hundred yards, and under certain conditions they are audible at least
half a mile away. The song is also variable, showing "every gradation
from a loud and vehement clear-cut phrase, through softer, sweeter and
more varied subsong to a very tender, quiet warble, and finally a 'whisper song' of sibilant notes which may be audible no more than a few
inches from the bird." European wrens also have "vocal duels" in which
two birds alternate phrases of their songs (Armstrong 1955, 52, 57, 78).

The wren is characterized as the "pretty, sweet, dapper Songster"
with a cheerful nature, who "throws out his notes with so much alac-
rity and pleasure" (Armstrong 1955, 52). To the human ear, the bird's
voice—"loud, clear and vehement"—sounds like a happy song; hence
the Breton name for the wren is "cheerful," "merry," or "lively one."
The Pawnee Indians also call it "the laughing bird" and "a very happy
little bird" (Fletcher 1904, 171). So intense are its sounds that the tiny
bird's "wings and tail appear to vibrate with the vehement spate of
notes" of its song, which has "remarkable volume" (Reade and Hosking
1967, 225). The little wren's voice has even been called "shattering." At
close range, its utterances "can be felt on the ear-drums as a physical
impact" (Armstrong 1955, 53, 57). A 1993 field guide describes the
wren's song as "a prolonged, excited and rapid verse high up on the
scale and with a vibrant quality" (Jonsson 1993, 380). It is significant
that the word "verse" crept into a text intended strictly for species
identification and not for poetic appreciation.

As with its song, whose beauty, ebullience, volume, variety, and
length belie the singer's minute physical dimensions, the wren's reputation for vigor, courage, and audacity contrasts with its smallness. Salient characteristics chosen for the 1993 revised classic field guide (in
which brevity is vital) to enable bird watchers in Britain and Europe to
identify the wren quickly are not only its "astonishingly powerful
song" but also its "extremely active and pugnacious" behavior (Peterson, Mountfort, and Hollom 1993, 171). The "spunky little bird" is "fa-

miliar as a pert, feathered vehemence" (Armstrong 1955, 22, 23) and is recognized as a feisty creature, aggressive in defense of its territory and its offspring, even against large predators. Shakespeare's Lady Macduff asserts that

> . . . the poor wren,
> The most diminutive of birds, will fight,
> Her young ones in her nest, against the owl.
> —*Macbeth* Act IV, Scene 2

The wren is observed to be spirited and restless, seldom still, possessing "overflowing vitality" (Armstrong 1955, 23), and is known for being "active and bold," "always scooting around" with a "bustling manner" (Hare 1952, 31; Bruun 1967, 119). It has a "noisy, perky, bossy spiritedness" (Parry-Jones 1988, 154) and even demonstrates "pugnacity" (Nichols 1883, 329). Field ornithologists report its unusual habit of "an almost continual bobbing of its head" (Terres 1980, 1047), noting that the wren "often bobs and bows" (Peterson 1961, 220) or "habitually teeters and bobs" (Ehrlich, Dobkin, and Wheye 1988, 440), and frequently flicks its tail. Characterized as a cheerful and endearing bird and a prolific and solicitous parent, the wren is also believed to possess cleverness and cunning disproportionate to its minuscule body. An Irish maxim reveals that "the fox is the cunningest beast in the world barring the wren" (Ingersoll 1923, 119).

The wren's scientific name, *Troglodytes troglodytes,* refers to its perceived nature as a cave-dweller (from the Greek *trogle,* "hole"; *duo,* "to plunge into"), due to its construction of a nest in the form of a cavern with one very small and narrow aperture through which the bird gains entrance (Hazlitt 1905, 2:665; Jobling 1991, 238). Certain symbolic perceptions of the wren, as will be seen, arose from this characteristic. According to legend, troglodytes were prehistoric reclusive creatures who lived in caves. The wren's name is related to its habits as well as its nest. The Greek *troglodytes* signifies "creeper into holes, or cave-dweller" (Terres 1980, 1047), with the Greek *dytes,* "diver," indicating "the bird's diving into cover" (Choate 1973, 187) or its "constant seeking for cover" (Gruson 1972, 201). "Troglodytes, the Den-Diver," was the term used by Aristotle for a creature that would bolt quickly into "the nearest den or hidey-hole" when disturbed (Lembke 1992, 50). Aristotle knew the wren as an inhabitant of "copses and holes," a bird that typically "skulks out of sight" (Pollard 1977, 37). True to its name, the wren "prefers rocks and crannies in cliffs or rock walls and the caverns under tree roots. It will poke and peer under things and will disappear and reappear almost like magic" (Archbold 1990, 88). It is a denizen of the undergrowth, preferring thick cover. Most typically observed creeping along the ground rather than flying, the wren is closely associated with the earth, where it frequents crevices or disappears into the vegetation of a forest or garden. Artist Robert Bateman, who painted the species, has special fondness for wrens because, he says, "they draw your attention to the world at your feet, a world that is easy to overlook" (Archbold 1990, 88).

NAMES

Widely known throughout the British Isles by affectionate names such as Jenny, Jenny Wren, Jinnie, Jinny Wren, Jenner Hen, Katy- or Kitty-wren, and Kitty-me-wren, or, in Ireland, Sally, the bird is also called Wran, Wranny, Wrannock, and Wirann. From its unusual short cocked-up tail and tiny squat body come names like Jenny Crudle, Bobby Wren, Puffy Wren, Cut, Cutty, Cutty Wren, Cutteley Wren, Cuddy, Scut or Scutty, Skiddy, Stag, Tope, Stumpy Dick or Stumpy Toddy, and Stumpit. Other folk and local nicknames stemming primarily from its diminutive size include Cracket, Crackey, Crackadee, Crackil, Chitty, Chitty Wren, Jitty, Puggy Wren, Dickey Pug, Tiddy Wren, Tidley Wren, Tom-Tit, Titmeg, Titter Wren, Titty Todger, Tit-Wren, Titty Wren, Tinty, Runt, Tom-Thumb or Thumb-Bird, and Two Fingers. (Other possible origins for some of these names are mentioned in chapters 4 and 5). A Polish word for wren signifies "little oxen eye," and some Russian names mean "little nut" or "little nettle." The bird is also known as Juggy Wren, Gilliver Wren, Vraun, Sheely, Moonie, Guradnam, and Jimpo (Swainson 1886, 35; Greenoak 1979, 242; Hare 1952, 182–83; Ralfe 1905, 37; Montagu 1831, 570; Morris n.d., 133; Bolte and Polivka 1918, 279–80; Lockwood 1993, 33, 42, 48, 50, 51, 68, 89, 122, 135, 146, 149, 155, 157).

In the Shetland Islands, the wren is a "wee brown button" (Armstrong 1955, 235–36). One song refers to the hunted bird as "Rolley." Local names identify it as little god or god's bird. In Ireland and Scotland, the wren is graced with elegant titles such as Our Lady's hen, the Lady of Heaven's hen, or St. Mary's hen. In France it is referred to as the Bird of God or God's hen. The Piedmontese call it the "chicken of the Lord." These religious names celebrate the belief that the wren was present at the birth of Christ, making a nest in his cradle and bring-ing moss and feathers to cover the holy child (Langstaff and Langstaff 1985, 129; Greenoak 1979, 242; Swainson 1886, 35–36; Bonwick 1986, 225; Gill 1932, 424; Rothery n.d., 59).

KING OF ALL BIRDS

Aristotle called the tiny bird "senator" as well as "king" (Evans 1903, 153). In many languages, names for the wren attest to its image as a royal monarch. The Latin name, *regulus,* "king," originally referred to another bird, the goldcrest, whose gold colored feathers on the top of its head suggest a royal crown. In common usage that bird has been inaccurately called golden-crested wren, though it is actually a kinglet. Early Greek wren traditions undoubtedly involved that species, but at some inde-terminable time, the wren became its substitute. The two birds share some attributes, notably their very small size, though of course the wren lacks the golden feathers on the crown. The confusion between the two stems from the fact that the word wren was commonly applied to other birds of similar small size. The same situation occurred in America, when artist John James Audubon painted the kinglets, close relatives of the Old World goldcrest, and referred to them as golden-crowned and ruby-crowned wrens rather than kinglets (Holmgren 1988, 176).

The Greeks call the wren *Basiliskos,* "little king," and the Latin name for the bird is *Regulus.* The French use *Roitelet,* "little king," *Roi des oiseaux,* "king of the birds," *Roi de froidure,* "cold weather king," and *Roi de guille,* "lively king"; and the Spanish call the wren *Reyezuelo,* a diminutive form of "king." In Italian, the wren is *Reatino,* "little king," *Re di siepe,* "king of the hedge" or "king of the bush," or *Re di maccia,* "king of the scrub"; and in Swedish it is *Kungs fogel,* "king's fowl." The Danish word for the tiny bird is *Elle-konge,* "alder king," or *Fugle Konge,* "fowl king." The Germans use *Zaunkönig,* "hedge king" or "fence king," *Dornkönig,* "thorn king," *Mäusekönig,* "mouse king," or *Schneekönig,* "snow king." The Dutch word for the wren, *konije,* means "king," *winter-koninkje* specifies "little winter king," and *niederländisch Tuinkoningje* signifies "Dutch garden king" (Swainson 1886, 36; Hazlitt 1905, 2: 665–66; Gill 1932, 360; Ó Cuív 1980, 59; Bolte and Polívka 1918, 279). In Welsh, the word *Bren* means "wren" as well as "king," and in Teutonic the word for wren, *Koning vogel,* means "king bird." A. W. Moore states, "Indeed the wren was called 'King of Birds' by al-

The tiny wren's fabled victory over the eagle relates to the title "King of All Birds." Drawing by Betsey MacDonald.

most every European nation" (1971, 137): from the ancient Greeks and Romans to the modern Italians, Spaniards, French, Danes, Germans, Dutch, Swedes, English, and Welsh (Gaster 1964, 561). "For 2,500 years, and probably much longer, the wren has been king, if only in name, in Europe" (Armstrong 1958, 138).

The paradoxical designation of the wren as royalty allegedly dates "as far back as the days of the Druids" (Gibson 1904, 152). According to Brian Ó Cuív, the Hiberian Druids knew the wren as "the Augur's favorite bird" and represented the tiny creature as "the king of all birds, hence he was called by the vulgar Breas-en, king bird; Righ-beag, little king; Ri-eitile, flying king" (1980, 58–59). The regal role of the wren is important in understanding the symbolism of the bird as well as the wren-hunt ceremony, which, as will become increasingly clear, involve the juxtaposition of opposites—the phenomenon of inversion, or reversal. For, as a noted authority on the wren, Edward A. Armstrong, has pointed out, "one could hardly discover any bird whose appearance and behaviour less suggest a claim to royal honors" (1958, 137). The incongruity of the wren as king is expressed by Henry Van Dyke in a poem:

> Where's your kingdom, little king?
> Where's the land you call your own,
> Where your palace and your throne?
> Fluttering lightly on the wing
> Through the blossom-world of May,
> Whither lies your royal way,
> Little king?
>
> (Martin 1914, 197)

Although no indisputable scientific evidence connects the wren to the Druids, ingrained tradition firmly upholds that linkage. It is widely assumed that the Druids—Celtic priests, spiritual guardians, prophets, judges, and healers—revered the wren and designated it the king of all birds. They regarded it as "the symbol of the Word of God" (Rothery n.d., 59). The "ominous character of its song" made the wren sacred (Spence 1947, 46). The Druids understood its language and believed that through its musical voice and actions, the future could be foretold. The direction from which the bird called was highly significant. Medieval Irish wren lore preserved in a fifteenth-century manuscript perpetuated the definite predictions that could be made according to the direction from which the "little bold face cries to thee." If "from the east, a pilgrimage of religious people are coming to thee, inflicting their roughness upon thee. If the wren cries from the south-east, vain-glorious fools are to arrive. If from the west, they are strangers to you." In like manner, every point of the compass as well as each position of the bird when its voice is heard portends a different result. When the wren "calls from off the ground, or a stone, a cross," or "at the feet of the bed," certain events will follow (Abercromby 1884, 66–67). "If it call from many crosses, it is a slaughter of men, and the number of times it alights on the ground is the number of dead it announces, and the quarter towards which its face is, from thence are the dead it announces" (Ó Cuív 1980, 46). There is evidence that the goldcrest was also a prognosticator in medieval Ireland (Ó Cuív 1980, 44).

So important were wrens in Druid augury that the birds might have been maintained in captivity, domesticated (or, more accurately, tamed) for use in this prophetic role. Ó Cuív points out that "wren is an English word derived from drean, i.e. Draoi-èn, the Druids bird; it was also named Draolèn, i.e. Draioi-ol-èn, the speaking bird of the Druid." The "Welsh word for wren is dryw which is also a word for 'druid'" (1980, 57–59). The Manx word *dreain,* "wren," may be derived from "druai-eean, the druid's bird" (O'Curry 1991, 46). Or it is possible that the word for wren, *drui-en, draoi-en,* or *druai-eean,* is the source for the derivation of the word "Druid," although the reverse is more likely (Moore 1971, 137–38; Cooper 1992, 252; Spence 1971, 156). *Dreoan* comes from *dreo,* meaning "wren," also "druid" or "soothsayer," from proto-Celtic *drevo,* cognate with the English *true* (Henderson 1911, 96). For the Druids, the oak was the king of all trees and the wren, *drui-en,* was the bird of the Druids and the king of all birds, the soul of the oak (Graves 1989, 298). The little wren was once the central object of worship in some parts of Britain and Europe, and beliefs about the bird, with attendant ceremonies and traditions, were handed down from ancient times (Spence 1971, 156).

A deeply entrenched narrative of ancient origin accounts for the wren's unlikely status as king:

> In a grand assembly of all the birds of the air, it was determined that the sovereignty of the feathered tribe should be conferred upon the one who should fly highest. The favourite in the betting was of course the eagle, who at once, and in full confidence of victory, commenced his flight toward the sun: when he had vastly distanced all

competitors, he proclaimed with a mighty voice his monarchy over all things that had wings. Suddenly, however, the wren, who had secreted himself under the feathers of the eagle's crest, popped from his hiding place, flew a few inches upwards, and chirped out as loudly as he could, "Birds, look up and behold your king!"

(Swainson 1886, 36)

Folklorists classify this tale in which "wren wins by cleverness" as "The Election of the Bird-king" (Aarne and Thompson 1928, 39). Johannes Bolte and Georg Polívka explain that it is a characteristic feature of the beast fable that the honor of kingship is granted to either the biggest and most powerful or to the smallest and most delicate creature. Just as dwarfs, Tom Thumb, or the Clever Little Tailor defeat strong giants through trickery, so the smallest bird wins the upper hand over the eagle, the old, original ruler of the birds (1918, 279). Plutarch attributed the wren-eagle tale to Aesop, referring to "Aesop's wren that was carried up on the eagle's shoulders, then suddenly flew up and surpassed the eagle" (Bolte and Polívka 1918, 279), but the story is not included in surviving collections of Aesop's fables.

An interesting possibility is that Aesop's fables may be traced back to earlier Mesopotamian sources, notably to Sumerian tales dating from the early second millennium B.C. and even before that time. One such tale that involves the tiny wren juxtaposed with the gigantic elephant survives in an ancient Sumerian text. In that narrative "the elephant boasts about himself, saying 'There is nothing like me in existence.' The wren answers him: 'But I, in my own small way, was created just as you were,'" and thus "puts the proud elephant in his place" (Gordon 1958, 10). Some scholars speculate that Aesop's fables were derived from stories classified as "Sumerian animal proverbs and fables," like the one just cited. If this is true, the wren-elephant story may be the source of Aesop's once-existing tale of the wren-eagle rivalry, which gave rise to later forms of the tale.

There are various versions of the wren-eagle story, as, for example, the one that indicates that the wren hid in the eagle's tail feathers or under one of the bird's wings. According to Grimm's fairy tale, "The Wren," the bird had crept into the breast feathers of the eagle (Zipes 1987, 549). A slightly different slant is that "the wren won by perching on the eagle's crest and thus rising higher than the eagle" (Lewis 1926, 77). Or, alternatively, "the eagle is shown as having easily won and from the heights proclaimed himself king, when to his surprise he heard a small voice above him saying, 'No. No. Not yet.' From the safety of these few yards above, it challenged the eagle to 'come up here,' but he was too exhausted, and the wren became king" (Parry-Jones 1988, 154).

Sequels to the legend indicate that after the wren was officially proclaimed king, the enraged eagle grasped his rival in his claws and dropped him to the ground. Although the wren was not badly hurt, he lost part of his tail in the fall (or the vengeful eagle plucked it out), and ever since has lacked half of that appendage. A variation relates that the angry eagle gave the wren such a stroke with his wing that from that time on the wren has never been able to fly higher than a hawthorn bush (De Gubernatis 1872, 2:208; Swainson 1886, 36). The eagle cursed the wren, disabling the little bird so that "it can never fly over a hedge, but always goes through it" (Tegid 1911, 99). In another version the eagle took revenge by putting a "spell of enchantment on the wren," as a result of which "wrens shall not be able to fly higher than the gable end of a small house, and most of the time their flight shall carry them no further than from the hole in one wall to the hole in another" (Ó Cuív 1980, 60). These tales correspond to the empirical observation of the wren's habit of making short, low flights—a behavior that made it far easier to hit the bird or stone it to death in the annual hunt.

A different twist is that the other birds, disgusted at the wren's trickery, from that day forward "have driven the wren from all open spaces and forced him to take shelter in the hedges" (Potter and Sargent 1974, 296) and have "condemned the wren to seek its food in crevices and low herbage" (Armstrong 1992, 2). A similar tale indicates that because he fears the wrath of the other birds whom he deceived, the wren "hides himself under the bushes and trees and has become a very furtive bird" (Gaster 1915, 301). Thus there are multiple explanations for the wren's characteristic behavior of frequenting low places such as underbrush, hedges, and crevices and remaining out of sight.

A Welsh sequel to the fable of the wren's outsoaring the eagle relates that the other birds were sorrowful about the outcome of the contest and cried bitterly. They decided to drown the wren in a pan full of their tears, but this plan was foiled by the owl, who clumsily upset the pan and spilled the tears. The birds swore vengeance against the owl, and ever since he has not dared to go out during the day but procures his food at night when all other birds are asleep. "Thus," the tale concludes, "the wren was saved, and continued king of the birds." Another Welsh account relates that in the flying contest the wren fell to the ground and was injured. The others were concerned about the accident and made a broth to cure the wren, "but the blundering owl upset the pot." In the Cornish version, it is butterflies who fill the bowl with their tears, in their fear that the wren will devour them, and it is the wren's negligence that upsets it. As a result, the other birds "lay upon her a curse, namely that she should never be able to fly over a hedge or bush as high as a milking-pail without alighting on it, and so giving the moths and butterflies a chance to escape" (Gill 1932, 421–23).

As recorded by the Brothers Grimm, the other birds were angry at the wren for using tricks and cheating to attain his status as king. "So they made another condition: whoever could descend deepest into the earth would be the king." The little wren, undaunted, "looked for a mousehole, slipped down into it," and declared "I'm the king!" Now even more angry, the birds decided to imprison the wren in the hole and starve him out. The owl who was posted as guard, however, fell asleep, allowing the tiny bird to escape. The owl was duly punished for her negligence, and ever since the wren "does not like to show himself because he fears for his neck if he is caught. He slips in and out of hedges, and when he feels very safe, he sometimes cries out, 'I'm the king!' And this is why the other birds mock him by calling him the king of the hedges" (Zipes 1987, 549–50).

Thus the eagle-wren legend explains not only the wren's truncated tail but also its characteristic flight pattern, feeding habits, and peculiar behavior on the ground. A song from Brittany, "The Wren's Wedding," accounts for the eagle's absence at a social function by implied reference to the legendary competition. The wren invites all the birds to her wedding, reminding them to bring presents because she is very poor—an old Welsh custom that prevailed even when the couple was not actually needy. "All the birds turn up except one, understood to be the eagle on account of his jealousy about the kingship." A Breton proverb, "The eagle flees before the wren," also alludes to the unexpected outcome of the wren-eagle battle (Gill 1932, 401, 419).

In almost every part of Europe some form of the wren and eagle fable exists. Variants of the wren-eagle dichotomy also occur elsewhere, as in North America among the Ojibwas and in the Confucianist tradition in which the association between the two birds results in fledglings of the eagle sometimes turning into wrens. The wren-eagle story was already well known in antiquity. References to the antagonism between the two birds occur in Pliny's *Historia Naturalis* and Aristotle's *Historia Animalium* (Balme 1991, 271; De Gubernatis 1872, 2:108; Gill 1932, 419; Bolte and Polívka 1918, 279). Christine Hartley believes the legend "can be easily traced back to Taliesin, the sun god in the British pantheon," for whom the wren was a sacred bird (1986, 123).

The wren and eagle play a role in the Celtic masterpiece *The Mabinogion.* In the story from that work entitled *Math son of Mathonwy,* the hero, Llew Llaw Gyffes, received his name for his skill in shooting a wren. Later, when Llew was slain in his human form—or was transformed by magic—he flew away in the form of an eagle. (His wife, Blodeuwedd, met a similar fate, being transformed into an owl.) The symbolism of the wren hunt can be linked to this tale: "The wren is the spirit of the Old Year killed at the Winter Solstice. The New Year rises up like an eagle, just as Llew Llaw Gyffes' soul becomes an eagle, and the wren rides up on the eagle's back just as one year runs into the next" (Fife 1991, 155).

Plutarch used the wren-eagle legend to teach a moral lesson: after describing some outstanding contemporary personalities, he pointed out that "such then, are the men to whom young statesmen should attach themselves and cling closely, not snatching glory away from them, like Aesop's wren who was carried up on the eagle's shoulders, then suddenly flew out and got ahead of him" (Armstrong 1958, 135–36). A seventeenth-century iconography also features the rivalry between the eagle and the wren in order to draw conclusions about human behavior. A woman dressed in royal robes holds a wren in her right hand and rests her left hand on the head of an eagle standing beside her. The accompanying text explains:

> Among the prodigies that happened the day preceding the death of Caesar, this little bird, called Trochilus by Aristotle . . . was seen flying toward the senate house, with a branch of laurel in its mouth, and many other birds following it. For this reason the wren was assigned as a symbol to empire, and called the king of birds in preference to all others. It is reported that the eagle frequently contends with the wren for superiority; and tho' it is well-known that the former is much greater in power and might than the latter, yet the wren is here placed in the most distinguished situation; which denotes, that ingenious and brave men, of whatever station, who, by their merit in art or in arms raise their reputation by some memorable exploit, have an equal claim to honour and preferment with those of the most distinguished rank.
>
> (Rowland 1978, 187)

In these tales, by exalting the tiny bird's cleverness and cunning in outwitting the large, powerful eagle, or in having prior knowledge of an important event or possessing special abilities, a human model is set up, implying that it is possible for a brave or talented but humble person to rise in status and obtain honor equal to those of superior rank. The idea inherent in this avian version of the David and Goliath story is still operative today. For example, "in Ireland, the wren is considered the 'king of all birds.' While not mighty, the little wren is, nevertheless, ultimately triumphant because it is clever. The Irish may think of the wren as a symbol of themselves" (Zeleny 1985, 66).

Folklorist Jawaharlal Handoo contrasts cultural attitudes as they are expressed in animal tales with attitudes found in the real world and suggests that the views of human societies toward animals or birds are inverted in folklore. He proposes a model:

Animals in real world
Small/weak = unwise = defeat   Big/strong = wise = victory

Animals in folklore
Small/weak = wise = victory   Big/strong = unwise = defeat

Handoo explains that in the real world it is generally believed that a big animal or bird is physically strong and is usually victorious in any kind of task or struggle. However, in folklore this attitude is inverted, and tiny or physically weak animals or birds are shown as wiser than the big animals and birds and are essentially victorious in their tasks and struggles against them (1994, 38). While this model represents an interesting kind of generalizing, I would like to point out that it does not take account of the empirically observed qualities of the animals in question. Specifically, as my study will show, there are many unusual characteristics and behavioral traits possessed by the wren that fit that bird for its winning role in the wren-eagle struggle. To a considerable degree it is through human awareness of the wren's peculiarities that this biological species is perceptually transformed into a creature that can defeat a much larger and more powerful bird.

As might be expected to follow from the wren's victory over the eagle, there is a corollary to the wren's achieving high station: the knowledge that he is king of birds has made the wren "the proudest and most conceited of the feathered kind. Tiny though he is, he hops about on the dead branches of trees, trying in vain to snap them with his weight, and piping with petulant anger, 'How strong it is!' or, . . . 'it must be steel, steel, since it does not break!'" (Swainson 1886, 36). For his accomplishment of defeating the eagle, the "cheeky little wren" acquired a reputation for impudence and audacity (Parry-Jones 1988, 154).

Some ambivalence toward the wren may derive from contrasting interpretations of the bird's behavior in the contest for the highest flier. The wren's cunning can be viewed as "a way of achieving great things with an economy of effort, and a rational and honest use of the achievements of others." But the same trait and actions can cause the wren to be seen as "a cheeky and dishonest 'upstart' who naively believes he can fool others and win status for himself through his ruse" (Carr-Gomm and Carr-Gomm 1994, 127). Building on the work of others may be wrongful exploitation of their achievements, and mocking others' pride by outwitting them at the final moment could be considered unfair. Thus the wren's cleverness may be construed as evil as well as good—an ambiguity that adds to the inconsistency and complexity of the wren's often contradictory symbolism.

Shakespeare, in *Richard the Third,* makes use of the wren-eagle contrast to comment on circumstances that seem topsy-turvy: "The world is grown so bad / That wrens make prey where eagles dare not perch" (1.3). Thus the noble great and the humble small have switched roles, an example of the wren's association with reversal, according to which the bird represents incongruity in ideas or events. Juxtaposition of the wren with the eagle to emphasize the contrast between the two is one of the many ways in which the tiny bird is used to symbolize opposite attributes. The huge, majestic eagle, often observed soaring gracefully aloft through the open air, is universally known as the highest flier among birds, the king of heaven, symbolic of the sun and the powers of the sky. The minuscule, chunky wren, on the other hand, belongs to the earth, and often disappears from sight, creeping in holes or crevices near the ground. The wren has been viewed as being closely in touch with chthonic forces (like the snake who in heraldry is often pictured in an eagle's talons). The wren's magico-religious role, including its oracular abilities, undoubtedly springs from its connectedness to the earth. The minute brown bird is associated with fertility of the soil and with the plough. In the conflict between the wren and the eagle, therefore, each bird represents "one of the two fundamental principles consciously or subconsciously recognized by mankind for untold ages"—the eagle being king of the heavens above, the wren belonging to the earth below (Armstrong 1958, 139). Analyzing the wren-eagle dichotomy, it becomes clear that the wren represents the "powers of darkness, most evident at midwinter," whereas the eagle symbolizes "the powers of light and life, growth and goodness." Thus the wren-hunt ritual "may be interpreted as asserting belief in the triumph of all that is favourable to humankind's well-being" (Armstrong 1992, 2–3).

During the wren ceremony in one district of France, the inhabitant elected king for the occasion held on his wrist a wren accoutred as a hunting hawk, "its head covered with a hood such as is used in falconry, and silk tassels on its feet" (Thomas 1906, 272–73). Because the hawk is an avian predator closely related to the eagle, this example also reflects the contrast between the tiny, gentle, ground-dwelling wren often hidden in the underbrush and the large, fierce bird who conspicuously masters the air in search of prey. As just recounted, the wren has a connection with the owl, who blundered in upsetting the pot of tears that was intended to drown the wren or the bowl of broth made to cure it, or fell asleep when posted as guard at the wren's hole when the bird was supposed to be "starved out," thus allowing the prisoner to escape. A Breton legend also focuses on the wren-owl association, relating that once upon a time each of the birds gave one of its feathers to the wren, who had lost his own. Because the selfish owl alone refused this act of charity, henceforth it was condemned to be always cold and solitary, being required to leave its abode only at night. If it was seen going about in the daytime, the other birds would pursue and persecute it (Swainson 1886, 124).

In an expanded form of this tale, when a messenger was needed to fetch fire from heaven to earth (or, some say, from the lower regions), the "weak and delicate" wren cheerfully undertook the perilous mission. In doing so, it scorched away all its plumage, causing each of the other birds, in gratitude, to present the brave little benefactor with one of their feathers. The denuded wren's acceptance of a feather from each bird explains why "the plumage of the Wren is so bizarre" (Tegid 1911, 101). The owl's refusal to give a feather to the wren angered the other birds so much that they detested him and no longer would admit him to their society. So he had to keep aloof from them by day and leave his "melancholy hiding place" only by night (Swainson 1886, 124). Because the "curmudgeonly owl" would not donate a feather, the other birds always "mob him whenever they see him" (Gill 1932, 419). (Birds actually do harass an owl they find resting in a tree during the daytime.) A behavioral source of the wren-owl association might also be that a favorite habitat for both birds is the ivy bush. Aristotle noted that the owl and the wren were "at war" (Balme 1991, 223). The wren's symbolic opposition to the owl, like its opposition to the eagle (both noted by Shakespeare), represents a contrast in size and habits—the two huge raptors versus the tiny insect-eater. In the case of the owl versus the wren, there is also the opposition between nocturnal and diurnal habits.

The duality represented by the eagle and the wren is an example of complementary pairs that occur in many legends and are the key to the interpretation of various customs involving pairs of opposites. The conflict between chthonic-lunar and solar ideas is frequently encountered in symbolism. A desire to establish equilibrium between two great contrasting principles that can be symbolized by the sky bird being opposed to the "chthonic creeping creature" underlies certain festivals, such as New Year celebrations (Armstrong 1958, 140). This concept applies to the wren-hunt ceremony, which typically takes place near the winter solstice, close to the end of the Old Year. Interestingly, the contrast between the two birds is still used to illustrate opposite poles of the avian kingdom. A twentieth-century poem praising the birds of Scotland, for example, begins with love for "the eagle soaring high in pride, / The wren so blithe and small" (Macdonald 1901, 211). A biographer wishing to demonstrate the broad scope of W. H. Hudson's intellect wrote that he "had the philosophic mind that ranged now with the wings of an eagle and then with the alert eagerness of a wren" (Roberts 1924, 89). And the description of an ornithological work in a 1991 book catalogue states that the volume covers "the whole gamut of bird life from eagles to wrens" (Graf 1991, 23).

The incongruity of the wren's exalted status in comparison to those creatures that seem much more deserving of royalty is also expressed in Grimm's tale "The Wren and the Bear." The bear, upon asking the identity of the bird who was singing such a beautiful song in the woods, was told by the wolf, "That's the king of the birds. . . . We must bow down before him." But the bear was skeptical, and when taken to the wren's nest, which he expected to be "the royal palace," he was contemptuous of the young wrens and insulted them by telling them, "You're not royal children in the least. You're a disgrace!" War was declared, and in the ensuing battle the forces of the wren were victorious over those of the bear. Finally, the mighty bear was forced to apologize to the young wrens, telling them they were indeed "a credit to the family" (Zipes 1987, 374–76). The familiar message is one of delight in the rise of the downtrodden over the proud. The tale also reinforces or explains the wren's high-spirited arrogance, which seems incongruous in relation to its size.

SPECIAL STATUS

Aristotle mentions that the wren, whom he characterizes as "industrious" and "gentle in character," is known not only by the title of "King"

but also "Old Man" (Pollard 1977, 37). That nickname reflects the respect and affection with which the bird has often been regarded
throughout the ages. The image of a beloved creature persists today, and
raising the topic of the wren in England during fieldwork always elic-
ited a smile and comments such as, "What a delightful and lovely bird!"
As one author of a British bird book stated, "The good-will of all men
goes out to Jenny-Wren" (Woodward 1928, 29). Most people in Britain
and Europe are familiar with the tiny bird, and country folk know it as
a year-round resident, for it is nonmigratory except in the extreme
northernmost part of its range. Wrens generally maintain their territory through all seasons, and thus are noticeable at times when most
other birds are absent or inconspicuous. The wren is one of the most
common and widely distributed breeding birds in Britain and Ireland,
and according to a survey by the British Trust for Ornithology, the species ranks third in abundance, with only the skylark and the crow being present in greater numbers (Mead 1984, 34).

In some areas the wren was believed to have "a drop of God's
blood" (Henderson 1911, 98), which gave the bird's blood curative
properties (Ó Cuív 1980, 63). In keeping with the power, respect, and
esteem accorded it, the tiny bird was given sacred status by certain holy
persons who held it in special regard. St. Dol, for example, upon realiz-
ing that his fellow monks were being disturbed in their devotions by
the noises made by numerous birds in the woods next to the monas-
tery, called all the birds together and imposed silence upon them. He
then dismissed them and forbade them to return. However, "an excep-
tion was made in favor of the wrens, whose presence cheered without
distracting the inmates" (Swainson 1886, 42–43).

Stories of saints reflect actual records of wrens laying their eggs
in such places as the fold of a curtain, a coil of rope, in a pair of trousers
hung out to dry, or on farm machinery that was in daily use (Armstrong
1992, 17; Parmelee 1959, 162; Ó Cuív 1980, 64). St. Calasius, being over-
come by heat as he labored in his vineyard one day, removed his frock
and hung it on a nearby tree. He was amazed to see a wren fly into the
folds of his garment and lay an egg there. "The saint was so delighted
that he spent the night in prayer and thanksgiving to God" (Swainson
1886, 42–43). St. Malo had the same experience with a wren laying her
eggs in his cloak: "Knowing that God's care is not far from the birds,
since not one of them falls on the ground without the Father, he let his
cloak lie there, till the eggs were hatched and the wren brought out her
brood. And this was the marvel, that all the time that the cloak lay

there, there fell no rain upon it. And whoever came to hear of it, they glorified the power of God, and they praised God's own pity in man" (Waddell 1934, 55).

(Secular sources also reflect the wren's unusual egg-laying habits. For example, a 1995 newspaper baseball quiz included a question about why the pitcher "sits in the dugout between innings with only one arm inside his jacket." The answer was that "wrens are nesting in the other sleeve" [Smith 1995, E10].)

PROHIBITIONS AGAINST KILLING THE WREN

Throughout the British Isles and areas of Europe not only saints but also the general populace were reluctant to disturb the wren. Strong injunctions, learned at an early age, protected the bird from being harmed or injured in any way throughout most of the year. For centuries the wren was esteemed as a sacred bird and was associated with good luck in these areas, where, except for once a year during the ceremonial wren hunt, it was cherished and protected. Tradition dictated that it was unlucky to kill a wren and that the bird should not be molested (Rowland 1978, 185; Armstrong 1958, 142, 152). As poet William Blake wrote in *Auguries of Innocence,* "He who shall hurt the little wren / Shall never be beloved by Men" (Mason 1988, 28).

Taboos that prohibit harming the wren, its nest, or its eggs clearly demonstrate the sacrosanct status of the bird and its influence in determining thought and action. The prohibitions reveal the retributive power possessed by the tiny wren and correlate with the sacrificial role that such a tabooed species may occupy. In Wales, "from the nursery upwards" people "were taught to respect and protect the bird and [were] threatened with the most dire calamities" if such teachings were disregarded. Children were warned of severe penalties to be suffered by anyone who disobeyed the injunctions. "Whosoever rob the wren's nest shall never have health in his life" was a well-known Welsh adage (Peate 1936, 1). Another Welsh saying held that "to destroy the nest was to forfeit eternal salvation" (Armstrong 1958, 142, 152). The perpetrator's punishment was spelled out in terms of a rhyme: "Whoever breaks a wren's nest / Shall never know the Heavenly rest" (Davies 1911, 224). It was also believed that "whoever destroys a wren or its nest shall never see the face of God" (Fisher n.d., 4).

"To kill a wren in some parts of France was regarded as a crime which might 'bring down the lightning'"—the culprit's dwelling being thus destroyed. Even touching the bird in its nest meant that the offender would be struck by lightning (Roheim 1930, 324). (The wren has a close connection with lightning, which will be discussed later.) In Wales, belief held that "if you kill a wren your house will be burned down. Anyone who kills a wren or harries its nest will break a bone or meet with some misfortune within a year." In Brittany, tradition dictated that "children will suffer from the St. Lawrence fire in their face if they touch the wren in its nest" (Roheim 1930, 324). Or tampering with the nest could mean suffering from "pimples on face and legs" (Hartley 1986, 121). In Cornwall, a person who killed a wren was shunned by his fellows, and parents were known to ban their children from playing with such a boy. Abnormally small children were often accused of having killed a bird or destroying its nest, causing their growth to be stunted: "Kill a robin or a wran, / You'll never grow to be a man" (Dean and Shaw 1975, 132).

Another admonition predicted: "The fingers of the man who kills a wren will gradually shrivel away and finally drop off!" (Swainson 1886, 42). A Sussex man was warned "if I ever took a Juggie's [wren's] eggs I would be sure to get a crooked finger" (Opie and Tatem 1989, 452). Such a transgressor might also be punished by having his cattle "suffer in their feet" (Roheim 1930, 324) or give bloody milk (Frazer 1963, 621). In Scotland, "a popular rhyme called down curses on those who robbed the bird or chased it: Malisons, malisons, mair than ten, / That harry the Lady's of Heaven's Hen." The same traditions existed in England (Spence 1947, 45). There, anyone who killed a wren or destroyed its nest "would infallibly, within the course of the year, meet with some dreadful misfortune" (Moore 1971, 138). A pastoral verse published in 1770 by George Smith, a poet in whose barn "a wren has young ones bred," warns:

> I never take away their nest, nor try
> To catch the old ones, lest a friend should die;
> Dick took a wren's nest from his cottage side,
> And ere a twelvemonth past his mother dy'd!
> (Brand 1849, 3:194)

On the positive side, it is fortunate "if a 'cutty' builds a nest in your hayrick," and in Scotland "a wren around the house brings good luck" (Opie and Tatem 1989, 452; Armstrong 1958, 169).

Such convictions about the wren's capacities to punish or reward human beings demonstrate not only the power attributed to the tiny bird, but reflect general faith in the reciprocal relationship between humankind and nature that was once taken for granted. Not long ago, I was reminded of the effects of the absence of such belief in the modern world when I went to visit a woman who had just moved into a house in which some sweetly singing Carolina wrens were nesting in the eaves. While I was there, a friend of this new country-dweller stopped by, and, noting the birds' presence, he immediately advised her to destroy and knock down the nests of the birds for no other reason than that he viewed them as intrusive.

THE PAIRING OF THE WREN WITH THE ROBIN

The wren is often closely associated with the robin, sharing some of the divine qualities attributed to that familiar and beloved red-breasted bird. Many prohibitions include both wren and robin. An Irish proverb indicates the sacrosanct status of the pair: "The robin and the wren are God's two holy men" (Ingersoll 1923, 117), and the Kentish equivalent states: "Robins and wrens are God's best friends" (Stenning 1950, 275). Strangely, there has been a common belief (evidently still held by some people) that the robin and the wren are male and female, respectively, of the same species, and are wedded (Armstrong 1958, 169). The love-smitten robin serenades his lady wren:

> Cock robin got up early
> At the break of day,
> And went to Jenny's window
> To sing a roundelay.
> He sang cock robin's love
> To little Jenny Wren,
> And when he got unto the end,
> Then he began again.
> (Munsterberg 1984, 332)

"The Marriage of Cock Robin and Jenny Wren" describes the nuptials in verse:

> Then on her finger fair
> Cock robin put the ring;
> "You're married now" says Parson Rook;
> While the Lark amen did sing.
> (Armstrong 1958, 172)

Details of the courtship, wedding, and the couple's subsequent fate appear in a rhyme from oral tradition:

> Says Robin to Jenny, "If you will be mine,
> We'll have cherry tart, and drink currant wine."
> So Jenny consented—the day was named,
> The joyful news the cock proclaimed.

Other birds participated in the ceremony and provided food. Then

> The jovial party dined together;
> And long did Robin and his mate
> Live in the happily married state,
> Till, doleful to relate! one day
> A hawk with Jenny flew away;
> And Robin by the cruel sparrow
> Was shot quite dead with bow and arrow.
> (Munsterberg 1984, 333)

According to W. B. Lockwood, the first explicit record of this interspecies marriage was published in 1787. But a poem dating to about 1400 mentions an alliance between the robin and the wren in which, although the two are not described as spouses, their relationship is intimate and loving. He suggests that the pairing of the two may be related to the fact that "Robert redbreast," a name probably derived from Latin *ruber*, "red," was given to the bird. Both this name and its later form, robin, are masculine, a fact that "ordained that the redbreast had to be a cockbird." Lockwood hypothesizes that "Cock Robert," as a male figure, required a hen, and of the available familiar small birds "only the wren possessed the requisite virtues: alliteration, or near-alliteration, with Robert, and rhyme with 'hen.' So the wren became a bride, and in due course her name was suitably qualified: 'Jenny' wren (first noticed as 'Jinny wren,' in 1638)." This author concludes that the superstition did not give rise to the verse, but rather the verse created the superstition. He points out that a late usage of a couplet published in 1939—"The robin and the wrens / Be God Almighty's friends"—represents a transition in which "the verse was used for enforcing a taboo against taking eggs from a robin's nest; it therefore links up with the wider issue of the 'luck' or 'sacredness' associated with these birds, and their 'marriage' is almost forgotten" (1989, 237–39).

A familiar verse expresses the high regard in which the robin-wren couple is held and the dire penalty for transgressing against either bird:

> The robin and the wren
> Are God Almighty's cock and hen.
> Him that harries their nest,
> Never shall his soul have rest.
> (Macmillan 1926, 114)

The two birds are coupled in numerous admonitory rhymes, such as:

> Kill a robin or a wren,
> Never prosper, boy or man.
>
> The robin and the redbreast,
> The robin and the wren,
> If ye tak' out of the nest
> Ye'll never thrive again.
>
> Cursed is the man
> Who kills a robin or a wren.
> (Armstrong 1958, 168)

In Cornwall, there is this variation:

> He who hurts the robin or the wren,
> Will never prosper sea or land,
> On sea or land will ne'er do well again.
> (Buday 1964, 104)

And in Essex folklore, "Robins and wrens are God Almighty's shirt and collar" (Buday 1964, 103).

The wren shares the robin's reputation for solicitude toward the dead, as demonstrated by its legendary kindness in covering with moss the body, or at least the face, of any lifeless creature it finds. This "Babes in the Woods" theme in which a robin covers the bodies of two young children with leaves is expressed in John Webster's familiar lines:

> Call for the robin redbreast and the wren,
> Since o'er shady groves they hover,
> And with leaves and flow'rs do cover
> The friendless bodies of unburied men.
> (Hazlitt 1905, 2: 520)

Christmas card with "Babes in the Wood" theme depicting robins and
wrens. Courtesy of Patrick Armstrong for the Estate of
Edward A. Armstrong.

A Christmas card, probably dating to the Victorian era, shows a poignant scene in which a robin and two wrens seem to be covering a doll that is half-buried in the snow.

Lines from a Welsh wren song reveal: "Robins of every color are about the wren; / Robins thrice turned are on his head for a covering" (Fisher n.d., 3). Evidently this couplet expresses a connection with the two birds' legendary acts of covering the dead.

In folklore the wren and the robin are both credited as fire-fetchers—another example of their perceived association. As previously mentioned, an old legend relates how the wren braved the dangers of hell to bring fire to humankind. This beneficial role undoubtedly explains the forms of retribution for injuring the wren that involve fire. As will become evident, the wren's association with fire is represented in certain elements of the wren ceremony.

According to a Welsh explanation of the pairing of the robin and the wren, it originated because both are "under a curse." The robin cannot fly through a hedge, but always goes over it, and the wren cannot fly over a hedge, but always goes through it (Trevelyan 1909, 113). This legend underscores the complementary relationship between the two species. The wren and robin are also perceived as opposites in their contrasting symbolic roles as the Old and the New Year.

At the time of the winter solstice, the pairing of the wren and the robin has a special significance that explains their depiction on Christmas and New Year's greeting cards. The coupling of the two birds is directly related to the progression of the seasons and to the annual wren hunt. The robin, representing the coming New Year, sets out to kill his father, the old King Wren, whose reign must end: "The murder is committed, the robin's breast is stained with red and the way is clear for the cycle to repeat itself" (Garai 1973, 79). A Victorian-era New Year's greeting card depicts the wren and the robin, symbolizing the Old year and the New. The robin, with brilliant scarlet breast, perches on a holly bush beneath which red flowers bloom, occupying most of the space, and the small brown wren appears in one corner, surrounded by mistletoe. The card contains an appropriate verse, entitled "The New Year":

Turn it o'er,
That page is done.
Years are flying
One by one.
Work, pray, and hope,
In youth and age,
And God's own hand
Shall turn the page.

Another interesting example is a card dating to 1895, depicting "The Kindly Robin." The illustration portrays an immaculately dressed male robin with red vest and top hat along with his stylishly outfitted wife and child. The robin is placing a red berry into a tattered hat held out by a beggar in the form of a ragged male wren with an eye patch and a crutch. His little mate with her cocked-up tail is hunched over and poorly attired. The wrens have no child with them to match the robin's bonneted offspring. It is not hard to imagine that the forlorn and dilapidated wren couple represents the Old, dying year. The prosperous robin, as the bright New Year, can afford to be "kindly"—a trait generally applied to that well-loved bird. The robin's charity toward the wren seems to be a recurrent theme in folklore. For example, the two birds are associated in an old nursery rhyme that tells "how when the wren fell sick, the robin brought her food and wine but when the wren got better, she was less than grateful: Robin being angry hopped upon a

Victorian New Year's postcard featuring robin and wren. Courtesy of the Royal Society for the Protection of Birds.

A·HAPPY·CHRISTMAS·TO·YOU.

THE KINDLY ROBIN.

"The Kindly Robin." From the John Grossman collection of
antique images.

twig / Saying 'Out upon you! Fie upon you! Bold faced jig!'" (O'Sullivan
1991, 33). Interestingly, an actual instance of robins' nurturant benevolence toward wrens is recorded. A man picked up two newly fledged
wrens and, intending to take them home, wrapped them in a handkerchief. But they escaped as he was walking through the woods. Three
days later, he discovered the same young wrens in a robin's nest, where
they had been accepted by the parent birds and were being fed together
with the nestling robins (Skutch 1987, 176).

Robins in many poses are commonly found on Christmas cards.
One particularly striking card shows a dead robin lying on its back, as
on a bier, with the line: "May yours be a joyful Christmas" (Hart,
Grossman, and Dunhill 1990, 20). Other cards with similar pictures but
different mottoes read: "Sweet messenger of calm decay and Peace Divine," and "But peaceful was the night, wherein the Prince of Light,
His reign of peace upon the earth began" (Buday 1964, pl. 30). Such
cards seem strangely morbid and difficult to comprehend today, but
were once popular. They may illustrate the general idea of killing birds
around Christmastime, or they may signify the sacrificing of a favorite

Cock Robin and Jenny Wren on a Christmas card. From the Brian
Paterson collection of antique images.

bird at the solstice to represent the winter death of all life and the hope
of resurrection embodied by Christ's birth. The explanation also may
lie in the idea that "the robin, a symbol of peace, was killed by celebrants of the inside-out Feast of Fools" (Buday 1964, 20) in keeping
with the reversals of behavioral norms—including killing robins and
wrens—that once took place during the interval between Christmas
and New Year's Day.

Today, robin and wren figures still appear at the holiday season,
though their original meaning has undoubtedly been long forgotten by
greeting card designers as well as senders and recipients. A contemporary Christmas card, printed in England and sold in the United States
in 1992, features a male robin and a female wren dressed in clothes appropriate to the sexes. The illustration is a Victorian reproduction entitled "An Offering of Friendship." The lady wren standing demurely
by her basket of red berries presents two of those berries to the red-
vested robin wearing a top hat, whose portrayal greatly resembles the
"kindly robin" described above. Here, the wren reciprocates the robin's
generosity, or she may be flirting with him as a prelude to courtship.

A craft book of Victorian Christmas items to be pressed out and assembled that was published in both New York and London in 1992 includes a greeting card depicting the robin and the wren (Ponder 1992, 27). A 1993 Hallmark Christmas gift-wrapping paper entitled "Christmas Naturals," featuring gold images of the robin and the wren, perpetuates the pairing of the two species. The birds face each other and are pictured on a dark green background containing mistletoe, holly with red berries, and pine boughs. The robin, though, is not the European species but the quite different American robin (actually a thrush) and is in fact a perfect match for the illustration of that species in Peterson's *Field Guide*. Although the wren hunt was not a tradition in the New World, the ancient symbolism stemming from British and European roots has been imported and perpetuated.

The sacrosanct status of the wren protected the little bird throughout most of the year, but the stringent taboos were set aside annually in those areas where the wren hunt was traditional. At that special time, prohibitions were replaced by highly complex rituals that grew out of ancient beliefs and involved the ceremonial death and display of the wren.

THREE

THE WREN HUNT

We were all day hunting the wren;
The wren so cute and we so cunning.
He stayed in the bush when we were running.
—Waterford Wren Song

IN LIGHT OF THE DEEP reverence with which the wren has been regarded in certain areas, it appears at first completely incongruous that the species was nevertheless ruthlessly hunted and killed in those same places on certain annual occasions. Although wren hunts took place on other dates in the calendar year, such as Christmas Eve, Christmas morning, or on specified days before Christmas, New Year's Eve, New Year's Day, Twelfth Day, and even Valentine's Day, the typical time for the ceremony in the British Isles was St. Stephen's Day, 26 December, the day traditionally associated with killing the wren.

RITE AND CEREMONY

The hunting of the wren, with its attendant ceremony and procession, is a ritual of great antiquity that varies slightly according to geographical areas. Also called "wrenning," "shacking the wren," "going on the wren," and "Jenny hunting" or "jenty hunting," the custom generally involved searching for the wren and killing it, followed by the carrying out of various rites with regard to the bird's corpse.

Typically, on the appointed "wren day" a group of boys and men went out armed with sticks, beating the hedges from both sides and throwing clubs or other objects at the wren whenever it appeared. Eyewitnesses described the hunting of the wren in Ireland in the 1840s:

> For some weeks preceding Christmas, crowds of village boys may be seen peering into hedges in search of the tiny wren; and when one is discovered the whole assemble and give eager chase to, until they have slain the little bird. In the hunt the utmost excitement prevails,

shouting, screeching and rushing; all sorts of missiles are flung at the puny mark and not infrequently they light upon the head of some less innocent being. From bush to bush, from hedge to hedge is the wren pursued and bagged with as much pride and pleasure as the cock of the woods by more ambitious sportsmen.

(O'Sullivan 1991, 32)

Similarly, on St. Stephen's Day in the Isle of Man, "numbers assemble by daybreak, with long staffs, with which they beat the hedges and bushes, till they start one of those smart little birds from its evening roost. They then pursue it with great shoutings, from bush to bush, till the little creature is so tired as to be taken by the hand or knocked down by the stick of one of its barbarous pursuers" (Roeder 1904, 51–52). In Sussex, knobbed sticks about eighteen inches long called libbets were thrown at the wren. Sometimes the tiny bird's assailants used stones to dispatch their victim, relating the wren's killing to that of the first Christian martyr, St. Stephen, who was stoned to death. Swords and pistols were said to be the customary weapons in certain areas of France, and in Wales tradition called for hunting the wren with bow and arrow (Armstrong 1958, 142–44). The person who killed the wren was believed to have good luck all year and was looked upon as "the great man of the day" or "temporary leader" (Hole 1975, 13; Paton 1942, 107).

Once the wren had been slaughtered, it was displayed in prescribed ways prior to being carried about and taken through a neighborhood from door to door. On the Isle of Man, the wren hunt was a particularly prevalent tradition, probably reflecting the fact that the island was "a stronghold of Druidism" (Hartley 1986, 93). The hunt persisted into the 1930s or later, and vestiges of the rite still occur there. The custom, which "has been a pastime in the Isle of Man from time immemorial," was described in 1731 by George Waldron in an account that has been frequently quoted by subsequent writers: "On the 24th of December, towards evening, all the servants in general have a holiday, they go not to bed all night, but ramble about till the bells ring in all the churches, which is at twelve a-clock; prayers being over, they go to hunt the wren, and after having found one of these poor birds, they kill her, and lay her on a bier with the utmost solemnity, bringing her to the parish church, and burying her with a whimsical kind of solemnity, singing dirges over her in the Manks language, which they call her knell; after which Christmas begins" (1731, 49–50, 126). Other reports of the wren hunt on the Isle of Man do not place the event on Christmas Eve, and there is a general feeling that Waldron may have been mistaken about the date. Joseph Train, writing in 1845, indicates that although in Waldron's day the wren hunt reportedly was observed on 24 December, it has taken place "for a century past" on St. Stephen's Day (1845, 2:124).

One account specifies that the dead wren was "fixed upon the top of a long pole to which is suspended a red handkerchief, by the way of a banner, and in that manner it is carried round the town in triumph" (Roeder 1904, 52). Or the wren was "afixed to a pole with wings out-stretched" (Armstrong 1958, 154). But most sources describe a more complex way of displaying the little corpse. The true Manx tradition, which persists to some degree in the present version of the rite, dictated that the dead bird was "suspended by a leg from the junction-point of two hoops of willow or other flexible wood with their ends fastened together to form two circles, and intersecting each other at right angles." Ribbons or paper streamers, tinsel, or foil might be used for decoration, but "the essential part of the equipment" was "bunches of such greenery as could be got at that time of the year—often holly or ivy," which were "fixed round the receptacle." Thus people referred to "the Bush" and "the Wren-bush," and would ask with regard to the wren procession, "Are you goin' round with the Bush this year?" (Gill 1932, 368).

The Manx participants, or "wren-boys," singing "Hunt the Wren," went to people's homes seeking money. When a coin was given, the donor received a feather plucked from the wren. Each feather was preserved as a protective charm in the purse or in the house or was kept in the fishing boat as a talisman against shipwreck or other evils for one year. For that purpose, according to an early observer, "many a jack-tar conceals them in his bosom" (*Farghar's Sixpenny Edition* 1853, 4). Sailors from Scotland also "used to catch and pluck a wren before set-ting out on a voyage, divining from the way the feathers fell whether the herring fishery would be successful or not. Probably they acquired these notions from the Manx fishermen" (Armstrong 1958, 154).

Sometimes on the Isle of Man the bearers of the wren obliged all persons they met to purchase a feather and to wear it in their hats for the day. The wren's feathers were considered effective in guarding against witchcraft. At the end of the day, the featherless wren was in-terred at the seashore or other wild area or, accompanied by ceremony and the singing of dirges, buried in the churchyard. After the interment,

Manx Wren Boys in Ramsey, 1904. Courtesy of Manx National Heritage.

the people who had gathered for the burial formed a circle and danced to musical accompaniment. The evening might conclude with playing games (Frazer 1963, 622; Swainson 1886, 37, 39; Armstrong 1958, 152, 153; Ralfe 1905, 39; Gill 1932, 357–58; Moore 1971, 134).

An interesting detail about the bird's final resting place connects the rite to the Druids. One of the areas on the Isle of Man in which the wren's burial is known to have taken place is the churchyard of the chapel, Kil-Ammon, in the town of Baaltin (now Baldwin). In 1836, the modern church of St. Luke was built over the ruins of that ancient chapel. According to popular belief, "a Druidical temple" occupied the same site "in early ages" (Paton 1942, 102; Kermode 1885, 164; Stenning 1950, 274).

Manx resident Mona Douglas described her version of aspects of the "curious spectacle" of the wren procession as it occurred during the early 1700s: "An elaborate wren bush was carried by a man so lavishly decorated with holly, ivy and other greenery that he almost seemed part of the bush." Inside the traditional crossed hoops of wood "hung the pathetic small body of a wren, stripped of feathers," these having been "given to the principle [*sic*] persons of the town 'for luck.'" Douglas's account reveals an additional feature: "Behind the dead wren in its elaborate cage, another man, dressed in women's clothing, carried a second, much smaller cage woven closely of green rushes, inside which was another wren; and this one was alive." Carrying "torches of flaming pitch," the whole party proceeded, singing "We'll Hunt the Wren," as they marched along to Kirk Malew. In Malew churchyard, they "sought out a secluded corner" to dig the wren's "small grave." While the bird was solemnly interred, everyone sang "O Colb ec Shee" (O Body at Rest). Then "came the turn of the living wren. Its small cage was hung inside the Bush where the dead wren had been and the people formed into a big circle with the Bush in the centre and performed the Hunt the Wren Dance, a prominent feature of which is homage to the Wren. At the end of the dance this living wren was set free, and as it flew away the Bush was broken and burnt on the grave of its former occupant, and the ceremonies were over for another year" (1963, 2).

This description echoes the concept prevalent in Manx lore that the wren is annually reborn after being killed:

> In Manx the wren is called Dreean or Druid bird because it is sup-
> posed to be a magic creature like the Phoenix who had to die and
> come to life again every year. The Phoenix used to set fire to its own

nest and perish in the flames, to rise again in new life from the ashes; the wren had to be hunted or stoned to death and buried in the churchyard by torchlight with a proper funeral procession and long ago it was believed that the bird's spirit would immediately pass into the body of another younger wren and fly away from the grave to be free and safe for the coming year—for nobody would harm a wren except on St. Stephen's Day when it was ceremonially hunted.

("How to Hunt" 1965, 11)

Religious authority, Douglas reports, was hostile to the ceremony. When the group bearing the sacrificed wren arrived at Kirk Malew, she writes, "they were *not* received by the Vicar.—He took good care to absent himself from the proceedings, for they were frowned upon by the church at that time as being Pagan and superstitious. In an earlier day the older church might have been wise enough to capture this ceremonial, as it had captured many another survival of ancient rites, dedicated it to St. Stephen, and so achieved the happy compromise of perpetuating an old custom but giving it a Christian aspect." She indicates that "in the early eighteenth century, when Puritan influences were strong in the Manx church, the clergy kept well aloof, knowing they would be unable to stop the proceedings anyway. What the clerical tongue didn't see the clerical tongue need not preach against, so everyone was kept more or less happy" (1963, 2).

Eyewitnesses on the Isle of Man described some of their observations of the wren procession: "The little wren was placed on a stick between two boys, on a piece of fir-tree tied with ribbons for a sign of their good going (success), and in remembrance of the good luck it brought in days long ago. There was a third boy, and he was covered with a net, and his face made black, and a bunch of leeks tied together to make a tail behind his back. He carried a long pole for a stick, and he kept time with the tune" (Paton 1942, 107). An account from the town of Ramsey provides an added feature that associates the wren procession with luck in fishing. Marching in front of the person carrying the wren's bower was a man wielding a stick in his hand "to belabour the doors" of the houses along the way. "Part of a fishing net [was] wrapped round him, formed behind into a sort of pocket, in which dangle[d] two or three herrings" (Kermode 1885, 162).

Another account from a Manx participant in the latter part of the nineteenth century indicates: "Getting your stang [pole] ready was a job that took some time. It was made of a strong stick about three feet long, with a wooden hoop fastened on one end. The hoop had to be wood and tied on to the stick. No iron was allowed in the make-up. A network of string was worked on the hoop, and into this network selected evergreens were woven, so that it looked like a bunch of evergreens on a stick. Then a lot of ribbons of fancy colours were fastened on, and in the center, a dead wren. The young girls were keen on getting a piece of these ribbons to tie their hair as it gave them good luck for the ensuing year" ("Manx Museum Folk Life" 1950, 3).

In one case the boys carried the wren about "in the middle of a green bush so big that you couldn't have got your arms round it; this was fixed on a long pole which was sloped over the bearer's shoulder, and the wren was hanging by a string in the middle." A Manx resident wrote in 1868: "A party of wren-hunters came to my house carrying the dead body of the pretty bird in the interior of a little bower made of evergreens tied with ribbons. I gave them some pence, and received three feathers." Another said the body was erected "on a perch between osier twigs, decked out with ribbons and evergreens" (Gill 1932, 369). Gill points to a possible connection between "these trappings . . . and the gigantic images constructed of osiers or covered with grass in which the Druids enclosed their victims" or with "the leafy framework in which the human representative of the tree-spirit is still so often encased" (1932, 369). These evergreen boughs, which in the nineteenth century surrounded the bird's body on the Isle of Man as well as in Wales, have been gradually replaced in the island ceremony by artificial materials, though some fresh plants are still used.

In different areas, the wren was carried about in a stable lantern decorated with ribbons or in an elaborate wooden "Wren House" with doors and windows. In Wales the "Wren-bearers" constructed a receptacle in the form of "a little square box . . . made of interlaced skewers pasted over with coloured paper, with streamers of paper attached to it. An opening was left in the box to give patrons a peep at the dead victim" (Gill 1932, 371). Some wren houses had a square of glass at either end for viewing the tiny corpse, and sometimes the house was surmounted by a hoop or circle. The structure containing the wren was called "'Noah's Ark' and it was borne by four men on poles fixed to the corners—as elsewhere, burlesquing the size and weight of the bird" (Armstrong 1958, 150). Other variations involved fastening the wren with its wings extended to the top of a long pole that was held aloft in a procession during which marchers beat drums and carried colored banners (Armstrong 1958, 150, 155).

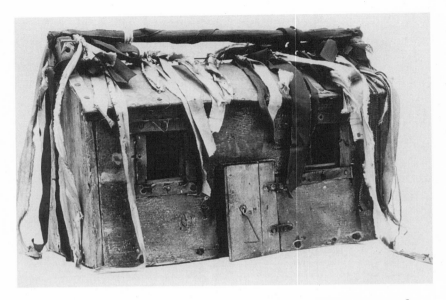

Wren House from Marloes, Pembrokeshire, ca. 1848. Courtesy of
Museum of Welsh Life.

In Pembrokeshire, Wales, one man who went out with the wren
was invited each year to enter the home of an old farmer and his wife in
the early morning and to sprinkle water over them as they lay in bed.
The doorsteps were also sprinkled in this form of blessing connected
with the wren ceremony. In North Pembrokeshire, for a three-week
period beginning with Christmas, farming operations were suspended
and the plough was carried into the house and placed under the dining
table. During this period parties of men went from house to house and,
on being invited in, sat around the table and drank warm beer. They
wetted the plough with beer before partaking of it themselves, thus
indicating that they had not forgotten it and that it would soon be put
to use. These bands of men generally carried with them a wren and sang
variations of the wren song (Gill 1932, 374). Thus farmers incorporated
the plough, a symbol of their work, into the wren ceremony, just as the
Manx fishermen adapted the wren ritual to their seafaring life.

Another Pembrokeshire tradition dictated that after hunting the
wren "four men carried handles on each side, supporting something
like a bier. On this was a nice box with a wren, or sometimes two or
three wrens in it, and it was decorated with coloured ribbons and flow-

ers." At each house they would sing and ask for drink and cakes. Associated with this tradition was the practice of "sprinkling people with 'New Year's water,'" a custom also known all over South Wales. In Pembrokeshire, young men went from house to house bearing the wren in a little box with glass windows, gaily decked with colored paper. It was carried by means of handles at the corners, "after the manner of a hand-barrow." Candles were stuck to the sides to "illuminate 'King Wren,'" and wren songs were sung whenever the procession halted. At Haverfordwest, the men who carried the wren sang a song that began with the line "Our King is no small man" (Gill 1932, 374–77).

A Welsh custom involved parties who carried the wren and made nighttime visits to recently married couples. They sang:

> Here is the Wren
> If he is alive,
> Or a sparrow
> To be roasted.

And then the husband admitted them to the house and regaled them with beer and food. Thus "the wren's virtue as an antidote to evil influences in general was here specialized to further the chief end of marriage—fruitfulness" (Gill 1932, 377–78). Because of this association with fertility, "the wren-party's visit" was "something which married couples should welcome" (Owen 1959, 68).

In Ireland the slaughtered bird was exhibited on an ivy bush decked with ribbons of many colors or in the middle of a mass of holly and ivy on the top of a broomstick, a pole, or on sticks shaped like a cross. Money was collected from householders who might alternatively contribute food for the participants' evening feast. A small container, such as a hollow turnip, a match box with a glass cover, or a decorated wooden tray, could also be used to display the dead bird. Verses about the wren were sung to the accompaniment of sounds produced by homemade skin tambourines, and sometimes the wren boys danced. Often the men participating in the wren ceremony wore straw masks, animal skins, or horns, or disguised themselves as women. Hobby horses were also included in the procession. The acts and rhymes of wren boys and mummers were so similar that they were smoothly meshed in many parts of Ireland (Armstrong 1958, 154–57, opp. 160; Evans 1967, 279; Glassie 1983, 74).

Accounts by Irish participants indicate that St. Stephen's Day, or the "Wran's Day," was an eagerly anticipated occasion that "put a great finish to Christmas." There was "an air of freedom and wildness about it." Although "the Wrenboys wore skirts, there was never a girl among them." The group of boys called "the wran" dressed up in "a rig-out" that was kept secret until the time of the procession. Every street had its own wran, and all "would do the round of the town several times during the day—dancing all the time, knocking at doors and collecting money." Sometimes, along with "a few coppers" given to the leaders, handfuls of apples would be thrown to the boys. "A drummer and some fifes, and maybe tin whistles and a melodeon" provided music. In the evening "all the wrans would join together for one big parade around the town" (O'Leary 1988, 84–86, 88).

Participants were usually welcomed in people's homes and provided with refreshments. Traditionally, they collected money and the proceeds were divided or used for a "spree" that night (Armstrong 1958, 157). Although the wren boys often urged people to "give us a penny to bury the wren," they actually spent it on a treat for themselves (Opie and Opie 1961, 288). The wren's carcass was sometimes thrown away in the evening, but custom dictated interring it as a mark of honor at the house where the wren boys had been best treated during the day or, conversely, burying it at or near the home of inhospitable people (Armstrong 1958, 157). According to one source, at a house where the wren boys received no money, they buried the wren "on the doorstep, which was considered a great insult to the family and a degradation" (Wilde 1899, 177). Even worse, if the "wrenboys buried their wren at your door, you were in for a year of foul luck" (Glassie 1983, 112). Such conflicting ideas about the wren's burial conferring honor versus signifying insult reflect the transition from the original status of sacredness to the secular mode in which the bird would be seen as merely a repulsive corpse. Vacillation between the two viewpoints undoubtedly expresses the confusion that results when people whose altered ideologies are incongruous with previous faiths continue ancient rites into modern times.

Irish wren boys who were refused admission "cast sarcastic luck over both crop and beast" (Glassie 1983, 112). It is also reported that in Ireland if the "Wren Boys" or "Droluns" were refused contributions of money or drink, they might demonstrate their displeasure by producing "rough music" (Crippen 1923, 132). Such retribution was in the form of "a rude cacophony," which "directed mockery or hostility against individuals who offended against certain community norms."

Sometimes elaborate rituals included "raucous ear-shattering noise, unpitying laughter, and the mimicking of obscenities" (Thompson 1992, 3). In Wales, if the wren party was not admitted into the house and entertained, members expressed their disappointment in a malediction: "Come raging wind, in fury frown, / And turn this house all upside down" (Gill 1932, 378–79). On the Isle of Man if no offering was given to the wren party or if the door of a house remained closed, "a derisory verse of 'Poor house says Robin a Bobin' might well be sung" (Caine 1987, 16). Or "if an immediate acknowledgment, either in money or drink, is not made, in return for the civility of their visit, some such [allegedly] nonsensical verses as the following are added":

> Last Christmas I turned the spit,
> I burned my fingers (I feel it yet),
> A cock sparrow flew over the table,
> The dish began to fight with the ladle.
>
> The spit got up like a naked man,
> And swore he'd fight with the dripping pan;
> The pan got up and cocked his tail,
> And swore he'd send them all to jail.
> (Hervey 1848, 189–90)

According to one source, the French hunted and killed the wren "devotionally on Twelfth Day" and then collected contributions in a stocking (Bonwick 1986, 225). Some of the wren customs recorded from France varied somewhat from those practiced elsewhere, although they still embodied the themes of sacrifice and royalty. At Carcassonne, for example, a "Wren-fête" was held on New Year's Day. Each year on 31 December, the champion of the previous year's fête took charge of summoning with a fife and drum band the young people who would take part in the activities of 1 January. Armed with a pole, the party went to the woods to try to knock down a wren. The first to succeed was crowned by the preceding year's champion, and the bird, surrounded by a garland of oak-leaves, was placed at the end of the longest perch that could be found. On 6 January the new *Roitelet* (kinglet), decorated with a Maltese cross and holding in his hand a scepter adorned with a garland of olive, oak, and mistletoe, attended mass with his companions. Following that, he went to wish a happy New Year to the municipal magistrates. If no wren had been obtained, the former *Roitelet* tossed last year's bird into the air and whoever caught it was proclaimed king (Gill 1932, 380–81). A similar custom prevailed in two other French towns, where "the inhabitants, on New Year's Day, brought a wren in solemn procession to the Prior, as their seignorial lord, in token of their fealty" (Lockley 1960, 324).

This concept of the wren as "a token of tribute" to high-ranking religious or civil authorities was also included in other French ceremonials, especially spring festivals held to encourage the association of young men and women. In one case, the prior of an abbey promised to give thirty pots of wine to the young men in exchange for bringing him a live wren. But unless the wren had nine feathers in its tail, the bargain was negated. The prior also agreed to pay a certain sum of money if a wren was brought to him at Christmas or on New Year's Day. Sometimes there was the stipulation that the wren must be "captured by an unarmed hunting party, to be produced as tribute on New Year's Day." The captor of the wren became "King of the Fête." During High Mass the "King" presented the bird to the prior, "the young people affirming at the same time that they had obtained the wren by legitimate hunting methods and not by means of a gun or a bow and arrow." In one town, newly married couples had to "visit the steward of the estate on the next Trinity Sunday after the wedding, bearing on their shoulders the large wooden receptacle in which grapes were crushed, with a wren inside" (Armstrong 1958, 145–47). In all of these situations the wren was ceremonially presented or exhibited to persons of higher rank. Such customs emphasize the great value that society attributed to the wren, reinforcing its kingly status, and indicate that the authorities sanctioned the various observances involving the bird.

At Ciotat, near Marseilles, the annual wren ceremony held at the beginning of Nivôse (23 December) involved a large assemblage of men, armed with sabers and pistols, who went to hunt the bird. The dead wren was suspended on the middle of a long pole, which was then carried by two men on their shoulders as if it were a heavy load. After the procession paraded through the streets of the city, the bird was weighed on a big balance before the men feasted. The celebrants called the bird *putois*, "polecat," or *Père de la bécasse*, "woodcock's father," because of the resemblance of the tiny brown bird's feathers to the plumage of the woodcock, which they believed was generated by the polecat (Gill 1932, 381–82; Swainson 1886, 42). Interestingly, a Yorkshire name for the wren is "woodcock pilot" (Hare 1952, 183). Lockwood indicates that this name for the wren was formerly applied to the Goldcrest because that bird was "said to precede the returning Woodcock by a couple of days" (1993, 169). The French also called the wren *Boeuf de Dieu* (beef of God) (Brand 1849, 3:195), probably in reference to sacrificial eating of the carcass.

Although the wren hunt generally involved killing the bird, this was not always the case. In Scotland the "Deckan' o' the Wren" ceremony meant catching a wren on New Year's morning, adorning its neck and legs with ribbons, and allowing it to go free. Similarly, in several areas of France the live wren caught in a hunt on Christmas Eve was presented to the priest, who blessed the bird and then released it from the church pulpit with a rose-colored ribbon attached to it following the midnight Mass. The man who caught the bird was exempted for one year from the olive tithe and was called "King of the Holidays." If women succeeded in capturing the wren, they were entitled to deride the men who had taken part in the hunt and to daub their faces with soot or mud when they caught them (Hole 1984, 163; Gill 1932, 382; Gaster 1964, 562). In Nivernais custom dictated that one of the landowners must go every year and "kneel bareheaded without sword or spurs on the threshold of the principal gate of Champ d'Ioux." While in that position he set free a wren that had been brought there for him to release (Thomas 1906, 270).

In Pembrokeshire, at Epiphany, "a little boy, with coloured paper streamers pinned to his cap, brought in a cage a wren caught for the purpose and afterwards let go" and repeated the lines "Come and make your offering / To the smallest, yet the king" (Gill 1932, 430). Or a live wren in a "Wren House" might be taken to various homes, especially those of young couples who had been married during the previous year (Hole 1984, 164).

In addition to the hunt, the procession, and the ceremony, the wren custom has been dramatized in a so-called wren play. One such play, entitled "'The Wren Boys: or the Moment of Peril,' an original drama in two acts" that had previously played in London, was performed in a Belfast theater in 1848. In act 2 "the wren boys enter confusedly, one bearing a bush with a wren in it," and sing:

> The wren, the wren, the king of all birds,
> St. Stephen's Day was caught in the furze;
> Although he is little, his family is great,
> I pray you, good landlady, give us a treat.

These lines were followed by the chorus (Swainson 1886, 37–38).

A traditional wren "folk play" that may have originated in England was enacted in Ireland. For that event the wren boys, usually young men over the age of twenty, were dressed in a grotesque manner, acting the part of "Fools in the Procession." Often the bladder of a slaughtered cow or pig, inflated and mounted on a stick, was carried by one of the men, who used it to "playfully strike onlookers." Participants often disguised themselves in such attire as "goat skins with the horns on the wearer's head." Sometimes there was "a wooden horse with two Wren Boys under it, capering about and performing various antics." Boys might be outfitted as brides and men were often costumed as women or dressed in straw. In some areas, a character called "The Wren" demanded "a trate" just as the wren boys do in their song. Members of the party were decked with ribbons and carried banners and poles. "The Wren Man, who carried the dead wren in a holly bush fastened to a pole, also wore a special costume." Some men carried swords, and mock battles were "staged between those bearing swords, the Fools and the strawboys." Such performances are believed to be derived from ancient Dionysiac ceremonials that embodied death-and-resurrection rites characteristic of the ancient civilizations of the Middle East. The folk play was probably originally a spring fertility rite that eventually was attached to the Christmas festival and then became associated with the wren procession (Armstrong 1958, 157–59). The hunting of the wren may be in certain ways "a parallel to the Mumming plays, in which the champion of darkness is slain and the world brought back to life" (Whitlock 1979, 97).

The typical wren hunt occurred in England, Wales, the Isle of Man, Ireland, and France—areas where Celtic tradition was firmly entrenched. As one source points out, these are the places "where Celtic blood is still strongest" (Potter and Sargent 1974, 296). In England, the ceremony was practiced in so many widely separated counties that it can be assumed "the practice was once current in almost every part of the country." The "archaic wren-myth" from which all the customs and their vestiges must have arisen "was probably current in Southern Gaul and Celtic Britain" (Gill 1932, 428–29). The ritual can be "tentatively traced back to Neolithic times" (Whitlock 1979, 96).

Although, as we have seen, there are some regional variations in certain details of the wren hunt, the basic pattern of the ritual, reflecting the same prevalent perception of the tiny bird, is identical wherever it occurred. Records of the wren hunt throughout time and over various areas are not detailed enough to allow analysis of the ways in which slight variations in the ceremony might be related to different characteristics of particular cultures. Armstrong, a scholar who made a thorough study of the ritual, conceded the impossibility of using a historical approach to the wren hunt and had to settle for merely mapping its distribution graphically (1958, 141–66). His analyses of wren songs reveal "the homogeneity of French and English wren traditions" and the correspondence between the rites in the two countries (1958, 149). Armstrong was generally unable to relate various elements of the wren hunt to specific societal traits, though he did comment on the French custom of ceremonially presenting the wren to persons of higher rank. He hypothesized that in this case, the "wren ceremonial represents the vestiges of a cult honoured by folk whose observances were tolerated by their superiors. If so, the ritual represents an early, submerged stratum of culture" (1958, 147). Another theory holds that the involvement of church officials and noblemen represents "vestiges of pagan springtime ceremonies calling for the offering of a live bird to the gods, or rather to the people's priest-chieftains in their role as mediators, in the course of cultic activities intended both to propitiate the gods and to celebrate or ensure the return of life to nature in the springtime" (Wentersdorf 1977, 193).

For the purposes of the present study, it is the general pattern of the wren hunt, not the regional variations, that has significance for analysis. Variations over time have not been documented in any detail. It is extremely difficult to date folk customs like the wren hunt by historical methods, and it is impossible to determine their time of origin or the point at which any aspect died out, for a tradition is a living process with neither beginning nor ending. A "national tradition, the body of group life-experience expressing itself, never fully dies but alters as any organic structure will change" (Stewart 1977, 10–11). As Armstrong explains, the multiplicity and inconsistency of the accounts dealing with the origin of the wren hunt indicate that it is a very ancient ceremonial whose beginnings have been forgotten (1958, 169). But the basic images found in the ceremony are "timeless in that they exist out of historical time or context in religion and cult." Those images are "true," in the sense that they sprang from elements of people's consciousness relating to interactions with their fellow creatures who shared the native environment. They also act as "cosmic symbols," representations of "natural laws" that were once part of the pattern of human existence" (Stewart 1977, 44).

Over the years, the wren hunt was gradually transformed from a sacred rite to a folk custom that had lost its religious meaning. And somewhere along the path of its transition, the rites that were once the domain of adult men were relegated to adolescents and children. At one point, perhaps at the time of transition, both men and children participated. E. Kermode wrote that on the Isle of Man many parties consisted of "grown-up men" whose "chorus of loud rumbles in hoarse, gruff voices . . . startle the nervous systems of the astonished inmates" of the houses outside of which they sang. "There is something very ludicrous in the queer contrast between the deep, rough basses of those men, and the shrill piping trebles of a party of children engaged in the same occupation a few doors off. It is like a chorus of bull-frogs in contrast with the squeaking of a company of mice" (1885, 161). It appears that when ceremonies are "no longer regarded as solemn rites on the punctual performance of which the welfare and even the life of the community depend, they sink gradually to the level of mummeries and pastimes, till in the final stages of degeneration they are wholly abandoned by older people, and, from having once been the most serious occupation of the sage, become at last the idle sport of children" (Flaherty 1992, 49–50). Armstrong claims that in the wren hunt, "the last degradation of male ritual has not been reached—the performance of the ceremony by little girls" (1958, 152).

Although the process of relegating the rite to children seems to fit the case of the wren hunt, the situation may not be so simple. Children, with their inferior and marginal position in the social hierarchy, may have special significance, as such groups often do in seasonal rituals when they represent status reversal. Social powerlessness may indeed make it appropriate that children play a critical role in liminal calendrical rituals such as the wren hunt. Furthermore, the annual wren ceremony marks the transition from one season to another. The notion that prosperity and good fortune in the ensuing months were dependent on demonstrating generosity during the transition period was firmly entrenched in the beliefs of many European societies. This idea explains the practice of children (and beggars) making the rounds of villages at that time, when people gave more freely because their future success depended on their charity (Flaherty 1992, 51).

Marcel Mauss, in his classic study of societal exchanges, *The Gift,* cites an old European custom in which "masked children go from house to house begging" for food and "none dare refuse them." This form of presenting goods in response to solicitation, as exemplified in the wren procession, may reflect or be a remnant of what the noted sociologist calls the ancient process of "contractual sacrifice," in which "the gods who give and repay are there to give something great in exchange for something small." "Sacrificial destruction," Mauss notes, "implies giving something that is to be repaid." His theory indicates that "alms are the result on the one hand of a moral idea about gifts and wealth and on the other of an idea about sacrifice" (1967, 13–15). Thus the sacrifice as carried out in killing the wren may have a related symbolic counterpart in the householders who provide goods and money to the wren parties.

In some areas, including parts of rural Ireland, the wren hunt was practiced largely in its traditional form until the mid-twentieth century (Palmer 1991, 129). Even in the decades prior to that, however, loss of old beliefs, industrialization and the consequent alienation of people from nature, and changing attitudes toward animals had begun to seriously erode the rites. Perhaps because of the difficulty of capturing a wren, but also due to humanitarian concerns, replacements were used. Now and then, when a wren could not be obtained, "or would be objected to for some reason, a robin or some other small bird [was] substituted" (Armstrong 1958, 155). According to a Manx historian, "a luckless sparrow" could be used by the wren boys who "endeavor to palm [it] off on the simple householder and his family (whose knowledge of ornithology may be but limited), as a very fine specimen of the wren species." He explains that "the beautiful golden wren is preferred to the common one; but I have seen a common sparrow do duty instead of either, when a wren could not be procured" (Kermode 1885, 160–62). In some areas of Ireland the tail feathers of a robin or wren were substituted for the bird itself, which prompted one commentator to observe that "in a severe winter a robin with a tail is rarely seen" (O'Sullivan 1991, 32).

Armstrong notes that "where the killing of the wren is disapproved the [Irish] Boys carry a potato with feathers stuck into it to resemble a wren, or some other object, such as a celluloid budgerigar" (1958, 155). A stuffed wren or one made of straw also might be used (Foley 1963, 62). In recent times on the Isle of Man a dummy made of feathers or just a bunch of feathers enclosed within the wooden hoops have been substituted for the wren (Stenning 1950, 274; Hunt 1954, 70). An Irish informant revealed that in his area the wren boys carried "an ensign with a bird, with a picture of a wran on it." He explained: "They had no natural bird. It wouldn't be easy, you know, gettin' a wren; a wren is a very hard wee bird to catch. But they'd have often a wee bird on a picture there on a box. The money would go in that box" (Glassie 1983, 72–73). Describing St. Stephen's Day, when "the children of the country go on the wren," as "one of the most festive, fun-filled days of the year," a contemporary book about Christmas in Ireland provides patterns and instructions for making a wren out of construction paper (Zeleny 1985, 66–67).

An elderly Manx man questioned in 1950 said, "I well remember Hunt the Wren when I was young. It was really something to look forward to." But because "a good number of people protested against killing the wren for this occasion, the last years I played Hunt the Wren we had no bird. With no bird on the stang the play seemed to lose its value as an omen of good luck. I think it was on account of when there wasn't a wren on the stang there were no feathers to give away for luck, for when the people of the house gave money to the boys they expected a feather plucked out of the wren" ("Manx Museum Folk Life" 1950, 3).

Two firsthand accounts from the Isle of Man illustrate the deterioration of the custom in recent times. One informant revealed that "Hunt the Wren was a great time for some old people. And when we were on the road between Baaregarrow and Cronk-y-Voddy we would be met by a character called Willie the Fairy who had a double-barrel gun, and when we went to a house that he thought he would get a drop of whiskey from, he would accompany us and fire the gun. And if taken into the house and treated well, when he came out he would let off the second barrel. And by the time we arrived at the hotel in Glen Helen, Willie would be in very good form to tell some of his fairy tales" ("Manx Museum Folk Life" 1959, 4).

Another narrative related:

The Hunt the Wren was common enough in my young days. I've done a bit of that myself. The last one I saw round St. Johns way was fifty or so years ago [about 1909]. The children from the Glenfaba Mill came round I remember. There was a gang of us young fellows one night decided we'd go out on the Hunt the Wren for a bit of fun for ourselves. A few of us had had a pint or two of ale, and we hadn't a real Hunt the Wren. We got a big gorse bush and I remember there was an old dead cat in it, and an old dead fowl. A woman we knew had put ribbons on it and that was what we were carrying with us. We were going to a few houses and the people were giving us something just so as to get rid of us. We were carrying on and making a great deal of noise and not everyone wanted that.

The party then went to a home whose owner, "Old Gale," had three daughters and a nephew asleep in the house, and they sang "Hunt the Wren," substituting the name of the owner's nephew in the Robin the Bobbin song in order "to annoy him." "He was awful mad but didn't dare come down after us. At last Old Gale himself came down from the house shouting and waving a big stick. We stood our ground, though, and when he saw who it was he dropped his stick. 'I thought it was them Foxdale fellas,' he said. After that we all got asked in—that was what we wanted" ("Manx Museum Folk Life" 1959, 4–5).

Welsh folklorist Trefor Owen admits that ancient customs like the wren hunt, whose origin and purpose were forgotten, often became "excuses for collecting money or drink." But he explains that such ceremonies have acquired a specific social function in recent times. The Christmas holidays mark the end of the year—"the season for relaxation when the work on the land made the least demand on the countryman." Rituals like the wren hunt, "containing age-old features of forgotten significance, gave an approved means of entering the houses of neighbors in a culture in which there were few public assemblies— at least in the heart of winter—in which the convivial spirit of the season could be released." Such celebrations, with the procession and singing of verses, "institutionalized the house-visit" and thus were continued for that reason after their religious import had been lost. Going from door to door to seek gifts of drink, food, and money helps to reinforce and maintain feelings of community among country folk and represents a new way of celebrating the winter season that reflects changing social conditions (1959, 68–69).

HUMANE CONCERNS

The issue of cruelty has influenced the evolution of the wren hunt in modern times. Early observers as well as contemporary writers frequently characterize the wren hunt as inhumane or barbaric, and the thread of compassion is often woven into many firsthand accounts. Mary Corbett Harris, for example, related that her mother, who observed the wren hunt as a child in Wales, remembered "how upset she was about the wren" (1980, 76). Writing just after the turn of the century, P. G. Ralfe recalled that "tender-hearted householders" on the Isle of Man "refused their contributions to parties with a dead bird" (1905, 39). (This is in contrast to the 1970 statement of a Manx resident: "My father remembered the [dead] wrens, and one man he knew would not give the children any money unless they had a dead wren, in fact he bought some of the dead wrens from them" ["Manx Museum Folk Life" 1970, 4].) An Irish woman admitted that on St. Stephen's Day during her childhood the girls often "made sure the boys didn't actually kill a wren" as they were supposed to do (Parry 1972, 35). In recent times a more humane practice called "Feeding the Wren" was established in Ireland to supersede the wren hunt. A live wren is caught and placed in a cage, where it perches on top of a bush, and "money is solicited avowedly for the starving wren" (Wernecke n.d., 50). Sympathetic feeling for the "little eagle-conquering wren" who has been martyred is expressed in the final verse of a 1964 Irish poem portraying "The Wren-Boy":

> He knows dominion now
> And leaves behind
> The heavy spade, the ponderous plough
> For glory in the mind
> And blood; a man whose pride
> In stick and drum commemorates
> The bird that died.
>   (Kennelly 1989, 78)

In England, the wren hunt was "put down by authorities" at about the middle of the nineteenth century (Dyer's 1876, 314). The elaborate wren-hunt customs of France were "abolished at the Revolution, revived at the Restoration and again suppressed after 1830" (Armstrong 1958, 145). The Welsh custom persisted "down to the nineties of the nineteenth century, and possibly later" (Peate 1936, 1). The Irish hunt was forbidden "on the score of cruelty" in 1845 (Morris n.d., 133), but "still linger[ed] on" in some areas (Swainson 1886, 38). The custom of killing the wren continued to flourish in many regions during the closing years of the nineteenth century, and in some places it persisted well into the first quarter of the twentieth century, in spite of opposition. W. Walter Gill wrote in 1932 that "the Wren-custom cannot safely be termed extinct in Ireland" (1932, 402). Accounts written in the middle of the twentieth century indicate that the Irish custom of hunting the wren still continued (Opie and Opie 1961, 288; Iles 1989, 74), but there is no way to determine at what point the killing of birds was eliminated from the ceremony. A 1994 autobiographical memoir of childhood holiday celebrations in Ireland recounts the excitement of observing the oddly costumed wren boys who made exhausting treks through snow-covered country to collect donations, but the author gives absolutely no mention of the wren itself and provides no reference to the bird's meaning in the event (Taylor 1994, 122–28).

Among the voices raised against slaughtering the bird in Ireland was that of William Drummond, author of *The Rights of Animals*, published in 1838. He explained that it is understandable that some animals might be "objects of antipathy, and consequently of injurious treatment, on account of their uninviting appearance or their real or imaginary noxious properties." But the idea that animals "of the most beautiful and inoffensive kind should be thus regarded, and persecuted to death from motives of political or religious bigotry, may seem to the humane reader a folly and wickedness too enormous to merit credit. . . . What shall we think of the 'most diminutive of birds' being hunted and stoned, for a supposed political offense of one or two of its progenitors above seven score years before it was born?" He relates the prevalent Irish tradition that when James II's forces were about to surprise King William's army early in the morning some wrens, attracted

> by the fragments of the preceding night's meal, alighted on the head of a drum which had served for a table, and the noise of their bills in the act of picking awoke the drummer, who instantly beat to arms, and saved William's army from defeat. The wren accordingly has been, ever since, a prime favorite with the Orange party, and an object of persecution to the friends of James, who on an appointed day have organised bands of ruffians, young and old, who go forth armed "with staves" to beat the hedges, and with stones to pelt this innocent and elegant little bird. St. Stephen's is the day preferred for this manly achievement; as if those engaged in it were ambitious of personating in a small way, the murderers of the first Christian martyr. Had the little birds that actually awoke the drummer been taken in fact and executed, their punishment would have been sufficiently truculent; but to visit the offence, supposing it to be such, on all their race, is an enormity unmatched even by that of the amiable youth, who, in the insurrection of 1798, hanged a drake, because the hand of the Creator had adorned its beautiful neck and head with the national colour, the eye-refreshing green of the "emerald isle."
>
> (1838, 142–43)

Drummond refers here to a legend that is one of a number of similar explanations that were grafted on the old wren custom and that will be discussed in the next chapter.

In the middle of the nineteenth century, John Brand wrote that in England the wren is "to this day hunted by boys . . . merely for *amusement and cruelty,* . . . so that there the practice has not even the excuse of superstition; and the poor little 'king of birds' dies unwept, unhonored, and unsung" (1849, 3: 197). An early twentieth century admirer of the "pigmy bird" noted, "Happily for the preservation of this pretty, restless little bird, the stupid and wicked custom of hunting it at Christmas-tide is almost extinct, and will, I hope, soon be entirely so. In whatever way the custom originated, nothing good could come of it. Quite the reverse, it fostered a spirit of wanton destruction, which, unfortunately, is already too prominent a characteristic of the average boy, and it was a gross injustice to the smallest and least harmful of all our feathered friends" (Gibson 1904, 156–57).

RELATION TO ETHOS

Changing world views were intimately linked to the growing disapproval of the wren hunt. Our ancestors generally did not perceive the separation between religious concerns and ordinary life that is found in Western culture today. All activities were considered religious in the sense that they were part of the pattern of life. Nor was there a sharp distinction between natural and supernatural. Far back in time, when the wren ceremony involved the sacrifice of a sacred animal for a holy purpose, the ideologies that guided human life were totally different from those in the modern mechanized and secularized world. Today, when multitudes of animals are slaughtered without regard to any religious principle, but rather for utilitarian reasons alone, it is difficult to comprehend the connection that once existed in certain cases between sacredness and killing. Our separation from the living environment and our perception of humanity as above and outside of nature have estranged us from the basic beliefs that were once embedded in the wren ceremony. We are virtually divorced from the legacy of our forbears' dependency on nature and its seasons, and few in today's industrialized world hold the conviction that rites and ceremonies can change the course of nature.

The influential seventeenth-century philosopher and mathematician René Descartes argued that there is a profound separation between humankind and the animal kingdom. His ideas became fundamental to the ethos of the Western world, and, as the concept termed Cartesianism, they are still to a large extent ingrained in our culture. Descartes asserted that there is a sharp distinction between body and mind, physical being and soul, and man and beast. Unlike people, animals are composed of matter governed by mechanistic principles. They possess no consciousness, no language, no pain sensations, and no souls. Only human beings, specially created by God, have awareness, sentience, language, and immortal souls (1979, 74–76). Thus according to the resulting world view constructed by "Western Scientific Man" during the past three-and-a-half centuries, "the Scientist as hero confronts as his object and prey a world of nature from which all traces of mind or spirit have disappeared, leaving in their place what is understood to be nothing more than a vast and immensely complex machine. Mastery and possession of this enormous object" was "the proper destiny of scientific humanity" (Willis 1994, xxvi).

In contrast, there was once no sharp demarcation between animals and people; rather, the same spirit animated all forms of life. Animals could possess knowledge and capacities that were equal to or superior to those of people. Druid belief, "the product of a very long human tradition extending back to the Ice Age and beyond," embraced the idea of "interpenetration—of deity, man and earth seen as one." The "feeling for the earth penetrated by divine forces" and the intermingling of all forms of life was "still as vivid for the Celts as for earlier people. An intense sense of oneness with animal life was also present" (Bancroft 1987, 107). The Celts felt a sense of participation in and partnership with nature, and their art and poetry reveal an unmistakable strong "identification with the natural world in all its seasonal facets" (Rutherford 1993, 208).

Death was not the end of life, but led to rebirth, for there was the certainty of life in the next world, not only for human beings but for other living creatures as well. Animals, like people, possessed souls, and everything that died would be reborn. The soul would never perish, but after death would pass from one body to another. The Druids had a firm, unshakable belief in reincarnation and the transmigration of souls (Hartley 1986, 93). For the Celts, death "simply marked the halfway stage in a long life" (Fife 1991, 44). Their ethos embraced the idea of the "Eternal Return," a prominent belief among certain preindustrial societies, which represented the metaphor of birth, growth, death, and rebirth. The cyclical view of time reflected the rising and setting of the sun, the phases of the moon, the procession of seasons, and the life stages of plants, animals, and human beings. According to that belief, there is neither an absolute beginning or an end, but "eternal recurrence for all time to come" (Brockway 1993, 53). This idea is in direct opposition to the Judaeo-Christian belief in a definite beginning at the moment of creation and a predicted ultimate ending of the universe. The concept of cyclical time contrasts with the notion of linear time that is embraced by the modern Western world.

As early agricultural societies were familiar with the cycle of plant life, they drew the conclusion that all living things returned to the Underworld in the earth, where they would be regenerated. People knew that the engendering of life depends upon the taking of life. In the societies in which the wren hunt flowered, a single animal would be looked upon as the embodiment of the ancestral spirit of its kind. The life of that spirit was maintained through sacrifice by generation after generation: "The animal would be reverently sacrificed in order that it would live again. It embodied the soul of each individual in the group" (Bancroft 1987, 27–28).

To understand the wren hunt and similar rituals, it is necessary to consider the whole question of attitudes toward the individual as opposed to the species or group to which it belongs. Today, individualism flourishes both in the way human beings in the developed Western world think of themselves and, to some extent, in the way they think of animals. For most preindustrialized people such as the Celts, however, the individual life generally was not considered really distinct from the group, and thus was not the main focus of concern. "They related to life rather than to individual lives" (Stewart 1977, 37). Such a mindset would dictate that when a divine animal is sacrificed, "the life thus diverted from one channel will flow . . . more freshly and freely in a new one." The "slain animal will revive and enter on a new term of life with all the spring and energy of youth" (Frazer 1963, 579–80). An individual wren, then, would be thought of as incarnate in all wrens in existence. Thus the sacrifice of single birds would not harm the population. It was the species that received homage, not the individual. Because there is no death, the essence of "wrenness" would continue as the cycle of life goes on.

Currently, some segments of Western society generally attribute more value to certain individual animals, but the two viewpoints—primary consideration of the population or species versus primary regard for the individual—are a source of controversy in human-animal relationships. Those who place the emphasis on the interests of individual animals endorse or are members of various humane or animal protection groups, animal welfare groups, or animal rights organizations.

People who favor the population or species, on the other hand, sanction or belong to ecologically oriented organizations that endorse sacrifice of individuals to ensure the survival or well-being of a species whenever the interests of the two are in conflict. This broader viewpoint, which embraces the ecosystem or even the "biosphere" when confronted by a dilemma, is a modern parallel, perhaps, of the attitudes that originated and perpetuated the traditional wren hunt—in which living individuals were once gladly sacrificed for the good of the greater community, to promote the all-important fertility of the earth and the well-being of the entire complex of life. But the passing of the ages with the rise of human control over nature, resulting in changing ideologies and new educational systems, helped to shift the emphasis from the web of life to the individual strands in that web. With the loss of old beliefs, people gradually began to deplore the annual killing of wrens, and civil and religious authorities eventually banned ceremonies involving the ritual death of the tiny bird.

CONTEMPORARY ASPECTS: THE ISLE OF MAN

The custom of "hunt-the-wren," as the Manx people invariably call it, was extremely significant on the Isle of Man, and it was once carried out in all parts of the island. In 1903 and 1904, P. G. Ralfe found that there were still traditional hunt-the-wren parties in many villages and towns (1905, 39). Resident folklorist Margaret Killip states that the hunt, "possibly the oldest surviving custom in existence," persisted on the island "into the 1920s and '30s, even later in some places," and notes that it is still carried out in Peel (without live birds) (1975, 184, 186). The Manx people continue to take an interest in this custom and to perform vestiges of the ancient ceremony. I made a trip to the Isle of Man in order to talk directly to Manx informants about the wren hunt and to consult the archives there. Although I visited virtually all parts of the island and spent considerable time in the museum and library located in the capital city of Douglas, I concentrated most of my fieldwork on the town of Peel. There hunt-the-wren is "a Boxing Day tradition" that has "continued unbroken since early times" ("Peel Keeps 'Hunt the Wren'" 1973, 1).

My first stop was Peel Hill, perfect habitat for the wren and the prime area in that vicinity where the little bird was once hunted each 26 December. Then, as now, the "steep, shaded, and overhung bank," which according to ornithologist P. G. Ralfe is the wren's "favourite

Wren habitat, Peel, Isle of Man, where wrens were once "caught in the furze" on St. Stephen's Day. Photos by author.

home" (1905, 38), attracted members of the species. I was able to find and observe several wrens in their native haunts and to study their tiny brown forms with the characteristic cocked tails. I heard for myself at close range the loud and melodious song that has made the wren so conspicuous and noteworthy in spite of its minuscule size. From the inhabitants of Peel I learned that it was in this very location, in 1910 or 1911, that the last live wrens were caught for the wren ceremony. After that time, they told me, as had been reported in the *Peel City Guardian,* no wrens were captured for the official annual hunt. According to a Peel resident, in subsequent years the searchers bagged only hares instead of the increasingly scarce and elusive wrens. When the subject of hunt-the-wren is raised, Manx people are quick to point out that they no longer catch and kill wrens for the occasion. As one longtime resident expressed it, "Nobody thinks of killing a wren for the bush now-a-days, thank goodness!"

An eighty-seven-year-old Manx native whom I interviewed participated in the wren hunt at the age of ten and remembered, "By the time we were twelve or thirteen, we thought we were too grown up to do it. But when we were little, all the children looked forward to it. We made two wooden hoops, like a cross, decorated with streamers and with artificial flowers at the top. I went from house to house and usually got a penny. We sang and recited the words to the wren song when we knocked on the door, and sometimes collected a shilling or two. We didn't kill a wren, though. My father was death on that. He often went hunting and killed hares, partridges, and grouse, but he wouldn't shoot that little bird, he wouldn't kill a wren. It's tiny, a different bird."

Time and time again smiles spread over the faces of the people I talked with when they expressed their feelings for the wren: "It's only a little bird, a pretty little bird—poor thing!" Today the "token wren" used in the festivities is some sort of artificial representation. It may be a toy robin, "a Christmas tree bird painted brown," or an imitation that is usually a "migrant from Taiwan." A bunch of feathers often suffices. "There is so much ivy you don't see the bird anyway," one participant said. Currently, instead of the wren's feather, one of the colored paper ribbons from the wren's bush may be given as a token of good luck to anyone who gives coins to the children.

Even without the real bird that once embodied its meaning, "many Manx people still feel it has not been a proper Christmas if there hasn't been a 'Hunt-tha' at the door." As the "longest surviving Manx Christmas custom," it "still clings tenuously to life on St. Stephen's Day

Manx First Day Cover with Stamp Depiciting Wren Boys, Christmas, 1978.

morning in Peel" (Caine 1987, 15). As a tribute to the event, on 18 October 1978, the Isle of Man Post Office released a beautiful five-pence commemorative stamp for Christmas of that year. It features a colored drawing of four wren boys with their wren bush, encircled by a garland of holly. A Manx first day cover issued in 1980 features a portrayal of the wren and robin, with a stamp honoring each of the birds. Christmas cards sent by residents of the island still often depict the traditional wren boys.

A few enthusiastic families in Peel keep the ceremony alive by performing hunt-the-wren every 26 December. "The parents push their children into it," one informant said. But others maintain that the children enjoy the activity a great deal and look forward to it all year: "They like performing with their friends and feel they are helping to preserve the custom." Local newspapers urge participation: "Children are encouraged to make a 'Wren Bush' and learn the 'Hunt the Wren' song to keep up the old tradition of St. Stephen's Day" ("Hunt the Wren on Boxing Day" 1987, 19). Citizens are often reminded that "Hunt-the-Wren is an unbroken tradition on the Isle of Man" ("Ancient Game Revived" 1991, 11). Observers point out that "the Longhouse is usually packed with people for this happy occasion," and that there are activities for adults as well as youngsters ("Hunting the Wren" 1982, 10).

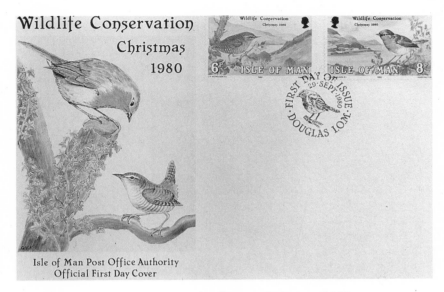

Isle of Man Post Office Authority
Official First Day Cover

First Day Cover, Isle of Man, Christmas, 1980.

When interest in the event lags, as it did in 1988, writers warn that hunt-the-wren will become "just another page in our history books unless the people of Peel and the Island make a determined effort to see that the St. Stephen's Day tradition of Hunting the Wren is encouraged." In that year, the idea was suggested that the custom was not supported by "local authorities and tourist organizations, probably because [it doesn't] fall within the tourist season" ("Hunt the Wren Must Be Preserved" 1988, 10). But in the past, organizations like the Peel Vikings, "determined to stop the decline," have sponsored the celebration ("Hunt the Wren Event" 1972, 2). Committees for the event are congratulated, for "what a pity it would be if we no longer saw the children with their gaily decorated poles and heard them chanting 'We'll hunt the wren'" ("Hunt the Wren Contest Success" 1973, 11).

A Manx teacher told me, "As soon as interest in the custom begins to wane and it becomes endangered, people here put more into it." He explained that his grandfather's generation "despised Manx things and had killed off interest in anything Manx. The language was not felt to be sophisticated enough, and was all but lost. Children were punished for speaking the native tongue. At that time, customs like the wren hunt were considered uncouth and were frowned upon. Now it's different. The island population is fifty-fifty, Manx and English, and

Old sketch from contemporary Christmas card, Isle of Man, depicting Wren Boys.

the Manx are afraid they won't be the majority. The Manx language is now taught in schools. And they're bringing back the hunt-the-wren tradition."

A woman from Douglas who is active in the event said that in her city there are now "forty people—musicians, singers, and dancers—doing hunt-the-wren. They make wren bushes decorated with ivy and ribbon streamers and use colored plastic birds. The numbers of participants are increasing all the time, and children are being taught Manx customs in school. The same is true in Ramsey."

Generally, no special clothes are worn for the contemporary wren ceremony on St. Stephen's Day, but when the dancing groups give demonstration performances at other times, as they sometimes do, costumes are used. Typically, on 26 December the youngsters, accompanied by a few adults, parade around the town of Peel singing and dancing at various stops along the way. Performances are also held in a community hall, the Viking Longhouse. The children do the dance they have been taught, and the spectators often join in. One routine consists of groups

Hunt-the-Wren Ceremony,
Peel, Isle of Man, 1990s.
Photos by Jane Killey.

Participants dance around the wren bush, Peel, Isle of Man.
Photo by Jane Killey.

of children and adults who hold hands in a circle. Someone stands in
the center supporting the wren bush. Each participant in turn dances
up to the pole of the wren bush and "shakes a fist at the wren," reflecting the Manx idea that the wren is an evil spirit. Dancers and singers
keep time to the continual beat of the dollan, a Manx drum.

Helg Yn Dreean, "a progressive ring dance for as many as will," is
described in *Dances of Mann* as the one "danced formerly by the Wren
Boys when the wren was buried by torchlight on St. Stephen's Night."
At one stage of this routine, participants "honour the bush." During
the performance, "half the boys would be dressed as women, with one
odd 'woman,' called the 'Ben-treoghe yn Dreean' (Widow of the Wren),
who wandered in and out of the dance, finally spinning round and
round with the 'bush.'" Today this dance has been transformed into a
"dance-game" for boys and girls in which an odd girl tries to capture a
partner at each progression. The girl who is finally left without a partner has to dance with the bush (Thie n.d., 13). The routine somewhat
resembles "musical arms" (or "musical chairs"). Singing the ancient
wren songs is an important feature, and children work hard ahead of
time to memorize the many verses of those traditional rhymes and
chants.

Dancer holding wren bush, Peel, Isle of Man. Photos by Jane Killey.

The events of hunt-the-wren are competitive. Judging takes place to determine the most skillful performance of the dance, the most authentic singing of the wren song, and the best decorated wren pole. The traditional form of two hoops crossing each other at right angles held up by a long stick must form the basis of the display. Manx informants said they were not familiar with other ways of carrying the bird, such as the use of wren boxes or wren houses. Colored ribbons are still required, and greenery, real or artificial, such as holly or ivy, should be attached. One winner's hoops were praised for containing "richly-berried holly" ("Hunt the Wren" 1972, 6). Feathers are added for luck— usually turkey feathers. Sometimes the token wren is scored as well; one former judge told me he took marks off for displaying a robin instead of a wren. The program is arranged so that prizes are awarded not just to the winners in different categories, but to all the children who participate. After the dancing, if weather permits, participants go out and sing at people's doorsteps, asking for money. The collection may be added to the dance club's treasury or the funds may be donated to charitable organizations. In 1971, the Peel hunt-the-wren raised money for the Manx Society for the Prevention of Cruelty to Animals ("Hunt the Wren Organized" 1972, 5). In 1993, contributions totalling £48.92

collected by the dancers in Peel between 10:00 A.M. and noon were applied to help defray the cost of a children's playground in that town.

With all of its changes over time, the wren-hunt ritual generally still includes singing of the ancient songs that encapsulate and preserve a tradition whose origins reach far back in time. Because "the folksong is an organic and unconscious development that persists independently of written material" (Stewart 1977, 50), much can be learned about the meaning of the wren ritual through study of the words of the associated songs. In many cases, surmises can be made that illuminate the complex and enduring symbolism contained in the rhymes. In some other instances, the phrases may defy analysis and remain cryptic—not because they are devoid of meaning, but because the key to that meaning is not readily available. Folklorist Alan Dundes asserts that "whatever is contained in a folkloric text is meaningful—even if we do not always have full insight into what the meanings may be. . . . Why would individuals bother to remember something and repeat it with such gusto if it had no meaning? It seems clear that if an item remains in tradition, it must have meaning for the carriers of the tradition" (1980, 39).

As explained by folklore scholar Jay Mechling, "Song texts are revealing because they are traditional and artistic. They come to change in response to the folk's thoughts and feelings. When the songs settle into relatively unchanging formulas and texts, we know that the songs are satisfying some sort of psychological or sociological 'needs' of the folk who hear them and pass them on through performance" (personal communication, 1995). The wren songs do indeed shed light on the deep symbolic meanings of the wren hunt as that ritual evolved out of people's perceptions of the wren and the bird's real and imagined relationship with both the human and the natural realm.

WREN-HUNT SONGS

Singing is an integral part of the wren hunt and wren ceremony, and there are many versions of the music and words of the wren songs, which express concepts and themes embedded in the rites. The most familiar of the verses that were sung to householders to solicit money or treats is:

> The wren, the wren, the king of all birds,
> St. Stephen's Day was caught in the furze;
> Although he is little, his family's great,
> I pray you, good landlady, give us a treat.

FIG. 78. The Song of the wren boys as sung in Cork city in 1946. Words and music transcribed by Mrs. J. O'Kelly.

Song of the Wren Boys, Cork city, 1946. Courtesy of Patrick Armstrong for the Estate of Edward A. Armstrong.

A Manx version promises blissful reward for generosity: "And if your trate [treat] be of the best, / In heaven we hope your soul will rest" (Kermode 1902, 191). And an Irish variant resembles a benediction:

> God bless the mistress of this house,
> A golden chain around her neck,
> And if she's sick or if she's sore
> The Lord have mercy on her soul.
> (Armstrong 1958, 156)

Other stanzas specify the singers' hopes for coins: "Knock at the knocker, ring at the bell, / Please gi's a copper for singing so well" (Armstrong 1958, 156); "My box, it would speak, if it had but a tongue, / And two or three shillings would do it no wrong" (Swainson 1886, 37); "I have a little box under me arm, / A tuppence or penny'll do it no harm" (Langstaff and Langstaff 1985, 128–29). An Irish song threatens revenge if the wren boys' desires are not satisfied:

> Money I want, money I crave.
> If you don't give me money,
> I'll sweep yous all to your grave,
> And bury the wren at your door.
> (Glassie 1983, 72)

And some lyrics reveal the singers' disappointment if not properly compensated: "But if you draw it of the small / It won't agree with the wren-boys at all" (Swainson 1886, 37).

Sometimes funds are solicited ostensibly to be presented to the wren itself, as in a song from Waterford:

> To Mr. —— we've brought the Wran,
> He is the best gentleman in the land:
> Put in your hand, pull out your purse.
> And give us something for the poor Wran!!
> (Swainson 1886, 37–38)

Giving gifts of value specifically to the bird relates to the old concept of honoring the wren as a sacrificial victim. The practice of sacrifice typically involved paying homage to the creature sacrificed, either before or after its death. In some cases, too, money was requested for the purpose of the wren's burial, implying the importance and solemnity of the coming interment: "A penny or two to bury the wran" (O'Sullivan 1991, 33).

In contrast, some songs merely express the desire of the participants for liquid refreshment: "A drop just to drink, it would drown melancholy" (Swainson 1886, 37). Or, more specifically, "A bottle of whiskey and a glass of beer" (Macmillan 1926, 162).

Certain verses detail the great effort hunters have put forth to catch the wren and the obstacles they encountered in the hunt:

> We followed the wren three miles or more,
> Three miles or more, three miles or more,
> Through hedges and ditches and heaps of snow,
> At six o'clock in the morning.

The lyrics proceed to describe finding and killing the quarry: "We hunted him up and we hunted him down, / And the best of the wran boys knocked him down" (Read 1916, 259). Lines of another song reveal how the wren was killed and then brought back for all to see, indicating that the sacrifice is for everyone:

> As I went out to hunt and all,
> I met a wren upon a wall,
> Up with me wattle and gave him a fall,
> And brought him here to show you all.
> (Langstaff and Langstaff 1985, 128–29)

The meanings of a very different type of song that describes turning the spit seem obscure until they are related to the wren lore they express. A Manx song reveals: "Last Christmas Day I turned the spit, / I burnt my finger (I feel it yet)" (Kermode 1902, 191). And an almost identical song from Wales explains:

> On Christmas Day I turned the spit,
> I burned my fingers, I feel it yet:
> Between my finger and my thumb
> I eat the roast meat every crumb.
> (Swainson 1886, 38)

These songs celebrate a magical quality of wrens. An old belief holds that when wrens are put upon a spit over a fire the stick revolves of its own accord: "It is much to be marvelled at the little bird called a Wren, being fastened to a stick of hazel newly gathered, doth turn about and roast itself" (Armstrong 1958, 176). One man told of actually witnessing this phenomenon in Rome, where "an eminent Cardinal . . . furnished the bird and a hazel rod for a spit" (Montagu 1831, 571–72). This tradition also involved the robin. On Candlemas the French country people would "kill a cock redbreast, run a spit of *hazel* wood through the body, and place it before the fire, when it at once begins to turn of itself." The hazel tree was "sacred to Donar," and was "regarded as an actual embodiment of the lightning," which explains the link between the bird and the fire (Swainson 1886, 17). The hazel is also known as the sacred tree of wisdom in Irish mythology. According to an ancient "calendar of the Trees," the Hazel tree comes at the turning of the year and in some circumstances can "represent the spirit or soul" of a slain victim (Stewart 1977, 32). Thus its relationship to sacrifice becomes clear.

A somber and foreboding Welsh song, with a corresponding meter that differs from the more lighthearted versions, is suited to the search, capture, and death of the tiny bird:

> Little wren is the man,
> About him there is quite a stir,
> There's an inquest about him
> To-night everywhere.
>
> He was captured, the rascal,
> Last night with rejoicings,
> In a snug, pretty chamber,
> And his brothers thirteen.
>
> The stronghold was broken,
> The young man was taken,
> And placed 'neath a shroud
> In a fair motley bier.

The idea of death and rebirth is poignantly expressed in a subsequent stanza:

> Jenny wrens have grown scarce,
> They have flown to the valley,
> But they will come back by
> The old meadow-paths.
> (Gill 1932, 389)

A song from the Isle of Man embodies the endemic concept of the wren as evil victim:

> Away to the woods, says Dick to Tom,
> Away to the woods, says every one.
> What to do there, ye merry Manx men?
> To hunt to the death the wicked witch-wren.
> (Gill 1932, 385)

Occasionally other traditions mingle with the wren hunt, as demonstrated in verses such as:

> Thou shalt have dinner of apples and flour
> That came from the orchard this morn of St. Stephen,
> Thou shalt have dinner of green leaves of bay
> That came from the garden so early this morning,
> Thou shalt have dinner on shining white stones
> That came from the brook after supper.
> (Gill 1932, 390)

The apples refer to wassail, a treat made with cakes, apples, and sugar that was enjoyed on Twelfth Night in Wales. When the wassail was taken to various homes, especially those in which the occupants were recently married, a wren was carried by the party. Verses sung by the wassailers indicated: "We have a remarkable bier, with wrens under the sheet, / And a fine orchard of apples in couples above it." Sometimes the wassail party took around a *perllan*—a small rectangular board with a circle marked in the center and an apple fixed at each corner. Within the circle was a tree containing a miniature bird. The participants sang a song that included the lines "And with us we have a *perllan* with a little wren flying in it; / He is the ruler of all birds." These two couplets exemplify use of the wren ceremony "in a modified and subdued form" as it was added to another custom—that of wassailing (Owen 1959, 59–60).

Various long, complex hunt-the-wren songs with many different verses are part of the ceremony on the Isle of Man and in other parts of the British Isles. These rhymes, consisting of repetitive questions and answers, refer to "Robin the Bobbin," as well as other names. In many Manx towns and villages, "the name of the principal farmer and most eccentric person in the parish were often chosen" for use in the chants (Kermode 1885, 163). Examples of these verses are:

> We hunted the wren for Robin the Bobbin,
> We hunted the wren for Jack of the Can;
> We hunted the wren for Robin the Bobbin,
> We hunted the wren for every one.
>
> > (Swainson 1886, 39)

And:

> We'll away to the woods, says Robin to Bobbin;
> We'll away to the woods, says Richard to Robin;
> We'll away to the woods, says Jack o' the Land;
> We'll away to the woods, says every one.
>
> We'll hunt the wren, says Robin the Bobbin.
> (Repeating as above)
>
> > (Kermode 1885, 162–63)

Interpretations of Robin the Bobbin range from sacred to profane: "Cock Robin represents the divine king who is sacrificed" to bring fertility to the land, or "Robin the Bobbin" could refer to a nursery rhyme character "with an enormous appetite that could not be satisfied" (Howard 1995, 36). In the latter guise, Robin the Bobbin starts out eating a crumpet, proceeds to eat a slice of meat, a pigeon, and a mare, and then even after consuming a tower, a steeple, and a belfry, still is not satisfied. In traditional rhymes, Robin the Bobbin is also known for shooting the wren with his bow and arrow. In some versions, Robin the Bobbin, or "Cock Robin," was killed by the wren but rose again (Iles 1986, 93–105). The use of "Robin the Bobbin" in wren song lyrics has some other rich and diverse meanings, and analysis of those meanings will be discussed in several contexts in chapter 4.

Subsequent verses of this chanting type of wren song involve extreme exaggeration and are very significant in articulating the deeper meanings of the wren ceremony. Embedded themes extol the huge size of the bird and the necessity for herculean measures to kill and cook it, as well as revealing the wren's association with royalty and the ultimate apportionment of its sacrificial carcass:

> I see him! I see him! says Robin the Bobbin
> [*these lines are repeated as above, and for each line
> that follows, "says Robin the Bobbin" is added*]
> Where is he, where is he? —
> In yonder green bush, —

How shall we get him down? —
With sticks and stones, —
He's dead! He's dead! —
How shall we get him home, —
We'll hire a cart, —
Whose cart shall we hire? —
Johnny Bill Fell's, —
Who will stand driver? —
Filly the Tweet, —
   He's home! he's home! —
How shall we get him boil'd? —
In the brewery pan, —
How shall we get him in? —
With iron bars and a rope, —
He is in, he is in! —
He's boil'd! he's boil'd! —
How shall we get him out? —
With a long pitchfork, —
   He's out, he's out! —
Who's to sit at the dinner? —
The King and the Queen, —
How shall we get him eat? —
With knives and forks, —
   He is eat! He is eat! —
The eyes for the blind, —
The legs for the lame, —
The pluck for the poor, —
The bones for the dogs, —
   The wren, the wren, the King of all birds, etc.
(Kermode 1885, 162–63)

A similar song includes a verse beginning "She's down, she's down, says Robin to Bobbin," followed by another verse with the lines "Then pounce, then pounce, says Robin to Bobbin" (Opie and Opie 1988, 368).

   A similar kind of wren song involving exaggeration also consists of an extended series of questions and answers. Typical of this style is a verse from Scotland:

Will ye go to the wood? quo' Fozie Mosie;
Will ye go to the wood? quo' Johnnie Rednosie;
Will ye go to the wood? quo' Foslin 'ene;
Will ye go to the wood? quo' brither and kin.

What to do there? [*quo' Fozie Mosie, etc. each time*]
To slay the wren, —
What way will ye get her hame? —
We'll hire cart and horse, —
What way will ye get her in? —
We'll drive down the door cheeks, —

I'll hae a wing, —
I'll hae anither, —
I'll hae a leg, —
And I'll hae anither, quo' brither and kin.
                         (Swainson 1886, 40)

A Welsh version beginning with "Wilt thou come to seek the little
wren" also describes apportionment of the sacrificed carcass:

A leg for Dibin and a leg for Dobin,
A wing for Richard and a wing for Robin,
Half the head for John Pen-y-Stryd
And the other half for all of them.
                         (Peate 1936, 2)

A song from Brittany describes the wren as a huge creature comparable
to a beef animal that must be prepared for sacrificial slaughter:

One day I went out for a ramble,
    And what did I catch but a wren!
When he was caught he was properly caught;
He was put in the cowhouse to fatten,
And there he grew fatter and fatter,
Till they sent for the butcher to kill him.
The butcher and all his assistants
Cried out at the tops of their voices,
They were simply unable to hold him
    When he saw the lad come with the knife!
                         (Gill 1932, 400)

A short Breton song seems to express the idea that the progress of the
hunter was difficult "due to the weight of the wren":

I went a hunting in the wood,
    (Never shall I get there!)

> And in the wood I caught a wren,
> (Never, never, *never* shall I get there!)
>> (Gill 1932, 401)

"The Cutty Wren" from Oxfordshire is also made up of repetitive questions and replies:

> Oh where are you going? says Milder to Malder
> We may not tell you says Festle to Fose—
> We're off to the wild wood, says John the Red Nose
> We're off to the wild wood, says John the Red Nose.
>
> And what will you do there? says Milder to Malder,
> We may not tell you, says Festle to Fose.
> We'll hunt the Cutty Wren says John the Red Nose,
> We'll hunt the Cutty Wren says John the Red Nose.
>> (Stewart 1977, 15–16)

These introductory interchanges are followed by questions and answers describing how the wren will be killed, brought home, cut up and cooked, and fed to the poor, as in the previous hunt-the-wren song.

A similar Pembrokeshire version asks:

> Where are you going? says the milder to the malder;
> Where are you going? says the younger to the elder;
> I cannot tell, says Fizzledyfose;
> To catch Cutty Wren, says John-the-red-nose.
>
> How will you get him? says the milder to the malder;
> How will you get him? says the younger to the elder;
> I cannot tell, says Fizzledyfose;
> With guns and great cannons, says John-the-red-nose.
>> (Swainson 1886, 41)

In Wales, actions in the Milder to Malder version involve "shooting the cutty wren" with "bows and arrows" and "great guns and cannons." The wren is carried home "on four strong men's shoulders" and is then cut up with "hatchets and cleavers." The body is boiled in "brass pans and cauldrons." She will be eaten by "the Poor of the Parish," who will also receive the "spare meat" (Gill 1932, 386–88).

In North Wales, after the indication "We will hunt the wee wren," another procedure follows:

> We will boil it for broth, says Owen to Hugh,
> We will boil it for broth, says Morgan to Pugh,
> We will boil it for broth, says John Jones and Son;
> And they did. And the broth drowned every-one.
>
> (Gill 1932, 393)

Undoubtedly the theme of drowning in broth derives from or is related to the story of the owl upsetting the broth that is part of the legend relating to the wren-eagle competition (see chapter 2).

In England, "Jenny Wren" is shot in the woods with "Powder and shot," and is hauled away "in a cart with six horses." Additional necessities are to "hire some ropes" and "buy or borrow a furnace" to "cook her" (Gill 1932, 393–95). A song from Devonshire expresses the same kind of imaginative exaggerations. The participants pretended to "hoist" the wren into a wagon, using actions and words as if it were some extraordinary sized bird as they sang:

> I've shot a wren, says Robbin to Bobbin;
>> Hoist! Hoist! says Richard to Robbin,
>> Hoist! Hoist! says John all alone;
>> Hoist! Hoist! says everyone.
>
> I'll take a leg, says Robbin to Bobbin;
>> Hoist! Hoist! says Richard to Robbin, etc.
>
> I'll take the head, says Robbin to Bobbin;
>> Hoist! Hoist! says Richard to Robbin, etc.
>
> I'll take a wing, says Robbin to Bobbin;
>> Hoist! Hoist! says Richard to Robbin, etc.

"And so the song goes on with a burden of affected labour and toil, as if the bird was almost beyond their strength to lift" (Kermode 1885, 168). The verses proceed with various characters heaving different portions of the wren into the cart. The meaning here is not that the bird is dismembered, but that all the participants must work as a team to lift such a ponderous carcass.

It is necessary to have a cart to fetch him home, a brewery pan to boil him in, special tackle to lift him, and so forth. Thus the "very least of British birds" was "treated as if he were some enormous animal, both in bulk and weight, and all the appliances spoken of, or used in the ceremonies connected with the wren, are of a size and importance altogether out of proportion to the size of the bird" (Kermode 1885, 167). Writing in 1869, W. Harrison noted, "It is a singular fact, that wherever we find this peculiar custom prevailing, it is always attended with appliances, as if the object sought for was one of extraordinary bulk or weight instead of being one of the most diminutive of our feathered tribe. . . . It may, perhaps, be accounted for by the desire to render every homage to so important a personage as 'the king of all birds'" (Paton 1942, 106). The burlesquing may also be a way to introduce "a grotesque component of levity," provoking laughter to protect the performers from ridicule (Armstrong 1958, 147), while allowing them to go ahead with a ritual that they feel compelled to perpetuate. Another relevant theory holds that such "inversions of scale are related to the humor of ambiguous boundaries—the humor of giants and dwarfs, stilts and costumes that shrink or enlarge a figure," and represent examples of "reversal" and "boundary play"—the testing of boundaries (Stewart 1989, 68). Additional interpretations of these curious rhymes will be discussed in chapters 4 and 5.

The beat and tempo of the wren songs are significant elements of the ceremony. To prepare for the annual event there was a prelude in which people would "thump staves on the floor of their village hall in rhythm, gathering speed to a frantic climax, and finally rush out actually to hunt a wren" (Stewart 1977, 17). The wren songs themselves are traditionally rendered in a quick-time tempo and are accompanied by percussion created by a drum and, sometimes, other instruments. Singers produce synchronizing beats by stamping vigorously or banging the ground or floor with a stick. A Welsh singer of wren songs who died as an old man in 1907 had always "stamped violently" in time with the words. A spectator remembered that "the tune went with emphasis and swing, the old man banging the floor with his stick at the accented notes, bringing out all his words very clearly and swinging his body in time to the tune" (Hunting 1914–16, 78). The Manxman also "expresses his gusto by hand-clapping" (Gill 1932, 396). Anthropologists have noted that percussion is often associated with rites of transition (see Lawrence 1985, 150–51, 181, 186–87), and this phenomenon may well relate to the meaning of the wren ceremony as it marks the boundary between winter darkness and the return of the sun.

On the Isle of Man it is "customary to gabble [the songs] at top speed," making the words "difficult to follow by one not previously familiar with them" (Gill 1932, 383). This is still true of the Manx song as it is now recited in the annual hunt-the-wren ceremony and in the contemporary recording of the wren song included in the "Dances of Man" audiotape that is commercially sold on the Island. Folk-song specialist Bob Stewart points out that "the compelling chant form of the melody of *The Cutty Wren* [such as the Milder to Malder version given above]—with its hypnotic call and response pattern—makes it "a powerful form of music" that helped in the retention through time of the poetry that is linked to it. This "leader and chorus" type of group expression "has the effect of continual rhythm and hypnotic magical reiteration," which makes it easy to "learn and participate in." The "pattern of the song is a progression of formalised questions and answers, worked by characters who have clear roles of relationship to one another," although their identity is not clear (1977, 17–18, 100).

This is, Stewart asserts, "a typical ritual pattern, one common to the magical rituals of both primitive and sophisticated peoples from the aboriginal hunting rite to the modern mass communication. Although everybody taking part knows the 'answers' to the questions, the real content lies in the accumulation of riddles created by the pattern of the ritual. The drawn-out progression and the rhythm and chant elements are typical means of focussing awareness on the matter in hand, widely used for many purposes today from education to formal liturgy, not to mention television commercials and popular music" (1977, 17–18). The stylized question-and-answer format is often used in rituals, for frequently the "mythology of life and death is greatly concerned with riddles and magical questions—the prize is usually eternal life and the penalty death and rebirth" (Stewart 1977, 33).

According to Stewart, the similarity between the construction of many folk songs and liturgical chants is significant. He suspects that "some of these songs *are* liturgical chants or ritual music," no matter how much they are altered in form. The similarity, he believes, "is *not* with the hymn-singing or congregational music of the present day or even recent centuries, but with much earlier forms" predating Christianity and used by the common people. "The symbolism of *The Cutty Wren*," he argues, "bears a close relationship to various forms of mythological, religious and mystical modes of thought." The "powerful vehicle of the music" combined with the "drive" of these symbols explains "the secret of survival through all changes of language and custom." Because the material itself is derived from "simple levels of awareness that are essentially non-verbal, the changes through time" do not pose a significant historical problem. It is the "basic reality of crude symbols that are consistent with an agricultural society" that "causes the songs to re-occur." That "way of life existed in Britain until the early years of this century, and in a few regions still survives." The songs "were usually collected from rural communities, and such material is not found or practiced in modern cities. The sacrificing of the wren was supposed to bring fertility. This would be a natural part of the life-cycle, where death leads to new birth through the ceaseless round of the seasons." The songs represent "the epitomizing of the processes by which the rural community lived." The wren hunt was "associated with the growth of crops," and the survival of the songs came "out of the land itself, through the humans who live upon it" (1977, 18, 22–23).

The wren song rhythm consists of "a throbbing three-fold beat." Although this form is "attributed to the symbolism of the Holy Trinity laid down very strictly for early church music," it is important to realize that "the ancient British religion was based on a three-fold system also." Thus there is a "natural continuity of symbolism expressed through the music and song of ordinary people." The "impact and vitality of *The Cutty Wren* is enormous. Its power is striking to the modern listener, no matter how far removed he is from the life-cycle which it represents." The "attraction of such material" lies primarily in "the life forces from which it grows. In the 'pagan' songs we can feel the essential flow of life expressing itself directly, a quality long departed from most formal religious music. There is no dogma or philosophy remaining to tie the mind, and we are free to respond naturally to the impulse of the rituals and songs themselves" (Stewart 1977, 22–23).

The "functions of the characters of *The Cutty Wren* are those of a principal officer (John the Red Nose)—who declares all final solutions and statements—and two teams of liturgists, Milder and Malder, and Festle and Fose. These two teams or choirs create the question-and-negation pattern which the principal officer grandly solves at the end of each verse." The "formalised characters of *The Cutty Wren* plot challenge and respond to each other. Their purpose is to hunt the Cutty (little) wren." But this bird "cannot simply be chased and caught—mere bows and arrows are not sufficient—big guns and big cannons are needed; carts and wagons will be necessary to bring it home, and hatchets and cleavers to cut her up. The repeated emphasis on something small that is also very great is a common type of mystical utterance or way of thinking." Stewart believes the song is religious, not political, and that the crucifixion of the hunted wren is "a direct link with the typical sacrificial forms of religion known to use the cross symbol, including Christianity" (1977, 18–19, 21).

Turning to another aspect of the wren-hunt songs, I find a fascinating linkage between the living wren and the ceremonial music that evolved to celebrate it. I believe that the traditional wren songs reflect the voice of the tiny bird itself. Members of the wren family are notable for singing exquisitely, "the male and female of a pair joining in antiphonal duets" (Skutch 1987, 154). "One wren's roundelay sets a rival singing" and then begins a long-continued musical performance with each bird "waiting for the other to finish its song before repeating it, note for note and trill for trill" (Woodward 1928, 31). Ornithologists have observed that "the vocal duels of European wrens often consist of counter-singing, the phrase of one bird being uttered in the pause after the other bird's phrase." The birds deliberately alternate their songs, as though each "liked to be able to hear his rival replying." These responsive songs play an important role in maintaining contact between birds (Armstrong 1955, 78). This habit, and the birds' remarkably loud and distinctive voices, would certainly have been noted by the country people who lived intimately with nature and were keen observers of avian behavior. It would be natural to imitate the wren's song pattern in connection with the ceremony centering on that species. And the extraordinary volume and forceful quality of the wren's voice are appropriately represented in the powerful strains of the wren-hunt music. The strangely incongruous energy and resonance embodied in the minuscule bird's voice, as mirrored in music, could impart hope and strength to vulnerable human beings living in a harsh and incomprehensible world governed by forces that seemed overwhelming.

As we have seen, many themes in addition to the blessings extended to the households visited by the wren boys and their solicitations for food, drink, or money are articulated in the various wren songs. The lyrics contain significant details of the hunting and killing of the bird—such as the wren's royal status, the search for the bird and its death, weapons used, transporting of the carcass, struggling under its enormous size and weight, fattening the bird for slaughter, the decorating and displaying of the wren's bier, plucking and distributing its feathers, the cooking and sacrificial eating of its body, and the disposal of the remains. Specific wren songs will be cited and analyzed in connection with the discussion of the particular aspects of the ancient ceremony that they serve to illuminate. The lyrics of the songs are, of course, essential keys to the puzzle represented by the wren hunt, and, as mentioned, they have played a vital role in expressing and preserving the deep-level meaning of the ritual. Analysis of these songs, an integral part of the discussion and interpretation of the wren hunt, will follow after the more recent, or superimposed, explanations have been addressed.

FOUR

ANALYSIS OF THE WREN HUNT

The culture of a people is an ensemble of texts, themselves ensembles,
which the anthropologist strains to read over the shoulders of
those to whom they properly belong.
—Clifford Geertz

BEFORE ATTEMPTING TO ELUCIDATE the underlying significance of the killing of the wren by chronicling the deep-level meanings that are attributable to the custom and analyzing its older, more complex roots, I will first consider various more recent, or secondary, explanations.

SUPERIMPOSED EXPLANATIONS

Classifying more recent explanations as superimposed does not diminish their important role in the wren's story or their significance to the beliefs of various societies at different times. The ingenuity with which these rationalizations have been fashioned and the fascinating parallels they draw between the tiny bird and those persons, elements, and forces with which it became identified comprise an exceedingly important part of the lore of the wren and of the ritual that surrounds it. Such explanations illustrate the great richness and variety of the wren's enduring symbolic power and the bird's almost limitless ability as a "signifier" to stimulate thought and evoke elaborate metaphor. Moreover, they shed light on the nature of human-animal interactions, illustrating the way in which people manipulate empirical observations about the form and behavior of animals to fit into preconceived belief systems, local legends, and various social frameworks. Through such explanations, human moral values are thrust upon nonhumans, who can then be judged and punished for human sins such as betrayal or made into scapegoats bearing human guilt. Thus hostility toward other species that is based on human projection in conjunction with perceptions about the other species' biological or behavioral characteristics is engendered and perpetuated. Outdated customs handed down over generations that are still enjoyable and entertaining can be justified at the expense of the animal even when it appears there is no logic in their practice.

Using Geertz's terminology for anthropological interpretation, these explanations might be termed "thin," as opposed to the "thick" description represented by deeper analysis of the hunting of the wren as sacrificial ritual. Borrowing this notion of "thin" versus "thick" from Gilbert Ryle, Geertz notes that the "thin" data represent "the sort of piled-up structures of inference and implication through which an ethnographer is continually trying to pick his way" (1973, 6–9). The "thin" rationalizations of relatively recent origin that surround the wren hunt are testament to the strength and urgency of the conflict between humankind and nature that this curious ritual embodies. That conflict involves the opposition between widespread feelings of reverence and humane concern for the wren and the hostile conduct toward that same bird when annually it became the victim of a deadly hunt. Not surprisingly, guilt caused by longstanding seasonal persecution of the otherwise beloved wren motivated conscious or unconscious search for rational reasons underlying such strange and seemingly contradictory behavior long after the original meaning of the sacrifice had been lost by the participants. As Armstrong stated, such "explanations are attributable to the urge folk feel to account somehow for a custom, the significance of which they have forgotten." The "multiplicity and inconsistency" of these rationalizations belie their depth and validity (1958, 153, 160).

The human tendency to rationalize group actions that would otherwise be inexplicable continues into the present day. For example, contemporary live pigeon shoots held annually in some parts of Pennsylvania have roots in that state dating to colonial times and extending far back into the population's cultural heritage. Now distanced from their ethnic background, which included the tradition of bird shooting, and in the face of vehement protests by animal rights advocates, certain groups of Pennsylvanians continue to enjoy the sport of shooting live targets, even though participants in the vast majority of such events elsewhere have converted to using clay pigeons. During my 1993 field research at one shoot, I found that when asked by observers why they remain so adamant in preserving the live-bird tradition, participants provide many well-rehearsed answers to support their actions. They call the pigeons "very dirty" and insist the creatures are "nothing

but vermin, only rats with wings." Shooters explain, "Pigeons crap
everywhere, even on cars" and point out that "they carry diseases."
They represent "a nuisance to farmers because they damage machinery.
They're a fire hazard in barns where their manure builds up and causes
spontaneous combustion." "Anyway," the shooters argue, "in cities they
spend millions of dollars killing pigeons. The light and power compa-
nies electrocute and poison them. So it makes much more sense for us
to shoot them here." Like any disempowered group, the pigeons have
to be segregated and perceived as perpetrators of evil to justify their
victimization.

Explanations for the wren hunt tradition have been created with
much ingenuity. The most commonly encountered one is the idea that
because the wren was sacred to the Druids, early Christian missionaries
hated the bird and thus encouraged their followers to hunt and kill it at
Christmas time in order to demonstrate rejection of druidical, or pagan,
connections. The enmity between Christians and the wren is often cor-
related with the fact that the bird "was displaced from high magical
status by Christianity" (Armstrong 1958, 161) and was condemned as a
symbol of heathen rites. Interestingly, one interpretation of the prohibition of killing the wren is that the custom represents "a relic of the
old pagan notion of his kingly inviolability yet struggling with the
Christian command for his persecution at Christmas" (Brand 1849, 3:
124, 197).

Clearly the Christian church could not tolerate vestiges of belief
in the notion of a sacred bird. Thus any lingering perceptions of the
wren hunt as a sacrificial ceremony were changed to make it merely a
secular campaign against a creature that must be hated in order to make
its killing intelligible. Vengeance was invoked as the motive for a misunderstood rite. It was even alleged that the wren has "a drop of the
de'il's blood in it" and thus deserved to be killed (Ingersoll 1923, 120).
Another vindictive explanation for persecuting the wren involves the
fact that the Druids once presided over courts of justice. If a verdict was
questioned, the priests replied that the wren had disclosed the truth to
them and the wren's testimony was final. Consequently, people grew to
hate the wren and cruelly hunted it (Ingersoll 1923, 120–21; Squire
1975, 417; Parry-Jones 1988, 154).

Religious guilt has been laid upon the wren in connection with
Christ, a saint, and an apostle. These explanations, however, are distinct
from and should not be confused with the identification on a deeper
level between the wren and the figures of Christ and St. Stephen, which

will be discussed later. To explain its persecution on a surface level, the wren has been blamed for betraying Christ while he was "hiding in the garden" when "by noisy chirping, [it] showed the place to the soldiers and servants of the high priest" (Swainson 1886, 38).

A more elaborate story relating the wren to Christ is also used to explain why the wren was an object of scorn:

> The soldiers were looking for Our Lord to kill him. He had to hide from them. One day he walked over a field where a man was sowing wheat, and drops of Our Saviour's blood fell on it, and by a miracle the wheat sprang up all in one night and was ready for reaping the next morning. On the next day the soldiers came by the same way in their search for Him. There was a robin in the bush in the wheat field and it saw the soldiers coming. It lay upon every drop of blood that marked Our Saviour's track and didn't leave a trace of it for the soldiers to follow, which is the reason that, from that day to this, the robin has a red breast. The captain of the soldiers asked the robin if it had seen a man passing that way lately.
>
> "Not," says the robin, "since that wheat was sown."
>
> "At that rate," says the captain of the soldiers, "we are on the wrong track." And he had his men turned round and was marching off with them when the wren came flying up and says:
>
> "The wheat was sown yesterday; the wheat was sown yesterday." And with that the soldiers were wheeled again, and [went] away out [in] the field and never stopped till they came up with Our Saviour. And from that day the wren was cursed, and ever since it has been hunted and persecuted.
>
> (O'Sullivan 1991, 30)

Allegations are made that when the first Christian martyr, St. Stephen, was about to make his escape from captivity, a wren prevented his flight by awakening one of his sleeping guards by flying on the man's face. Legend also relates that "when the Jews were in search of St. Stephen, they lost their labour for a long time, till, on passing by a clump of furze-bushes, they observed a couple of wrens flying in and out, and chattering in a most unaccountable manner. They had the curiosity to pull a bush aside and there they discovered the saint concealed" (Lewis 1926, 77). The stoning of the wren was said to be carried out in retribution for the bird's betrayal. It became analogous to the stoning of St. Stephen, whose execution took place on 26 December, the first saint's day after Advent. Thus the bird's death was interpreted as a "vengeful reminder of the manner of that martyr's murder by a mob" (Ingersoll 1923, 121). Another explanation simply traces the killing of the wren on that day to the fact that a wren of which St. Stephen had made a pet shared his martyrdom, having been stoned along with him (Douglas 1963, 2).

The slaughter of wrens on St. Stephen's Day has also been ratio-nalized as a memorial of the "massacre of the Holy Innocents" (Potter and Sargent 1974, 296)—the children slain by Herod after he learned of the birth of Jesus—an event that is celebrated on 28 December. Or the wren may have been categorized with various other animals who were traditional subjects for persecution on St. Stephen's Day. That oc-casion has been described as a "general shooting holiday" during which "the woods and fields echo all day with the desultory practice of 'sportsmen,' and the pigeon-shootings held for prizes" (Gill 1932, 380). Men felt they had the right to hunt on St. Stephen's Day, "license or no license," and there was a popular belief that game laws were not in force on that date (Wright 1940, 3: 276, 279). Not only bird shoots, but also the hunting of squirrels, foxes, cats, and owls once took place at that time (Coffin 1973, 41; Crippen 1923, 131). The saint's day is also associ-ated with the annual custom of bleeding horses to increase their strength and keep them healthy during the coming year. As expressed in rhyme: "If you bleed your nag on St. Stephen's Day / He'll work your 'wark' for ever and A" (Wright 1940, 3: 279). And:

> Ere Christmas be passed, let horse be let blood,
> For many a purpose, it doth them much good,
> The day of St. Stephen old fathers did use.
> (Hervey 1848, 188)

In Scotland, "shooting forays" were held on New Year's Day. The no-tion that blood must be shed around that time of year was widely ac-cepted, and the slaughter undoubtedly "had sacrificial implications" (Armstrong 1958, 144). Belief in some areas of preindustrial Britain held that the midwinter shedding of blood not only benefited the animal victim but also prevented future misfortune. Originally, this practice may have been a sacrificial rite in which the animal's blood was used to fertilize the earth. But that meaning was later forgotten and the focus changed to the animal itself (Bord and Bord 1982, 130). The bloodlet-ting of horses on 26 December, however, may in reality honor a differ-ent St. Stephen, a lover of horses who first brought the Gospel to

Sweden and was martyred there during the eleventh century. The two may have become confused, both inheriting a connection to pre-Christian midwinter festivals (Hole 1984, 38–39).

Another justification for the wren's yearly punishment also relates to a religious figure. It has been alleged that "when St. Paul was converted, the evil side of his character (or 'the Spirit of Destruction') went out of him and into the body of a wren. Since then, the birds have become so vicious that, unless they were killed, they would destroy every creature smaller than themselves" (Deane and Shaw 1975, 133). Interestingly, the involvement of St. Paul in this rationalization can be related to his short stature, for "he was as small among men as a wren is among birds" (Gill 1932, 423). An alternative explanation of retaliatory behavior toward the bird involves St. Moling of Ireland, who, according to the legend that "provides the earliest literary reference to the Wren Hunt," allegedly cursed the wren for eating his pet fly. The bird's punishment was that it must henceforth dwell in empty houses, live in damp areas, and be subject to destruction at the hands of young people in the annual hunt (Armstrong 1958, 160). Some implications of this episode are discussed in chapter 5. (Another legend gives an entirely different slant to the incident: St. Moling saw a wren eat a fly and then a cat ate the wren. Out of pity, he ordered the cat and then the wren to disgorge their prey. This event was construed as "the resurrection of the dead from their narrow graves" and "gave glory to Christ" [Bell 1992, 95–96]).

The Irish were said to have hunted the wren because they thought the bird was a witch (Lockley 1960, 323). The story was also told in Ireland that it was Fionn Mac Cumhaill, a legendary divine Celtic hero, who was betrayed by the wren. When Fionn's pursuers approached, the wren pinched his ear with its beak, and thus his presence was revealed. It was alleged that "the little nip was visible on Fionn's ear until the time of his death" (O'Sullivan 1991, 33). The wren is known as "Fionn's Doctor" (Matthews and Matthews 1988, 164), perhaps in association with this incident of blood-letting.

Patriotic themes take their place beside religious considerations in projecting guilt onto the tiny bird. Association of the wren with military events must have followed logically from suggestive qualities of its utterances. For, according to a leading scholar of bird music, the "great distinction" of the wren's "melody is its marked rhythm and accent, which give it a martial, fife-like character. Note tumbles over note, . . . and the strain comes to an end so suddenly that for the first few times you are likely to think that the bird has been interrupted" (Mathews 1936, 221). Its repertoire has also been interpreted as a "rattling warble of shrill clear notes in quick time" (Rowland 1978, 185). The bird's call is a loud, hard note that sounds like "click," "kip," "kip-kip," "chimp-chimp," or "tit-tit-tit." The alarm call of the wren is "a rush of sharp loud notes following thick and fast one after the other and resembling a rapid drumming"—sounds that, according to Francesca Greenoak, are reflected in the wren's names "Crackil" and "Cracket" (1979, 244). In times of danger "the little Wren often gives the alarm, by uttering rapidly its note of fear, 'shrek! shrek!' so quickly repeated that it sounds like a miniature watchman's rattle" (Morris n.d., 136–37). Because of the alarm sounds with which it greets trespassers, the wren is known as "the garden's sentinel" (Woodward 1928, 29). Thus a series of "warning stories" involving the wren arose from its perceived martial "drumming" or rattling.

One legend holds that in the late eighth century, when the Vikings were invading Ireland, Irish soldiers were betrayed by a wren as they were sneaking up on sleeping Viking raiders. The wren was alleged to have eaten bread crumbs left on a Viking drum. The "rat-a-tat-tat" of the bird's pecking on the drum woke the drummer boy, who sounded the alarm. Thus the Irish soldiers were defeated by the Vikings, and the wren has been persecuted for its treachery ever since (Zeleny 1985, 42–43). A similar explanation blames the wren for hopping on a drum at the siege of Doolinn, thus awakening the Danes and preventing the Irish forces from surprising them (Swainson 1886, 38). The account of the wrens' role in preventing James II's forces from surprising King William's army was given in chapter 3. In the same way, wrens are also said to have alerted Cromwell's forces "when the Irish were stealthily advancing on them" (Armstrong 1958, 160).

Still another "curious story" regarding wren hunting relates that "at the battle fought in the North of Ireland between the Protestants and Papists in Lunsuly, County Donegal, a party of the former would have been surprised by the Irish were it not for several wrens who awakened them by dancing and pecking on their drums as the enemy was approaching. For this reason the Irish mortally hate these birds, calling them the 'Devil's Servants' and killing them whenever they catch them; they teach their children to thrust them full of thorns; you'll see sometimes on holidays, a whole parish running like madmen from hedge to hedge, a wren-hunting" (Thompson 1989, 209).

The Manx people had their own version to justify the wren hunt:

In a time of war in the Island—and we had many in ancient times—
there were two powerful chiefs encamped some distance from each
other with their armies, and intended to have a battle in the morning. But one of those chiefs armed his men at midnight, and
intend[ed] to surprise the army by coming on them while asleep. But
a wren came and fluttered her wings and feet over the drum's head,
and the stir awoke someone near it who saw the wren, who thought
it was a sign of something which was to happen, and called up the
rest of the army, which was ready when the enemy was come, and
when they found them all in readiness, they were surprised themselves, and lost the battle. So the discomfited party made a practice
of hunting the wren, [which] became universal in the Island.

(Kermode 1902, 190–91)

A similar but oddly illogical tale from the Isle of Man involves the
"Manx Fencibles" who "were employed in suppressing the Irish rebel-
lion of 1798" and "were aroused in this way on a similar occasion."
Actually, the wren in that case saved the Manx forces from being "taken
unawares by the Irish" (Clague 1911, 13), so the explanation for the
vendetta against the bird is contradictory and exemplifies the confusion inherent in this type of rationalization. As one author commented,
the Manx fighting men had "a poor reason . . . for killing the amateur
drummers who saved their lives" (Paton 1942, 107).

A well-known Manx legend involving the fairy tradition and centering on the ocean that is so pervasive in Manx life is traditionally invoked to account for that area's marked seasonal hostility toward the
wren and the hunting of the bird, which "has been a pastime in the Isle
of Man from time immemorial." This "singular ceremony" is founded
on the tradition that

in former times a fairy of uncommon beauty exerted such undue influence over the male population, that she, at various times, induced,
by her sweet voice, numbers to follow her footsteps, till by degrees
she led them into the sea, where they perished. This barbarous exercise of power had continued for a great length of time, till it was apprehended the Island would be exhausted of its defenders, when a
knight-errant sprung up, who discovered some means of counter-
vailing the charms used by this siren, and even laid a plot for her
destruction, which she only escaped at the moment of extreme hazard, by taking the form of a *wren.* But though she evaded instant
annihilation, a spell was cast upon her, by which she was condemned
on every succeeding New-year's-day, to reanimate the same form,

with the definitive sentence, that she must ultimately perish by human hand. In consequence of this *well-authenticated* legend, on the specified anniversary, every man and boy in the Island (except those who have thrown off the trammels of superstition), devote the hours between sun-rise and sun-set, to the hope of extirpating the fairy, and woe be to the individual birds of this species, who show themselves on this fatal day to the active enemies of the race; they are pursued, pelted, fired at, and destroyed, without mercy, and their feathers preserved with religious care, it being an article of belief that every one of the relics gathered in this laudable pursuit is an effectual preservation from shipwreck for one year; and that fishermen would be considered as extremely foolhardy who should enter upon his occupation without such a safeguard.

(Train 1845, 2: 124–25)

Gill raises an interesting point with regard to the "individual birds" mentioned in this Manx legend. It is not clear whether "reanimate the same form" means that the fairy entered an individual wren or all the wrens. Because wrens were killed indiscriminately, it is uncertain whether the wren hunters hoped they could hit upon the particular bird that embodied the sorceress or whether they assumed every one of the birds contained the evil spirit and thus "sought safety by destroying all the wrens in the neighborhood" (1932, 367–68). Of course, the wrens, one or all of which embody the fairy, returned again the following year and were once again hunted.

According to a pattern found in many traditions, there is a periodic revival of the slaughtered animal. The alternating death and life of the wren can be compared, for example, with the California Indians' annual killing of the buzzard. Belief held that a woman had gone into the mountains and there been changed into the bird. Though the buzzard was sacrificed each year, "she came to life again and returned to her home in the mountains." As often as the bird was killed, its numbers were multiplied, but all sacrificed individuals were considered to be one and the same female. In Samoa, a similar practice dictated that each family had for its god a particular bird such as an owl. Yet the death of an owl did not mean the death of the god, who was still "alive and incarnate in all the owls in existence" (Gill 1932, 367).

As Kermode says of the wren on the Isle of Man, "The poor bird has a singular life of it in that singular island. When one is seen . . . scores of Manxmen start and hunt it down!" (1885, 160). The strong tradition of the "Fairy-Wren" on the Isle of Man and the revenge taken against her each year are reflected in the first stanza of a "We'll Hunt the Wren" song peculiar to that location. Known as a "Manx carol," the words relate to "the tit-wren" who "was selected as the victim":

> Away to the woods, says Dick to Tom,
> Away to the woods, says every one.
> What to do there, ye merry Manx-men?
> To hunt to death the wicked witch-wren.
> (Gill 1932, 385)

The story of the fairy who turned into a wren may be traced to the sorceress or enchantress, Tehi Tegi, who by means of "her diabolical arts" seduced the male population of the island and lured them to their death by drowning. When her murderous deeds were completed, she "converted herself into a Bat" and flew out of sight. Or the legend could be based on the story of a fairy named Cleena who did the evil work and who "resumes the wren-form every Christmas Day." All the associated legends involve an enchantress in the guise of "a storm-raising sea-witch who drowned fishermen." Her connection to the little land bird, the wren, persisted, becoming firmly entrenched in the lore of the Isle of Man. As described in an early account, "The Manx herring-fishers dare not go to sea without one of these birds taken dead with them, for fear of disasters and storms. Their tradition is that of a sea-spirit that haunted the herring-track attended always by storms, and at last it assumed the figure of a wren and flew away. So they think that when they have a dead wren with them all is snug" (Gill 1932, 361–63).

The idea of a woman taking the form of a bird is an ancient one, as evidenced by the Greek sirens of the sea appearing as birds with women's heads who "lured sailors to destruction with their sweet voices." In the Manx legends, the fairy or sea-spirit has the ability to bring about storms, but "immunity is conferred upon fishermen by a wren's feather" (Gill 1932, 364). Whereas in Britain, Ireland, and on the Continent, wren songs frequently refer to the bird as "he" and "the king," the Manx tradition focuses on the wren as a seductive and destructive female oceanic sprite. It is easy to understand that particular association among a people surrounded by the sea, whose livelihood depends on fishing. It is logical, too, that the unusually sweet and loud voice of the wren, which seems incongruous with its tiny body, might suggest that the bird was indeed the mysterious embodiment of a siren who attracted the island's men by her bewitching singing. Additionally, the wren's tiny, elflike proportions and its habit of appearing and disappearing as if by magic add to the suitability of the bird for that role. It is tempting to perceive the wren as a fairylike creature, and indeed the members of a group of Australian birds resembling the wren have been named "fairy wrens."

Spence argues that on the Isle of Man "the wren-spirit became confused nominally with Ran, the Norse goddess of the sea, whose name and legend must have been well known in any area so thickly settled by Norse folk as was Man." He believes that mix-up accounts for the fact that in Man the wren was regarded as female and that a maritime connection with the bird not found elsewhere exists there. Ran, according to Grimm, drew drowned men to her in a net, and to "fare to Ran" meant to be drowned at sea. Ran, who, according to Spence, gave her name to the Isle of Man, was believed to keep the souls of drowned sailors in pots turned upside down. Spence cautions that this "confusion concerning 'wren' and 'wran' in the Isle of Man has obviously nothing to do with the wren legend as we find it elsewhere and must be separated from it absolutely, as a local growth." The Manx legend reflects the myth of Ran, as it was known in the Island, and it "was blunderingly employed to 'explain' the hunting of the wren." The wren, however, "can have had no association whatever with the Norse goddess Ran" (1971, 157–58).

A different interpretation traces the roots of the Manx belief to the Celtic epic, *The Mabinogion*. Ward Rutherford suggests that the concept of the tiny bird being "regarded both as a transformed witch and a presager of disaster" derives from an incident in that work, related in *Math Son of Mathonwy*. According to that story, "Arianrhod is tricked against her will into naming the son she has disowned. She sees the boy, whom she does not recognize, shoot at a wren with perfect aim. He hits it in the leg 'between the sinew and the bone,' causing her to comment that he has a very skilful hand, so becoming Lleu or Lugh of the Skilful Hand. Since Arianrhod is one of the many witchlike goddesses of Celtic mythology it may well be she who had taken on the form of wren and who is thus wounded by her son. An injury inflicted on one who has undergone transformation invariably causes a reversion to their normal state" (1993, 97). And the fate of Llew's wife, Blodeuwedd, who was changed into the form of an owl, "to be harassed ever since by the other birds in punishment for her former misdeeds," may also be a source for the similar transformation of the Manx witch Tehi Tegi into a bird (Gill 1932, 423–24). Other significant wren transmutations have occurred. "One of the most dominant figures in British history," Taliesin, the Welsh bard who wrote *The Book of Taliesin,* was once transformed into a wren. One folklorist asserts that "the song and custom of 'Hunting the Wren' are undoubtedly linked with one of Taliesin's re-incarnations" in the form of that bird (Llewellyn 1926, 215–16).

Whatever the origins of the belief in an enchantress inhabiting the body of the wren, that legend, like others that recount the evil deeds of the bird, is a tale that "has been grafted on the Manx wren-custom in order to explain it" (Gill 1932, 364–65). Thus "the various popular legends regarding the origin of 'Hunting the Wren' may be safely ignored" (Gilchrist 1926, 78). As Welsh folklorist Llew Tegid points out, "The real explanation" extends "much further back" than the story of destroying the evil Manx fairy. Tegid describes an ancient Punjab ceremony in which a model of a snake is paraded to each home, honored by gifts of food to the bearers, and then solemnly interred. Similarities between this ritual and that pertaining to the wren lead him to suggest that the wren hunt is also "a religious ceremony from very primitive paganism." Yet "Christian Europe has been exercising its ingenuity for centuries in trying to invent some explanation, other than the right one, for a custom it can neither countenance nor eradicate." Viewed in this light, "there is nothing contradictory or inconsistent in the care and protection afforded the Wren, during the whole year, and the sacrifice made of it on one day. The killing of the *Wren* was a solemn sacramental religious ceremony" (1911, 111). The sacrificial roots of the wren hunt, as well as other possible origins and included elements that will be described, are undoubtedly far older and more profound than the superimposed, or "thin," explanations that developed to account for this strange tradition.

DEEPER ROOTS AND UNDERLYING ELEMENTS

Legends such as those just recounted involving Druids, Christ, various saints, religious figures, heroes, and military forces, which deal with the wren's betrayals and wrongdoings that merit human retribution, "are mere rationalizations of a ritual that appears to be older than Christianity" (Hole 1984, 166). As time eroded the old belief in the principle of sacrifice, people no longer understood the killing of a specially sacred and beloved animal for a divine purpose. Slaughter became mainly a secular affair, and when the deeply entrenched ritual of the wren hunt continued to be performed in spite of loss of its original meaning, there were many attempts to "make sense" out of such a tenacious, but seemingly strange and cruel, custom. Thus, as we have seen, various tales arose in later times to account for the alleged vendetta against the wren. These stories, which obscured the original meaning of the rites, were fused to the ancient wren traditions, causing confusion and adding new and complicated dimensions that expressed ambiguity toward a generally beloved bird that custom dictated must be killed. Explanations resting upon more recent historical or religious factors were elaborated to fit into an already established pattern and were superimposed upon it.

Evidence suggests an origin in the far distant past for the wren hunt, and its antiquity must be taken into account when searching for its roots and meanings. The ceremony undoubtedly originated "from a very primitive paganism" and may even date back to "a time before the invention of husbandry when animals were revered as divine in themselves" (Gaster 1964, 561, 563). Armstrong, who studied the ceremony in detail, concludes that "the Wren Cult reached the British Isles during the Bronze Age and was carried by megalith builders whose cultural inspiration came from the Mediterranean region" (1958, 166). Stewart proposes that the wren hunt songs originate "from a very ancient cult indeed, possibly the oldest recognisable religion in Britain of which specific elements may still be traced." The symbols of the lyrics, he asserts, "derive from even older faiths and unknown racial roots." The music and texts of the songs reveal "some startling parallels with ancient British myth and symbology, and with a religious system that is essentially pre-Christian." The symbolic elements of the wren ceremony, as expressed in songs, have been retained over long ages, and the origins of these "basic racial symbols" cannot be accurately pinpointed in time (1977, 15, 17, 18).

Certainly some of the wren songs appear to be very old, and many versions feature themes that reinforce the idea of the sacrificial role of the wren. The words never seem to refer to figures or topics involved in the later rationalizations, such as Christ and saints (except to mention St. Stephen's Day), or military exploits that entailed the wren's betrayal. A Manx wren song, as we have seen, does mention the "wicked witch-wren"—the fairy related to the fishing tradition on the Isle of Man. One could speculate that this thematic grafting on an ancient custom might have come about more readily in an area where the wren hunt has probably continued uninterrupted from ancient times and where it was a particularly well-entrenched tradition. A seafaring society would have felt an especially strong urge to relate the ritual to its main occupation and its concerns.

Many different explanations of the wren hunt have been set forth, and there is no single factor that can be isolated as the sole source for such an old, complex, and multifaceted ritual—except to say that it almost certainly arose as a sacrificial event. Symbolic analysis is rewarding in illuminating some of the probable roots and deep-level meanings of the ceremony that are consistent with many of its elements. Perhaps the oldest of these is totemism.

Totemism

A totem is a specially revered animal (or other natural object) serving as the emblem of a clan or family by virtue of a shared ancestral relationship and descent and through kinship ties. Totemism implies social and religious associations linking human and animal groups with a sense of brotherliness, goodwill, and interdependence between people and their totem. Ordinarily, the totem animal is neither killed nor eaten, but this taboo is lifted under special ritual conditions. Some scholars argue that all animal veneration, sacrifices, or food prohibitions are vestiges of totemism. Belief in totemism (which has been studied in greatest detail among Australian aborigines) involves mystical and spiritual connections with the designated animal and is characteristic of people who do not control nature but surrender to it, align themselves with it, and feel at one with it. Through totemism, people view nature as like them and themselves as like nature. Nature is safe because they are part of it, not a separate entity (Howells 1986, 179–86, 194). Totemism can be viewed as the "ritual expression of interdependence between the social order and the natural environment" (Leach 1974, 41–42).

Spence suggests that the sacred wren, as it was featured in the wren hunt, was in fact a totemic animal. Evidence supporting this interpretation is the practice of carrying the wren around the community so that everyone could partake of its divine influence. The customs of ceremonially eating the bird (or simulating this practice) and of ritually burying its remains are also strongly suggestive of totemism (1947, 45–46). "According to totemic theory," notes Ernest Ingersoll, "the wren was once regarded as sacred, and the Christmas hunting is the survival of an annual custom of slaying the divine animal, such as is found among primitive peoples" (1923, 120).

There is a close association between totemism and sacrifice, and it well may be that "the root origin of sacrifice" is to be found in the "totemic cult." In totemism "the totem or the god is related to its devotees:

they are of the same flesh and blood; the object of the rite is to maintain and guarantee the common life that animates them and the association that binds them together," reestablishing their unity. "The 'blood covenant' and the 'common meal' are the simplest means of obtaining this result." By eating the totem, the devotees become allied with one another and with the totem and may acquire the wisdom of the animal consumed. The object of sacrificial slaughter is "to make possible the devouring of the sacred and consequently forbidden animal" (Hubert and Mauss 1964, 2–3). The wren songs, as we have seen, specifically describe fattening the wren for slaughter, cooking it, apportioning its meat in ritually prescribed ways, and eating the flesh.

Gill also concludes that the wren sacrifice shows points of strong resemblance to some of the totemic rites that have been described by ethnographers and other observers in which feathers from the totemic bird became sacred and powerful, as the wren's feathers once were for the Manx fisherfolk. For example, a California tribe that revered the buzzard (vulture) held an annual festival in which the bird was ritually killed. The feathers were "preserved to adorn the sacred dress of the medicine-man," and the body was buried with mourning rituals resembling those for the loss of a relative or friend. Among two South American groups, "to put himself more fully under the protection of the totem, the clansman carries . . . an easily recognizable part of his totem with him" in the form of feathers. Members of Peruvian condor clans, believing themselves descended from the condor, wear feathers from this bird. And the Piaroans of the Orinoco customarily pluck a feather from the sacred toucan for each member of the family. These feathers are first attached to sticks outside the dwelling to scare away evil spirits and later are worn in headdresses. In analogous instances, fur from the sacred animal has magical qualities, as for a Central African tribe whose members wear for protection scraps of fleece from a sacrificed lamb (1932, 358–60).

Totemic animals warn their human counterparts of danger and provide information about forthcoming events (Heinberg 1995, 215)—two capacities that, as we have seen, were commonly attributed to the wren. Géza Roheim believes that the wren was probably once a totemic being, noting that "a prohibition against killing connected with an annual ceremonial slaughter undoubtedly looks like totemism." Additionally, "the killers of the wren are called 'wren boys,'" which could be interpreted as "youths of the wren totem." But complete explanations of the wren hunt, he warns, "go far beyond and below totemism" (1930,

324). And so they do. The concept of the sacred or divine king is one such explanation that correlates with certain prominent features of the wren hunt ritual.

The Divine King

The wren ceremony is a particularly intriguing example of animal sacrifice that can be interpreted as representing the ancient phenomenon of the periodic sacrifice of the divine king. In numerous variations of the lyrics that accompany the ceremony, the wren is referred to as the "King." Those who carry the wren in procession believe that "the wren is their king and they are his men" (Dyer's 1876, 314). The Welsh song accompanying the ceremony during which the wren was enclosed in a box with glass windows surmounted by a wheel with colored streamers attached gives the "King" all the homage required by his royal status. It ends with a reference to the New replacing the Old—signifying the succession of kings as well as years:

> Joy, health, love and peace,
> Be to you in this place;
> By your leave we will sing
> Concerning our King:
> Our King is well drest
> In silks of the best;
> With his ribbons so rare
> No king can compare.
> In his coach he does ride
> With a great deal of pride:
> And with four footmen
> To wait upon him;
> We were four at watch,
> And all nigh of a match:
> And with powder and ball
> We fired at his hall.
> We have travell'd many miles
> Over hedges and stiles,
> To find you this King,
> Which we now to you bring.
> Now Christmas is past,
> Twelfth Day is the last.
> The Old Year bids adieu—
> Great joy to the new.
> (Swainson 1886, 41)

One early source specifically connects the ceremonial killing of the wren with the death of an actual ancient British king at the time of the Saxon invasion (Swainson 1886, 41), but it seems evident that the royal association is in fact more general. The wren hunt may represent "a relic of the primitive custom of sacrificing the king who was the incarnation of the god, and upon whom the entire welfare of the tribe depended. By killing him ceremonially before his natural powers failed, the divine principle was released to take up its abode in the next king without danger to the people" (Hole 1940, 75). In his description of the divine king, Roheim explains the concept of the king doing penance for his people. The royal ruler was responsible for his subjects' guilt and thus became a scapegoat (1930, 311–20). Such "'sacred kings' lived a closely ordered life, with privileges and restraints outside normal behaviour and rules. At certain predetermined times, the king was killed by specific means. In each case, the dying victim was replaced by a chosen heir, often his murderer, who in turn died an unnatural death when his time came" (Stewart 1977, 36). At his demise, the old king imparted his strength to his successor, conferring upon him his royal power and semidivine status (Hartley 1986, 121). This tradition expresses the idea that the ritual death of a god "bestows strength on his killer" (Carr-Gomm and Carr-Gomm 1994, 129).

The idea of the sacred king, also known as the Cult of the Dying God, was a feature of some forms of pre-Christian religion in Europe and Britain. According to that belief, the spirit of god dwelled in the king, and the king imparted fertility to his kingdom. In Celtic tradition, the state of the land always reflected the kingly rule. If the king was in harmony with his obligations, the land flourished, but if he neglected his duties, the country became a wasteland. Under an unworthy ruler the kingdom would suffer from loss of productivity of the land, crop failure, dryness of cows, drought, and famine (Murray 1970, 161; Matthews 1989, 25–26). During the time of his power, the king was inviolate, but when a certain date came, he had to be killed, "lest the spirit of god weaken" and bring disaster to the people (Murray 1970, 160). Although in former times the king had been put to death at the first sign of disease, weakness, loss of sexual potency, or aging, that custom evolved into a practice in which, to avert the danger of gradual enfeeblement of the king's powers, he must be killed and his soul transferred to a vigorous successor *before* there was any impairment by decay (Frazer 1963, 309).

It was imperative to catch the soul of the dying god just as it left his body, because to chance losing it would mean the people's prosperity would be gone and their very existence endangered. Because the king's life and spirit were intimately bound to the health and productivity of the whole country, it was unsafe to wait for the slightest sign of the ebbing of his strength. This risk led to the eventual establishment of a fixed term for the king, after which he was killed while still in full vigor. The death of the king, with the passing of his power to his successor, was the only means to perpetuate divine life unimpaired in order to ensure the salvation of the people and even of the world. Traditionally, the body of the old king was dismembered by his successor, but when the pieces were gathered together he underwent a glorious resurrection in another world (Frazer 1963, 309; Graves 1989, 292–93).

Such a royal sacrifice becomes intelligible today by understanding that although Christian doctrine asserts that God died once and for all, earlier religious belief held that "god is perpetually incarnate on earth and may therefore be put to death over and over again" (Murray 1970, 128). The modern Christian does not depend upon "the oblation of blood which normally would be poured out partly on the altar and partly on the worshipper to reunite him with his god in a covenant relationship." Rather, this act can be "spiritualized in the guise of a heavenly offering made accessible by faith instead of by ritual" (James 1962, 76). Scholars sometimes view Christ as one in the succession of divine kings. His portrayal "in the Passion narratives was that of a mock king clad in a scarlet robe, with a reed in his right hand and a crown of thorns on his brow, subjected to brutal and ignominious veneration and mockery, like so many victims in this role in the long history of the sacral kingship." However the account of the Crucifixion is interpreted, "the fact remains that the Passion and death of Christ introduced into the Jewish Messiah tradition the ancient conception of the divine Saviour King suffering and dying for the salvation of mankind." Calvary was "the central event in a redemptive process" (James 1962, 72).

It is important to realize that "the role of the Sacred King was much sought after, and was never that of a forced or unwilling victim." The sacred victims were "highly honored and revered people." A sacrificed individual was "a *willing contributor* to the pattern of life. By his voluntary death he went consciously to the Other-world, and while there he was to attempt to learn from the [Earth] Mother, and to replay her wisdom back to his people. By performing a willed ritual cycle of deaths and rebirths, the pagan peoples aspired to harmonise with and contribute to the greater life-cycles that they felt evident around them"

(Stewart 1977, 37–38). The killing of the sacred king was a tradition that persisted in many forms, including the various substitute or "mock kings" whose murders, sometimes feigned, ultimately became associated with the Saturnalia celebration at the winter solstice.

The king represented "the faltering forces of nature in winter" that would perish with the coming of spring. The advent of winter signaled that the divinity of the king was waning. This weakness was dangerous to the people and was regarded as the reason for all the misfortunes of the previous year. As winter would lose the battle with spring, so the old king would lose the ritual struggle with the new incarnation of divinity. Thus he was sacrificed to redeem the community. His resurrection symbolized the birth of the New Year and the regeneration of life in the seasonal cycle (Orloff 1981, 17). Religious scholar Mircea Eliade explains, "It is easy to understand why the installation of a king . . . took place at the New Year," because "the king was believed to renew the entire Cosmos. The greatest of renewals takes place at the New Year, when a new time cycle is inaugurated." The rejuvenation effected by the New Year ritual is a reiteration of the cosmogony and "begins the Creation over again." For preindustrial peoples, the world had to be renewed annually according to a certain model or myth that was expressed through ritual (1975, 41–42).

At some indeterminable point in time, the ritual killing of the sacred king undoubtedly came to be symbolized by the execution of the wren, the "little king" whose revered status, analogous to the sacred king's inviolable period of rule, protected the bird against persecution except for an annual period of sanctioned slaughter near the solstice. During the ceremony at that time, a Welsh wren song urges: "Please turn the King in" (Owen 1959, 64). The "wren-king" became a "form of symbolism or substitution for the human sacrificial victim" (Stewart 1977, 19). The English romance *Merlin,* dating from 1450, contains the line: "Thus shall the Knyghtes of the rounde table go to avenge the deth of the wrenne" (Fife 1991, 155).

I find a fascinating likeness between the sacred king and the little avian king. Divine kings may have been once revered as "intercessors between man and god" who "were able to bestow upon their subjects and worshippers those blessings which are commonly supposed to be beyond the reach of mortals." They could, for example, "give rain and sunshine" and "make the crops grow" (Frazer 1963, 11). Because birds are also looked upon as links between people and god, beings who could communicate with both secular and sacred realms and mediate between them, the tiny wren, with its perceived magical characteristics, becomes an apt parallel to the human kings. A sacrificial victim, whether human or animal, represents a connection between the natural and the supernatural—a role that applies to both divine king and king wren.

Citing cross-cultural examples of ceremonies that involve the periodical death or periodical expulsion of an animal, often a bird such as the cock, Roheim places the wren hunt within the context of "a group of rites in which the aggressivity of a whole class is manifested against an individual, who has been raised to a position that . . . is higher than their own" (1930, 317). It is relevant that during the wren ceremony on the Isle of Man, those who carried the "King of the Birds" from house to house traditionally sang verses that ended with "We hunted the wren for everyone"—an indication that the rite, which was carried out by a few individuals, actually constituted a "vicarious sacrifice for the whole community" (Roheim 1930, 322–23). The wren hunt may be compared to the annual procession with the bear among the Aino of Saghalien and the Gilyaks of Siberia. In both cases, as with the wren, "the worshipful animal is killed with special solemnity once a year; and before or immediately after death he is promenaded from door to door, that each of his worshippers may receive a portion of the divine virtues that are supposed to emanate from the dead or dying god" (Gaster 1964, 546–48, 562–63).

During the version of the wren hunt carried out in certain parts of France, the person who was the first to strike the wren or who caught or killed it was "dignified by the title of 'King'" (Swainson 1886, 42). Following the wren hunt, there was a procession headed by the king, who carried the wren on a pole: "On the evening of the last day of the year the King and all who had hunted the wren marched through the streets of the town to the light of torches, with drums beating and fifes playing in front of them. At the door of every house they stopped, and one of them wrote with chalk on the door *vive le roi!* with the number of the year which was about to begin. On the morning of Twelfth Day the King again marched in procession with great pomp, wearing a crown and a blue mantle and carrying a sceptre. In front of him was borne the wren fastened to the top of a pole, which was adorned with a verdant wreath of olive, of oak, and sometimes of mistletoe grown on an oak. After hearing high mass in the parish church, . . . surrounded by his officers and guards, the King visited the bishop, the mayor, the magistrates, and the chief inhabitants, collecting money to defray the expenses of a royal banquet which took place in the evening and wound up with a dance" (Frazer 1963, 622–23). The fact that the man who killed the wren was called king may symbolically relate the wren ceremony to certain theories regarding the Hellenic games. For some scholars believe that those games were in some way "associated with the divine kingship and its ritual" and that "the victors at the games were the successors of kings who gained their royal status as a result of winning a ritual contest" (Spence 1947, 45).

Sacrificial Role

Animal worship and the associated sacramental killing of the embodied animal god are generally manifest in several different ways. When the revered animal is habitually killed, the slaughter of any one of the species involves killing the god, and this act is accompanied by proscribed apologies and atonement rituals. Or, there may be a special annual atonement ceremony during which a select individual of that species is slain with extraordinary displays of respect and devotion. In another kind of sacrifice, the sacred or revered animal is habitually spared, but is killed—and sometimes eaten—on specific, infrequent occasions, as with the rite of the wren sacrifice.

The custom of hunting and killing the wren is undoubtedly related to practices of animal sacrifice of pre-Christian origin, in which "the virtue of the thing sacrificed (believed to be Divine) is thought to be communicated to those taking part in the sacrifice, or to impart a fertilizing influence upon the fields over or in which the divided fragments may be carried or buried" (Macmillan 1926, 78). The world as it is known to humankind undergoes an endless cycle of creation and destruction—birth to death and birth again. Sacrifice rests on the principle that there must be death in order to have life, and is the natural outcome of the agricultural way of life in which new life is observed to spring out of a buried body. Symbolically, a living being must die in order for itself, and those it represents or embodies, to be reborn to another level of existence. One must die in the flesh in order to be born in the spirit. The soul does not perish at death, but passes from the body to another form. Killing one small victim—a part of the entity—is believed to release a force that brings about invigoration of the whole through sacrifice. The concept behind this practice is that violence is needed to stimulate the regenerative forces of nature.

The strips of colored cloth or ribbons that were attached to the wren or its bier during the wren procession are connected to the Celtic concept of sacrifice, for they undoubtedly represent "tokens in the tradition of offering and supplication" (Stewart 1991, 40) in an attempt to gain desired benefits from the slaughtered victim. This detail of the ceremony was taken seriously, as "every young lady, and even old ladies, used to compete in presenting the grandest ribbon to the wren" (Davies 1911, 65). The importance of the ribbons is reflected in various wren songs. A British song describes the paraded dead wren as having "a bunch of ribands by his side" (Swainson 1886, 37–38). And a Welsh version reveals that

> Ribbons all-colored
> Encompass the wren,
> Ribbons thrice-twisted
> Are his for a roof.

Slightly different lyrics describe "Ribbons all twisted / In place of a house" (Gill 1932, 389–90). And the lines from the wren song that describe "giving the 'eye' to the blind, and the 'leg' to the lame indicated the blessings derivable from the sacrifice" (Tegid 1911, 112).

In sacrifice, supernatural powers may be expected to give something great in exchange for something small. Yet there is meaning in sacrifice that goes beyond the desire to obtain certain blessings or to win god's favor. By means of sacrifice, communication is established "between the sacred and the profane worlds through the mediation of a victim," who "in the course of the ceremony is destroyed" (Hubert and Mauss 1964, 97). Sacrificed beings, whether human or animal, are generally considered willing victims. The process was not necessarily one of killing as an offering to a divinity or for supplication or thanksgiving. For the ancients, "ritual sacrifice was never intended to deprive creation for the sake of creation." Rather, it was a procedure in which the victim "threw off the burden of earthly dross and rose through a series of stages in his attempt to reach the divinity" (Bancroft 1987, 112).

In former times on the Isle of Man, "after the obsequies had been performed" over the grave of the wren, "the company ranged themselves in a circle, and danced to music provided for the occasion" (Cookson 1859, 27). The idea of gaiety accompanying a ritual death and the concept of a consenting, even joyful, sacrificial victim are almost impossible for people to understand today. Thus the encircling dance, accompanied by music and singing, that was held in conjunction with the ceremonial burial of the wren as late as the 1700s is often misunderstood as a mockery. Certainly by that time the ceremony may have been losing its original solemnity, but it nevertheless represented a survival of the old idea of the being who happily gave up life for a greater good. Perceiving little difference between the human and the animal world, early wren hunters would have projected upon the wren the image of the willing subject fulfilling its destiny, not the image of an object of wanton human cruelty. When the full significance of sacrifice is lost, only then is such a ritual killing perceived as a barbarous act.

The sources indicating that Jesus viewed himself as a willing victim of sacrifice and wanted his associates to understand him in that light were removed from orthodox Christian doctrine and deleted from the Bible. The original Acts of John contained a description of "the round dance of the disciples, led by Christ," as revealed by the Gospel writer himself. The narrative indicates that just before he was taken captive, Jesus gathered his disciples together and said: "Before I give myself over to them, let us praise the Father in a hymn of praise, and so let us go to meet what is to come. Then he bade us form a circle" for the dance, and "he was in the middle." And "after the Lord had thus danced the round with us, he went out" to be crucified "upon the thorn of the cross" (Pulver 1978, 169, 178–80).

Sacrifice meant "a sublime giving up in order to receive—the victim became the god in the same way that the Communion bread and wine *are* the body and blood of Christ." And for the community fulfilling the ritual, the victim was a "messenger whose association with the divinity would make him a link between that particular god and mankind" (Bancroft 1987, 112–13). According to the theory of René Girard, "The purpose of sacrifice is to restore harmony to the community, to reinforce the social fabric" (1977, 8). The sacrificed being is the "mediator who brings about the reversal from common danger to common salvation." The "unquestioned effect of the procedure is salvation of the community from evil and anxiety, which disappears with the doomed victim." Thus the "message" of the ritual is that the one singled out is going to his doom, whereas the rest of the group is safe (Burkert 1979, 67, 70).

The wren king is generally believed to be "a form of substitution for the human sacrificial victim. In the Christian ritual a substitution was also made for the body and blood, and the relationship of the symbology is very clear on certain points. The killing of the wren in folk custom was supposed to bring fertility to the fields and good luck to everyone, and a revealing key is the cooking and eating of it in a brass cauldron" (Stewart 1977, 19). A possible analogue to the slaughter of the wren is the ancient custom of the killing of the quail, a sacred bird for the Phoenicians. That "mystical sacrifice of a sacred animal" once took place at an annual festival at Tyre in February or March, just at the time when the quail returns each year to Palestine, "immense crowds appearing in a single night." This sacrifice commemorated the resurrection of Heracles, who had been restored to life by smelling of a quail (Smith 1972, 469).

The status of the wren in the areas where it was annually victimized made the tiny bird a fitting object for ritual death. The wren was a sacred bird, and sacrifice derives from sacredness. W. Robertson Smith, in his study of animal sacrifice, points out that a "reputation of natural holiness" gave certain species "a peculiar virtue when used in sacrifice." Totem animals are customarily sacrificed at an annual feast, with special and solemn ritual. The body may be buried, cast into a river, or eaten as a mystic sacrifice. "The sacrifices of animals not ordinarily eaten," according to Smith, "are not the invention of later times, but have preserved with great accuracy the features of a sacrificial ritual of extreme antiquity" (1972, 295, 466).

References to burial of the wren's body or its feathers after plucking, and most particularly the interment of its bones following the sacrificial eating of the carcass, are specific. An Irish wren song reveals: "We are the boys who came today / To bury the wren on St. Stephen's Day" (Macmillan 1926, 162). The lyrics of another wren song ask, "Where shall we bury the feathers?" and provide the reply: "In a grave mound" (Gill 1932, 410–11). An Orkney Islands version addresses the problem of disposing of the wren's bones after the bird has been shot and gives indications of the tremendous and incongruous power of those remains that can be nullified by fire:

> Whit will we do wi' his banes?
> Bury them in the land.
> They'll brak' men's pleughs.
> Cast them into the sea.
> They'll grow into great rocks.
> They'll wrack ships and boats.
> We'll burn them in the fire.
>   (Gill 1932: 399)

This concept of the necessity for disposal of what remains after a holy sacrifice undoubtedly stems from ancient belief that also motivated various subsequent injunctions relating to Christian communion. According to Roman Catholic and Anglican rules, the elements—wafer and wine—that are left over after the congregation has taken communion should be buried in a special way. Belief in the doctrine of transubstantiation means that the substance of the Eucharistic bread and wine is actually changed into the body and blood of Christ. Recognizing their sacred nature, such blessed elements cannot be simply discarded as refuse. In much the same way, the wren's sacrificed body or bones must be treated as holy objects. Burial of the wren's body would also ensure that it could not be consumed by scavengers. This practice relates to the Christian rule that sacred food must be rigorously guarded from animals and the host should never be left for "beasts and birds to devour" (Salisbury 1994, 65). Train's account of the Manx custom specifies that the dead bird was once ceremonially interred in the churchyard and that later "the sea-shore or some waste ground was substituted in its place" (1845, 2: 126–27). The wren, like the Christian host, was viewed as spiritual food associated with sacrifice that should be consumed only by humans.

The hair of a sacrificed animal, regarded as "the special seat of life and strength," has often been used as a means of divination or charm and represents a "permanent bond of connection" between the dead and the living (Smith 1972, 295, 324–25, 466). And sometimes the skin of the sacrificed animal was preserved as a token of the god, containing a part of the divine life (Gaster 1964, 544–45). In the case of the wren, the association of skin or hair with sacrifice and divinity transfers to the bird's feathers, whose magical qualities are part of many of the attendant ceremonies, and which themselves become valued protective talismans and charms. The attribution of such power "suggests that the sacrificed bird possessed divine influence" (Tegid 1911, 112). As noted previously, Manx wren boys distributed feathers for luck and protection against evil influences. According to Manx fairy legend, the wren's feathers were "preserved with religious care" (Train 1845, 2: 125). And Irish wren boys seeking money sang to the householder: "So now young lady shake up your feathers, / And do not think that we are beggars" (Macmillan 1926, 162). In a Brittany song, the miraculous nature of the wren's feathers is featured in lyrics that indicate even after "Four carts upon iron-shod wheels / Have carried his feathers to Nantes," enough are "still left in the house" to "furnish four fine feather-beds!" (Gill 1932, 400).

And in the Isle of Man wren song indicating that the bird's feathers would be "buried in a grave mound," the purpose is undoubtedly to engender new life with their capacity for regeneration. An English song reveals that the cook must be given the wren's feathers as well as the bones, but "the feathers will choke her," and finally, "the feathers *have* choked her, so the poor cook is dead" (Gill 1932, 393–95). Thus feathers are associated with death and, by implication, with subsequent rebirth. In another song, a feather is plucked by each member of the wren party after the bird has been brought home: "So they brought her away after each plucked a feather, / And when they got home shared the booty together" (Gill 1932, 410). These features may connect the wren ritual with another Manx custom, the sacrifice of a hen, which also involves a procession, mock mourning, plucking, burying, special use of feathers, a song, and a reward for the principal participants (Gill 1932, 410–15).

One Breton wren song is entirely devoted to the plucking of the wren. And during the ceremony in another area of France, the wren is plucked and its feathers tossed into the air. The feather motif is prominent in wren legends such as the one in which the other birds contribute feathers to the bare and needy wren, and in the sequel to the tale of the wren-eagle contest in which the wrathful eagle plucks feathers from the wren's tail. In certain areas of the world, among diverse cultures, feathers from a sacrificed bird have special power. This power is exemplified by the northern European rite in which roosters' feathers are plowed into fields during spring sowing to ensure a bountiful harvest and protect the crops (Orloff 1981, 39). It is also illustrated by the magical feather cloak worn by the Irish Druids (Gill 1932, 395, 420–21). The common phenomenon of feather preservation for use as charms or decorations rests on the observation that although birds die and their bodies decay, their feathers remain immortal. Additionally, such customs may relate to the concept dating from Paleolithic times that "the wisdom of birds was symbolized by, and transmitted through, their feathers" (Johnson 1988, 8).

The enigma of the slaughtered wren is all the more intriguing because, as a wild species, it does not meet the requirements of the classic object of sacrifice. Jonathan Z. Smith, an authority on sacrifice, states flatly: "I know of no unambiguous instance of animal sacrifice that is not of a domesticated animal" (1987, 197). Some characteristics of the wren, however, do fit closely into the image of a sacrificial victim. For example, Girard, in his study of violence and the sacred, presents the theory that the animal victims chosen were those "that display human characteristics. . . . The sacrificial animals were always those most prized for their usefulness: the gentlest, most innocent creatures, whose habits and instincts brought them most closely into harmony with man." Victims selected were those "most human in nature" (1977, 2–3).

The issue of the qualities of the sacrificed animal brings to mind the observations of the seventeenth century American pioneer woman and Sioux captive Fanny Kelly. She revealed in her memoirs that when the Indians killed a horse or held a ritual "dog-feast" to appease or conciliate offended deities, this sacrifice of a "faithful animal" was "invariably done by giving the best in the herd or the kennel" (1973, 90–91). The beloved and endearing wren meets the criteria for sacrifice in many respects. For few other wild creatures are so familiarly addressed and given a human name such as Jenny Wren. And interestingly, long ago the wren may even have been "kept domesticated on account of the auguries derived from it, which were employed by the Druids" (Ingersoll 1923, 119), who "divined the course of events from the chirping of tame wrens." The Irish also seem to have "domesticated the wren" for the "purpose of divination" (Spence 1945, 103–4). Armstrong points out that though the wren may not be "tameable," it may have been kept caged "for magico-religious reasons as geese were kept in enclosures by the Britons of Caesar's time" (1958, 161). A nineteenth-century ornithological work gives directions for furnishing the cages in which wrens were confined (Montagu 1831, 572), indicating that it was not uncommon to keep the species captive. Another authority on British birds asserts that wrens "may be kept in confinement" (Morris n.d., 135). That it might be possible to tame wrens at least to some degree is indicated by a contemporary naturalist's observation that "some are tame and come into summer camps for bread crumbs" (Terres 1980, 1047).

Thus there is convincing evidence for the wren hunt as a sacrificial rite. The bird was reverenced but killed at one season, its feathers were kept as talismans, its body was buried with respect, the chief human actor in the ceremony was regarded as a king, and the bird itself received a royal title. The wren, like other sacrificial victims, was treated with both honor and contempt. Also relevant to the wren hunt is the idea that "sacrifices are markers of boundaries in social time" and are associated with rites of transition (Leach 1976, 84). This precept fits the idea of the causal relationship between the killing of the sacred bird and the hoped-for seasonal change in the cycle of the sun at the time of the winter solstice that would ensure the return of spring. Also closely connected with the idea of sacrifice is the concept of the scapegoat, which relates to certain aspects of the wren hunt.

Seasonal and Scapegoat Rites

Boundaries between the sacred and the accursed are often fragile. The wren, like other animals who are generally esteemed, is a likely candidate for elaborate seasonal persecution as a scapegoat or sacrificial victim. Scapegoat ceremonies involve either periodic expulsion or killing of the animal. Although in most cases the wren was put to death following the hunt, in one Scottish ceremony, as we have seen, the wren was decorated with ribbons and then set free, and in Pembrokeshire, Wales, a live wren was carried around, so that people could make offerings to the "king," and then was released. Or a living wren was sometimes exhibited in a box with glass ends (Hole 1984, 164). In areas of France, too, a live wren was let loose, as was the original animal from which the term scapegoat was derived—the goat who was yearly sent forth into the wilderness bearing the sins of the Hebrews.

Inferring from its ceremonial nature and its enactment near the winter solstice, the wren hunt obviously belongs to the "category of rites which have as their object the banishment of evil influences at a seasonal crisis" (Armstrong 1958, 161). The sacrificial nature of the wren ceremony can be compared to other ancient rites involving the chasing, killing, and carrying in procession of a species of bird with a role as scapegoat associated with the New Year. Armstrong suggests the possibility that in ancient Sumerian prototypes of the wren hunt, the "dying down of the vegetation in winter may have been attributed to [a bird], or rather to that of which it was a symbol, and its destruction was regarded as giving magical aid to the powers of fertility associated with the New Year" (1958, 162).

Roheim also views the wren hunt as a scapegoat ceremony, one of many such rites in which an animal is held responsible for human guilt and, like the old kings, must atone for the presence of evil. Roheim cites European examples comparable to the wren ceremony; in one of these a cock is tormented and killed as a sinner, a "scapegoat not only for the sins but also for the anxieties of the community" (1930, 322). In another case, a goose is burdened with guilt for all the calamities that occurred during the past year and is sentenced to death (1930, 314). Similarly, the wren hunt, Roheim suggests, is a vicarious sacrifice in which according to the rhymes of the accompanying songs, the body is boiled and eaten. On the Isle of Man, feathers from the dead wren purchased with coins could protect the recipient from shipwreck for a year. Thus the anxiety dispelled through the "annual cathartic rite" of the wren ceremony was probably the fear of drowning; the hunt for the wren represented "a repetition of the perilous seaward rush of the amorous knights" (1930, 323).

With the rise of Christianity, the wren took on the symbolism of various religious figures—notably St. Stephen, Christ, and the Virgin Mary.

Identification with St. Stephen

In relatively recent times, the sacrificial role of the wren has been associated with, and on a deep level (not to be confused with the rationalization mentioned earlier) identified with, St. Stephen, through the general custom of being hunted on that saint's day, 26 December. "The martyr's day comes first after Christmas," Charles Jones points out, "symbolizing the idea that Christ's advent leads to His martyrdom" (1978, 297). In *Murder in the Cathedral,* T. S. Eliot aptly expressed this connection through Thomas à Beckett's Christmas sermon in which the Archbishop revealed that 25 December celebrates "at once Our Lord's Birth and His Death," and "on the next day we celebrate the martyrdom of . . . the Blessed Stephen." It is no accident that "the day of the first martyr follows immediately the day of the Birth of Christ" (1963, 48–49). It is fascinating that Beckett was born at the winter solstice in 1118 and murdered in Canterbury cathedral on 28 December, fifty-two years later. Shirley Toulson notes, "Many people believe that he deliberately chose to be a substitute for Henry II, by whose command he was killed; and that he was so well aware of the significance of his coming death that he actually arranged for the killing to take place on the cathedral steps at the time the solstice sun was setting" (1981, 102–3).

Stephen was the earliest deacon serving the Jerusalem church. According to Biblical scripture he was "a man full of faith and of the Holy Spirit," and was "full of grace and power," demonstrating "great wonders and signs among the people." Stephen was noted for "the wisdom and the spirit with which he spoke" (Acts 6:5, 8–15; 7:57–60). By preaching the truth fearlessly and criticizing people for resisting the Holy Spirit and for killing Christ, he made enemies who falsely accused him of blasphemy and stoned him to death as a heretic. Like Christ, even as he was dying, he prayed that God would not hold this sin against his persecutors (Farmer 1987, 391–92). His nobility makes him a tragic figure.

The association between St. Stephen and the wren is well established. It is interesting that Stephen Dedalus, the protagonist in James

Joyce's *Ulysses* and *Portrait of the Artist as a Young Man,* identifies with his namesake, St. Stephen. When Dedalus dreams that he is crowned king of Ireland, his procession includes a group of young men who chant the wren boys' rhyme (Glassie 1983, 130–31). The date of St. Stephen's Day is highly significant, with ancient implications indicative of death. As Jones points out, "the heart of winter" for Christianity was once the twelve days between the Nativity and Epiphany—"between the joyful birth and the magi's gifts—into which death seems to creep." Through the ancient rite of the annual killing of the wren on 26 December, which persisted into Christian·times, "the prehistorical winter slaughter" continued to haunt that day (1978, 297, 298).

The name Stephen is from the Greek, *Stephanos,* and signifies "crown" (Walsh 1991, 428). Thus metaphorically the saint is linked to the original sacrificial victim of the wren hunt—the goldcrest with its miniature golden crown who first became "king wren." There are other fascinating parallels between St. Stephen—who was characterized as being not only wise but also "eloquent and forceful"—and the tiny bird who was killed by stoning on the saint's day. The wren is "famed among men for wisdom, small though he be" (Klingender 1971, 366) and personifies not only "hidden wisdom" but also the "inner knowledge of God" (Hartley 1986, 121). The unusual forcefulness of the bird's demeanor and its remarkable vocal eloquence that are out of proportion to size—hallmarks of the wren that have already been described—make the likeness between saint and bird more striking. The method of their executions has underlying societal significance. For the concept of death by stoning serves to "divide the responsibility" for the martyrdom (Hubert and Mauss 1964, 129). The entire community participates in the killing.

Another aspect of Stephen's martyrdom relating his death to the killing of the wren is that, according to Acts 7:42 and 8:1, St. Paul condoned the stoning of Stephen because of Stephen's attack upon animal sacrifice (as well as other Jewish practices). Paul later changed his opinion, opposing the practice himself, not out of kindness to animals, but because he felt that such sacrifices were meaningless and because Christ had made the one sacrifice that counts and all other blood sacrifices were futile (Sorabji 1993, 179).

Correspondence with Christ

Though symbolically and calendrically related to St. Stephen, the hunted wren has an even deeper correspondence with Christ himself, being associated with both his birth and death. As noted previously, the wren was alleged to have been present at the Nativity and to have exhibited solicitous behavior toward the newborn Savior. The Manx wren hunt may have formerly taken place on Christmas Eve or Christmas morning, thereby mingling death with the celebration of birth. In an ancient poem containing the first Irish reference to the kingship of the wren, there is a reference to the wren being wounded and falling into the power of his enemies that is highly suggestive of Jesus' torture and Crucifixion. The bird reveals, "I have no rest, I have no protection from wood or branch, . . . everyone struck me a hard blow about the jaw and cut short my flight; I have been brought from kingship to death" (Ó Cuív 1980, 53–54). Some early sources specifically refer to the captured wren's death as a crucifixion—a practice "once actually carried out by country folk" (Stewart 1977, 19). Sometimes the wren "was crucified on a pole so that it appeared to be flying" (Howard 1995, 36). Descriptions of wren hunt processions quite commonly involve display of the bird's body with wings spread out in the form of a cross or fastened on sticks shaped like a cross. Cross symbolism pervades the wren hunt on the Isle of Man, where in the traditional rite the body of the bird is displayed in the center of two crossed hoops.

The cross has meanings with particular relevance to the wren ceremony. It has often been a "symbol from the neolithic to the present," representing "the year-journey and also the four cardinal directions." Because cross designs occur in Paleolithic cave art as well, it is probable that they are older than the Neolithic. Interpretations of the cross indicate that it "evoked whatever powers ensure the continuance of the cosmic cycle, to help the world through all phases of the moon, and the changing seasons." The cross can be a "symbol of life," a meaning that fits both "the older paleolithic calendrical associations" and "the later Christian idea of the cross as a symbol of Christ's sacrifice for the salvation of humanity" (Brockway 1993, 35–36).

The point of intersection of the cross may have special symbolic importance. Popular author Joseph Campbell offers one possible meaning for the cross, especially as it pertains to Christ's Crucifixion. Heroes, he suggests, at some time during their inevitable journeys, often confront an abyss. They may go into the abyss alive, as Jonah enters the dark cavity of the whale, or they may go in dead, as Jesus goes into the cross. Christ "goes through the cross, through the mid-point or sundoor." In so doing, he "leaves the four dimensions behind him" and proceeds to the world beyond (1990, 1: 1).

Something great in exchange for something small.
Drawing by Betsey MacDonald.

So the sacrificed wren, like the dead and mutilated Christ, is suspended at the midpoint between two crossed circles, the entrance to the Otherworld. Both wren and God, killed and ritually dismembered, will become alive and whole again through the process of rebirth and renewal. Death and birth are juxtaposed, becoming one and the same— tomb and womb. As René Guénon explains the symbolism, "At the center of the cross, all oppositions are reconciled and resolved; that is the point where the synthesis of all contrary terms is achieved" (1993, 81).

It is recorded that Irish wren hunters, hating the wrens, "thrust them full of thorns" (Thompson 1989, 209), an obvious reference to the nails piercing Jesus at the Crucifixion and, more specifically, to the crown of thorns. The Irish song that indicates destruction of the wren involves holly: "We knocked him down and we broke his knee, / And we brought him home on a holly tree" (Macmillan 1926, 162). In one song, the wren's body was "guarded in a holly tree" (Swainson 1886, 37–38), and in another version, the martyred bird was brought back "Dressed high upon my holly tree" (O'Sullivan 1991, 33). Many wren songs contain the refrain "Sing holly, sing ivy, sing ivy, sing holly" (Read 1916, 259). And one song locates the wren's nest in the holly tree, bringing together birth and death—the nest as the place of new life and death as represented by crucifixion on the holly tree:

> Rolley, Rolley, where's your nest?
> It's in the bush that I love best,
> It's in the bush, the holly tree,
> Where all the boys do follow me.
> (Langstaff and Langstaff 1985, 128–29)

The frequent occurrence of holly in wren songs is revealing, for the sharp-pronged leaves of that plant symbolize the crown of thorns as well as the nails that pierced Christ's hands and feet, and its red berries stand for the blood shed at the Crucifixion. The "holly tree" itself also represents Christ's cross, which is frequently referred to as a tree.

Additionally, the wren is identified with the crucified Christ in a symbolic way through corresponding wounds inflicted upon both. Jesus can be viewed as a sacred king, and the wounding of the sacred king is a symbolic motif reaching far back in time. Generally that king has received an "initiatory laming" by being pierced in the thigh (Mann 1985, 27). (Some sources assert that the real injury is to the genitals, the leg being a euphemism that avoids sexual connotations.) The spear wound delivered to Christ on the cross by the soldier Longinus—a ritual maiming—is sometimes considered to be analogous to this phenomenon, though that wound was made in his side. Thematically, the ritual wounding of Christ that was part of the Crucifixion has been related to the maiming of the legendary Fisher King, whose kingdom languished until he was healed: "The Maimed King suffers for his people. In his health lies theirs; and in his suffering, their ill" (Fife 1991, 155–56).

Thus there is a strong connection between Christ and the king of all birds. According to legendary narratives, the New Year Robin (alias the god Belin) shot his father the Wren (alias the god Bran to whom the wren was sacred), transfixing him "between the sinew and the bone" of his leg. Robert Graves explains that this is the same spot between the Achilles tendon and the ankle bone where the nail was driven in to pin Jesus to the cross "in the Roman ritual borrowed from the Canaanite Carthaginians; for the victim of crucifixion was originally the annual sacred king" (1989, 306, 318). Graeme Fife also points out that the foot of the wren (sometimes known as "Bran's sparrow") was "split through by dead-eye Llew Llaw Gyffes" in the same area as the nail was driven into Jesus' foot (1991, 155).

The story of Llew Llaw Gyffes, a Celtic divine warrior and solar hero or sun-god, appears in the Celtic classic, *The Mabinogion* (see chapter 2). When a wren lighted on the mast of the ship on which the young man was sailing, "the boy aimed at it, and hit it between the sinew of its leg and the bone" (Jones and Jones 1991, 66). "The Maimed King— Bran wounded in the foot, Llew Llaw Gyffes lamed like a smith"—is a "surrogate for the Saviour himself, of whom John says, in Revelation: 'For thou wast slain and hast redeemed us to God by thy blood.' The wound, which can be cured by some heroic act or spiritual triumph, holds out the all-important promise that death and disaster [are] never absolute, that redemption is never wholly unthinkable" (Fife 1991, 157).

The "laming" of the wren can be related to the leg wounds of the sacred kings and of Christ. For example, in Ireland, the captured wren "was tied, alive but maimed, to a pole . . . or tied by the leg" (Ingersoll 1923, 119). As previously noted, descriptions of the Manx wren ceremony indicate that the avian victim carried in the procession was hung by one leg in the center of the two crossed hoops (Hazlitt 1905, 2: 666). An Irish version of the wren song indicates that

> We followed this wran three miles or more,
> Through hedges and ditches and frost and snow,
> We knocked him down and we broke his knee.
> (Macmillan 1926, 162)

The reference to injuring the bird's knee (a term seldom applied to avian anatomy) suggests the maimed king and is another indication of the tie to Jesus. Probably the warning that if someone kills a wren that person will suffer a fractured bone during the course of the year (Brand 1849, 3: 195) represents a correspondence to the laming of the sacred king—an appropriate retribution for breaking the age-old taboo.

Association with Mary

Norman Iles, an expert on pre-Christian carols, accomplished some intriguing folkloric detective work regarding an ancient song about the wren. He determined that the song "Joys Seven" is actually an ancient traditional carol that had been "altered by Christian propagandists." They revised it to describe the joys of Mary, Mother of Christ, whom they substituted for the wren, the "pagan bird-symbol of woman," the subject of the original song, "The Seven Joys of Jenny." He demonstrates convincingly that the points made in the song cannot be logically applied to Mary, who would not have observed her son's Crucifixion with joy and did not see Jesus "read the Bible o'er" (it had not yet been written), as the lines of the altered version indicate. Most important, the joys attributed to Mary in the song are "not her joys at all. They are the powers of Jesus"—to "bring the dead alive," to "make the lame to go," to "make the blind to see," and "to wear the crown of heaven." The lines concerned with woman's joys, Iles argues, are much more aptly applied to Jenny Wren, whose sacrificed carcass traditionally "gave eyes to the blind, legs to the lame, and pluck to the poor," according to the wren songs. So he "restored the powers, the joys and the praise to her name" (1986, 172–75). Iles's argument is logical, for, as the lore of the wren makes clear, it was Jenny's death that regenerated the earth, thus redeeming all life, including human.

The Seven Joys of Jenny (Restored)

> The first good joy that Jenny had
> It was the joy of one,
> To see the power her nesty had
> To make to speak the dumb

Chorus:
To make to speak the dumb, b . . . boom,
And blessed may she be,
Both birdy, nest,—and loving song—
For ever night and day.

The next good joy that Jenny had
It was the joy of two,
To see the power her nesty had
To make the lame to go.

Chorus:
To make the lame to go, b . . . boom,
And blessed may she be,
Both birdy, nest—and loving song—
For ever night and day.

The next good joy that Jenny had
It was the joy of three,
To see the power her nesty had
To make the blind to see.

Chorus:
To make the blind to see, b . . . boom etc.

The next good joy that Jenny had
It was the joy of four,
To see the power her nesty had
To give pluck to the poor.

Chorus:
To give pluck to the poor, b . . . boom etc.

The next good joy that Jenny had
It was the joy of five,
To see the power her nesty had
To bring the dead alive.

Chorus:
To bring the dead alive, b . . . boom etc.

The next good joy that Jenny had
It was the joy of six,
To see the power her nesty had
To stand up stumps like sticks.

Chorus:
To stand up stumps like sticks, b . . . boom etc.

The next good joy that Jenny had
It was the joy of seven,
To see the power her nesty had
To raise man into heaven.

Chorus:
To raise man into heaven, b . . . boom,
And blessed may she be,
Both birdy, nest,—and loving song—
Forever night and day.

Here the bird is female—the familiar Jenny Wren. But the little bird's gender is ambiguous, for in other contexts it can be male as well. Sexual symbolism in the wren ceremony takes on several different aspects.

Sexual Imagery

Sexual elements have been identified in the wren hunt. The tiny bird, as related in the eagle-wren legend, flies highest of all birds and penetrates deepest into the earth and hides in the eagle's breast. According to Roheim's controversial but interesting notion, "flight is coitus" and "the penis is the small part of the body that penetrates deeper into Mother Earth." The contest between the eagle and the wren is "between the powerful body with all its muscles [the eagle] and the seemingly insignificant, yet all-important, member of generation [the wren]." This contest may be interpreted as "a regression into the uterus, a race in which the penis must always be slightly in advance of the body." The "king and the little king, eagle and wren, body and penis, are two aspects of a whole" (1930, 325, 326).

To illustrate the sexual connotations of the wren, Roheim describes the French wren ceremony in which a man who was elected king, after swimming under water, entered the town with a wren on his wrist, mounted on a wagon. People who had been married within seven years pulled on one side of the wagon and those who hoped to undertake matrimony soon pulled on the other, until one group won the tug-of-war, bringing the wagon over to its side. After the king and his wren received homage in the town, the king plucked feathers from the bird and threw them in the air. Additionally, a wooden wren was fastened to a pole nearby and each inhabitant had to shoot it with an arrow. Roheim interprets the man holding the wren in his hands as a representative of the phallus, symbolic of the returning impulse of procreation. His rite of swimming stands for "coitus with a complete return into the amniotic fluid" (1930, 327). The contest between the newly married and those who wish to take their place is interpreted as a struggle for the phallus, and hence the wren was customarily carried into the houses of newlyweds. In these ceremonies there is an ambiguous attitude toward the organ of generation. Its representative, the wren killer, becomes king, but only after killing the wren—that is, the phallus—and the wren has been shot at by the whole population. Through their actions, "the wren becomes a scapegoat; they disclaim their part in his sin. The small bird is the true emblem of royalty, the phallus is king of birds and men" (Roheim 1930, 326–27).

In a general discussion of the language of birds and their prophesies, Roheim postulates a phallic role and finds references to sex. He points out that because they fly skyward, birds are messengers of gods and mortals and their flight "recalls the flying or erection dream." He suggests that "those who believe in the language of birds, that is, practice bird omina, are affirming the *prototypical nature of genitality*" (1992, 178, 180). Feathers themselves—the object of considerable attention in wren-hunt ceremonies and accompanying songs as well as in legends about the bird—may have a phallic connotation. It is possible that "the Latin word for feather 'penna' might be etymologically related to the word 'penis'" (Dundes 1991a, 342).

"Robin," so often encountered in wren songs, may have a sexual connotation, for "in Cornwall 'Robin' means phallus" (Graves 1989, 397). The insatiable desire for food demonstrated by the nursery rhyme character Robin the Bobbin, described in chapter 3, can be interpreted as a sexual appetite as well. In his analysis of folk rhymes Iles, too, proposes sexual meanings for the wren hunt, offering some interpretations drawn from the familiar Robin-Bobbin song. He asserts, "It's a woman hunt. That's why the lads and men chase the bird for miles over the countryside." The men garland the dead bird and "then they carry her body back in triumph to the village. 'We've got one!'" He goes on to explain:

> Wren for woman, Robin for man, is the foundation of all bird-symbolism. The wren was chosen as the woman-bird because she has a jutting-out little tail, and a round nest with a hole in it, lined with moss inside. What more can any primitive man want? Robin was chosen as man's own badge because of his reddish breast. Dark red—

blood red—is the true phallic color; and the robin's the only bird that has something like it on display.

"Robin" became the favourite man's name. "Jenny" became the favourite woman's name. The birds were loved, for they were every married couple—though country people knew perfectly well, then as now, that robins don't mate with wrens. Feelings over-ride facts. . . .

But we still put robins on Christmas cards, and by so doing we keep the link with the Druids and with this chant. For robin was their king-bird, and the wren was the queen. So, on 25 December, the day of the sun's return, the king-deputy (Robin) led the hunt for his queen—for all women. The hunt was to help the sun rise again, for the sun was a male god and, like any other man, needed his virility confirmed. His return was not just a natural fact. It was a human one. It was linked with unconquerability and potency.

Robin leads the hunt as chief male member. And his two companions are also male members, men and more-than-men. They're called Robin and Bobbin or Dibbin and Dobbin, because they're a pair. They are the testicles—just as Robin, being phallic, can be called John the Rednose.

"Robin and his two partners," the "three men-in-one, hunt a woman. They pounce on her as she lies. . . . A woman—desire of a woman— will give eyes to the blind, legs to the lame, and pluck to the poor. Blind men, lame men, poor men, will go on the hunt." And "what's the end of the men's wren hunt? It's not her death. The chant goes on after she's been pounced on. It's 'How shall we boil her? In the brewer's big pan.' What that means is, 'How shall we settle her down? In the pudding club's pan.' For the brewer made things swell up, froth and ferment. In Ireland, the brewers even make a 'creature.' When the wren becomes pregnant, that's the rightful end of the hunt" (1989, 74–76). Here Iles refers to elements featured in some of the wren hunt songs quoted in chapter 3.

Traditionally, the wren hunt was always an event for males. I have rarely found a source that reported female participation. The old account found in *Manx Reminiscences,* for example, indicates that it was "old men and young boys" who pursued the bird (Clague 1911, 13). Train wrote that the wren was captured "by boys alone" (1845, 2:126). In Ireland, "the principals were young men" (Gill 1932, 403). The Irish wren boys were "usually lads aged 10–14, but here and there men up to the age of 30 [took] part" (Armstrong 1958, 155). Carrying out a hunt (in general) has often been compared to sexual conquest, the sexual act, and rape. The hunt may symbolize an erotic event, in which women become the prey: "From the thirteenth century to the end of the Middle Ages, women were described as deer and other animals who served as quarry" (Salisbury 1994, 158). An in-depth study of Cree Indian hunting reveals data that reflect similar beliefs in that society as well. Anthropologist Robert Brightman found that "Cree metaphors represent human male-female relationships as homologous with hunter-prey relationships. . . . From the point of view of male hunters, sex is a metaphor for hunting, and women are metaphors for animals." There is an "interchangeability of human women with game animals" (1993, 127).

In his work on the general history and meaning of hunting, Matt Cartmill notes that "the connection of hunting with masculinity runs deep," and "hunting has been a stereotypically male activity throughout most of western history." Some contemporary men say they like to go hunting so they can "drink beer, shoot at inoffensive animals, and talk about pussy." Many "think that their sport affirms their virility as well as their masculine identity" and feel that "hunting makes them sexier." Bumper stickers with slogans such as "Bowhunters have longer shafts" and "I hunt white tail year round" proclaim this association. One devotee of the sport identifies his reason for hunting as "intercourse with nature" (1993, 233, 234). Marti Kheel has also made a convincing analysis of modern-day hunting in terms of its metaphoric representation of male sexuality with woman as prey (1995, 85–125).

Interestingly, in a 1665 painting entitled *Rest on the Hunt*, artist Abraham Hondius has used bird symbolism to portray the masculine sexual connotations of bird hunting. As the scene is depicted, a woman is about to be seduced by the hunter when he pauses from the chase. The setting includes a live owl, which is tied to a pole in order to attract birds who approach and "mob" the predator so that the hunter can shoot them (a commonly used ploy for decoying birds). Hanging in the trees are cages containing pretty song birds, representing the hunter's "sweet talk." The man has just killed a bittern, an unusual species to hunt, a tall slender marsh bird that has strong phallic symbolism due to its habit of pointing its long bill straight upward to camouflage itself among the reeds. The same theme in literature is vividly expressed in Thomas Hardy's *Tess of the d'Urbervilles*, when Tess, suffering from the great wrong that has been inflicted on her by her seducer, compares her pain and exploitation to the agony endured by some wounded pheasants that have been shot by hunters and left to die slowly (1984, 273–74).

There is sexual imagery in the etymology of "wren." The word comes from the Middle English *wrenne,* deriving from the Old English *wroenna* (or *wraenna*), from *wroene* (or *wraena*), meaning "lascivious." The closely related Danish word, *vrinsk,* denotes "proud," and the Swedish *vrensk* signifies "uncastrated" (Swann 1968, 261; Gruson 1972, 200). In a study of the origins of words from nature, the authors point out that the wren's "cocked up" tail is a very prominent feature. Thus the sexual symbolism of the wren may be traceable to "the shameless elevation of the little tail" and to "the fact that the bird produces a large number of offspring" (Potter and Sargent 1974, 296). Another explanation is that the lecherous image "originated in observation of the polygamy of the males" (Leahey 1982, 775–76).

One British nickname for the wren, "cutty quean," means "bobtailed hussy, . . . an apt name for this bird that bustles, cocking its stubby tail and brazenly scolding the rest of the world" (Lembke 1992, 51). In an old traditional poem entitled "Robin Redbreast's Testament," the robin refers to the "Lady Wren" as "Ye little cutty quean," an epithet that means "naughty little girl, often used as a name for the wren" (Philip 1990, 96). Not only was the word *cutty* "once a term for a testy or naughty girl or woman," but also "a cutty-stool" was formerly "a seat in church where offenders against chastity had to sit." Other of the wren's sobriquets have connotations of sexual desire or lust. Kitty-wren reflects an Oxford English Dictionary meaning for *kitty* indicating "a young girl or woman, occasionally a light woman" (Wentersdorf 1977, 196). The Lincolnshire name "Gilliver Wren" (with a variant, "Julliver Wren"), signifies "wench" or "hussey" (Lockwood 1993, 68). British names like Dicky Pug, Pug, or Puggy Wren are also sexually suggestive, as "pug" is slang for prostitute or mistress (also for a dear one, sweetheart, or pet) and "dick" is used for penis.

A relevant application of the wren's sexual image occurred in Ireland during the Crimean War. Prostitutes known as "camp followers" in and around the neighborhood of the military base at Curragh, County Kildare, were called wrens. It was noted that "these creatures . . . do not live in houses or even huts, but build for themselves 'nests' in the bush" (Rowland 1978, 184–85). "Wren" is a slang expression for young woman or girl. (It had evidently lost its derogatory connotation when it was used to designate a member of the Women's Royal Navy Service, an auxiliary of the British Navy during World War I that was reorganized during World War II and subsequently incorporated into the regular Navy.)

Association with Royal Hunting Rites
and the Hunt in General

Sociologist Francis Klingender, in discussing courtly hunting rites of the Middle Ages, likens the wren hunt to the stag hunt. The hunted stag, he asserts, may have unconsciously served as "a symbolic substitute for the lord himself." As a sacred bird and "culture hero," the wren is the object of a ritual that is analogous to the royal stag hunt in which there is a ceremonial distribution of the slain animal among participants, just as there is reference to division and eating of the wren's body in the wren ceremony songs. "The veneration shown for the wren as a royal bird is paralleled by the chivalrous respect for the stag as the royal game and also by strict game laws . . . which made the hunting of the stag a royal prerogative." There is reason to suspect that when the head of the stag was presented to the lord, "it was his own severed head, or rather that of his animal-symbol." The courtly hunting ceremonial "retained much of the emotional intensity of the ancient totem sacrifice" (1971, 471–72). These comparisons reveal another facet of the victimized wren as representing the "king."

In a broader sense, it is revealing to note how the particular ceremony in which the wren is the quarry fulfills the criteria of the general category of the hunt. Hunting is defined as "the deliberate, direct, violent killing of unrestrained wild animals." It involves "confrontational, premeditated, and violent killing" and is "an armed confrontation between humanness and wildness, between culture and nature." The hunt takes place at the boundary where the "human domain confronts the wild" and "marks the edge of the human world." Creatures that can be killed easily without being chased are "not worthy subjects of a hunt" (Cartmill 1993, 30, 36, 250).

The wren must have presented quite a challenge to its pursuers. An old proverb advises, "Better a wren in the hand than a crane on the wing," but as Aristotle noted, the bird "is difficult to catch" (Balme 1991, 271). A Waterford wren song expresses the frustration that the wren hunters must have felt when pursuing the tiny and elusive creature:

> We were all day hunting the wren;
> We were all day hunting the wren;
> The wren so cute and we so cunning.
> He stayed in the bush when we were running.
> (Armstrong 1955, 5)

Even ornithologist Armstrong, using modern trapping methods to band the birds for his scientific studies, found "catching wrens difficult, time-consuming and exasperating" (1955, 5). Most significantly, by metaphorical extension of its original meaning ("to pursue and kill wild animals"), to hunt also means "to search after, seek" (Cartmill 1993, 250). In this sense, the original wren hunters were chasing something far more complex than a tiny bird. They were seeking wisdom, redemption, and the perpetuity of life through the ritual slaughter of a sacred being.

The wren hunt is also concerned with liminality, darkness, and the sun and demonstrates the phenomena of reversal, exaggeration, and transformation.

Associations with Liminality, Darkness, and the Sun

The close association between the hunted wren's death and the darkest period of the year allegedly traces back at least to the time of the Celts and probably much earlier. The placing of the ceremony near the winter solstice is far older than Christianity, and results from some of the same factors that centuries later determined that Jesus' birth would be celebrated at the identical magical season that is fraught with anxiety and hope. The Savior's birth comes a few days after the winter solstice, when the days are shortest, and his death is commemorated near the spring equinox, when the days and nights are of equal length. Thus, in a kind of symbolic inversion, he was born when the world is the darkest and died when it is heading toward the lightest. This reversal emphasizes the concept that death ultimately means light, for the Resurrection will follow. The concept of a divine entity dying and disappearing, only to return, is probably as old as humanity itself. It is significant to note that Christ's birth is generally said to have occurred at midnight—a liminal point in time denoting the change from night to day and demarcating successive days.

Another relevant factor is that for the Celts, "boundaries exerted an enormous fascination. . . . The merging boundaries between contrasting periods of time—for instance, noon or midnight—were felt to be haunted by unseen powers." Divisions of time such as phases of the moon or seasons of the year possessed deep meaning, and "the divisions themselves were moments in which time was transcended and the unseen world believed to be very close." An "essential aspect of the Otherworld was the subtle area of intermingling between two worlds, such as dawn or twilight, the river's edge, . . . and birth or dying" (Bancroft 1987, 94).

The winter solstice—the shortest day of the year, the day containing the least amount of light and the longest night—marks the moment of change, following which the interval of sunlight will become progressively longer. There is a perceived moment of hesitation, an interval in which the sun seems to pause before returning. That moment is characterized by hope that the sun will indeed come back. The time when physical life is least active on Earth seems to provide a stimulus for spiritual concerns to reawaken and become preeminent, especially concerns about the annual cycle and the hoped-for reappearance of life-giving vegetation. Human well-being and survival once depended on the seasonal cycles, and nature was known to be not only powerful but also capricious. For people in the preindustrialized world, the sun's disappearance meant loss of light and heat, foreshadowing death. For the ancients, the sun-god died each year at the winter solstice and was reborn the following day at the dawn of the New Year. In metaphoric terms, humankind has always regarded the time of the solstice as one of turning from darkness to light, and from death to rebirth. It is also the boundary between the old and the new, for almost universally, the marking of the New Year follows the solstice. Indeed, the shortest day is sometimes called "the day the year dies."

The period of the solstice is liminal, "betwixt and between" seasons, when uncertainties about the continuing cycle of the year result in rituals and sacrifices to ensure the return of the sun, bringing the increasing daylight and warmth that are necessary for sustaining life. It is relevant that sacred kings, and later the mock kings that were included in winter festivals, were put to death, literally or figuratively, at this dark season when the tiny "king of the birds" was also slain. Even in historic times, kings have been killed as well as crowned at the winter solstice; and although their deaths did not take the public form of ritual sacrifice, some people believe that they must be accounted for in those terms (Toulson 1981, 102).

The winter season brings "a frenzied movement against the inevitable flow of death and rebirth," and the liminal time of the solstice imparts "special anxiety tinged with pathos" (Jones 1978, 296–97). The wren boys' solicitation of money and sometimes food bears a relationship to traditional ways of coping with periods of uncertainty. For as described in chapter 3, Europeans gave more freely during the period of seasonal transition, not out of benevolence and charity, but because they believed future good luck depended on the generosity they demonstrated at that time. Thus people looking for handouts took advantage of the season.

Saturnalia festivals held at the time of the solstice and, later, the Christian idea of Jesus' birth at that special time of year, both trace their origins to pagan rituals involving the sun. Christ—perceived as a new

Son or new sun—came to transform the cold, dark season. In ancient times during the darkest days of winter, sacrifices were made to the sun-god to "ensure that, at the end of its long decline, the life-giving orb would not disappear forever over the rim of the horizon" (Beaton 1986, 49). The Druids once "worshipped the golden-crested wren, holding him sacred to the sun; and once a year they held a sacrificial offering to ensure immortality for the deity. In later days the wren became peculiarly sacred to the Virgin" (Hare 1952, 33). It is fascinating in this regard that a poem published about 1555, *Armonye of Byrdes,* relates the wren to the Mother of Christ, identifying her Son as interchangeable with "her Sun":

> Then said the wren
> I am called the hen
> Of Our Lady most cumly;
> Then of her Sun
> My notes shall run
> For the love of that Lady.
> (Hare 1952, 33)

On the Isle of Man, the value of the wren as a good luck talisman depended upon the bird being caught between dawn and sunrise. This timing would ensure "a good herring fishery the next season" (Townley 1791, 1:4). Such a short interval, hard to measure, is liminal in the strictest sense, and certainly would have been a difficult time to find and kill a wren. Such a refinement of detail in the hunt indicates that the Manx people, like those who preceded them, had an overriding concern with the position of the sun in regard to the ritual sacrifice. For all knew that the sun was needed for life and for the power of fertility, to oppose the realms of darkness and death. Another demarcation of time based on the sun that was important to the wren ceremony was documented on the Isle of Man by Kermode. In the Manx ceremony, "by noon the wren is almost featherless. When twelve o'clock arrives the different parties who have been perambulating with the birds, cease their labors, and divide the money received among themselves. . . . After that hour no one pays any attention to the custom, nor would a feather from the bird be considered worth accepting" (1885, 161). Thus the position of the sun had a profound effect on the power of the bird's feathers and determined the boundaries of the wren hunt and procession—marking the beginning and end of those rites.

Manx belief held that the wren was "a spirit of nature protective of man against the forces of winter, storms, and tempests." Thus the bird "had a solar connection," and "its dead body may have been considered as a species of solar talisman emanating solar virtues" (Spence 1947, 46). It is also evident that "the death and burial of the wren symbolizes the decease and obsequies of the old sun" (MacCulloch 1991, 221). The wren was a "drinker up of sun rays," the sun's enemy (Rothery n.d., 60). This idea certainly relates to the deeply entrenched legend in which the wren flies higher than his rival, the eagle, thus attaining a position closer to the sun than any other bird. In his study of Celtic religion, James Bonwick also points out that the wren "symbolized the sun, and was once sacrificed to Pluto. It perhaps symbolized the weak sun." The Druids "employed a wren to symbolize the sun's divinity" who escaped into a shrine "to save himself from his murderous pursuers" (1986, 225). It is significant that Llew Llaw Gyffes, who, with such perfect aim, shot the wren in the leg with an arrow, was known as a "sun god" (Squire 1975, 262, 264). In mythology, arrows often represent "the rays of the sun or sunbeams" by which darkness and cold may be conquered. The concept of "infallible skill in archery," encountered in many myths and legends, "is originally derived from the inevitable victory of the sun over his enemies, the demons of night, winter, and tempest" (Dundes 1991a, 336, 337).

It is fascinating to find that a Native American tribal tradition assigns to the wren the role of extinguisher of the sun. The Miwok tale "How Marsh Wren Shot Out the Sun" features a wren who once carried out his threat to "shoot out the sun with an arrow as sharp as his beak," making the whole world turn dark. An "orphan boy, Cha-Ka, the Marsh Wren" (a New World species related to the wren), made the sun's light disappear because he was angry at the other animals for treating him as "an outsider" and not giving him enough to eat. In the darkness that followed the wren's feat of archery, no one could see to find food, and everyone was starving. Finally, the hummingbird was able to fly up and find a hole in the sky, tear off a piece of the sun's fire, and bring it down to light the earth again (Edwards 1995, 87–91).

The association between the wren and the sun occurs in a certain Irish legend that indicates that there is a "ritual marriage between the sun-god and the soil." This marriage "betwixt sky and earth" is associated with "the idea of the divine king and queen" (Spence 1945, 118). The wren is connected with both the sun and the soil and is also identified as a divine king and as a queen, thus embodying all elements of this legend. As a ground-dwelling species, or even an underground creature due to its habit of creeping into holes and crevices, the wren is in direct opposition to the sun. The Greek sun-god Apollo was known to be enemy to crawling and subterranean creatures and this antagonism was expressed in the hunting of the goldcrest, or king of birds, at the season of the solstice in ancient Greece.

Graves notes that "in British folklore, the Robin Redbreast as the spirit of the New Year sets out with a birch rod to kill his predecessor the Gold Crest Wren, the Spirit of the Old Year, whom he finds hiding in an ivy bush" (1989, 97, 186). (A birch rod symbolizes fertility and also has the power to drive out evil spirits.) According to popular belief, the Celtic god Bran, or Saturn, hid from pursuit by his rival in the ivy bush disguised as a "Gold Crest Wren," but Robin always caught and hanged him. In the incident previously cited, it was the New Year Robin (or Belin) who shot his father the Wren (or Bran) in the leg (Graves 1989, 318, 397). These events offer one explanation for the references to "Robin" that appear in various renditions of the wren song, such as "Who'll hunt the Wren? cries Robin the Bobbin," and "We'll away to the woods, says Robin the Bobbin." They also underscore the interpretation that "the Wren Hunt represents a New Year ceremonial having as its purpose the defeat of the dark earthpowers and identification with the hoped-for triumph of light and life" (Armstrong 1958, 166).

Reversal

Prominent in the wren ritual, as previously mentioned, is the element of reversal, also called inversion, which characterizes many ceremonial observances, particularly those held during the winter solstice or the period between the Old and the New Years. At the most basic level, this phenomenon is embodied in the enigmatic seasonal persecution of a creature who is at all other times revered and protected by strong taboos. Reversal involves many of the actual and perceived traits of the wren itself and extends into the deep-level aspects of the ritual surrounding the bird. The symbolic inversion that is incorporated into many celebrations involves actions that are the opposite of what is supposed to characterize everyday life. In keeping with the spirit of the season, Irish wren boys comprised a "tumultuous party" wearing "ludicrous garments such as pyjama jackets and women's blouses, some with faces blackened" (Armstrong 1958, 141)—thus reversing night and day, male and female, and black and white. A boy might don a mask or wear his clothes inside-out as a sign of revolt against the normal order. One wren boy was described as being covered with a net, his face blackened, and having a bunch of leeks tied to him for a tail (Gill 1932, 370), reflecting human-animal and animal-plant boundary reversals. According to the performance studies of anthropologist Edward Norbeck, rites of reversal reflect "the antithesis of behavior at other times." Reversals are "institutionalized acts opposing everyday conventions . . . which certain individuals or whole social groups are encouraged, expected, or required to perform on specified occasions" (Abrahams and Bauman 1978, 193, 194).

Certain reversals may function to "transform the mundane into the sacred by disguising the everyday features of environment, society, and behavior, and . . . 'setting it apart.'" During the rituals, "participants are conscious of the extraordinary nature of their undertaking" through the alterations from ordinary conditions. Also, a sense of continuity is invoked through the "emphasis on opposition" (Myerhoff 1978, 230, 232). Reversal plays an instructive role in enhancing understanding of the normal order, for perhaps only when the system is violated do the partakers come to comprehend its structure. Inversions have been interpreted as the means of "letting off steam" by providing a "protest against the established order" and may act to "preserve and strengthen the established order." They may cause people to question the absoluteness of the cultural order and enable them to see certain features of that order more clearly, "simply because they are turned inside-out." Reversal rites are expressions of the idea that "man both orders and disorders his environment and his experience." An especially important form of symbolic inversion is that used to mark a boundary (Babcock 1978, 19, 22, 27, 29, 31).

At the heart of the wren ceremony are boundaries—between the Old Year and the New, between the winter and the hoped-for spring as represented by the lengthening days, and ultimately, between death and life. Anthropologist E. R. Leach sheds light on the connection between time, reversal, and the fertility of the earth. He points out that "since harvest is logically the end of a sequence of time, it is understandable enough that, given the notion of time as oscillation, everything goes into reverse." Ceremonies accentuate the notion that "the beginning of life is also the beginning of death" and reflect the idea that "we would all like to believe that in some mystical way birth and death are really the same thing." Religious ceremonies and particularly sacrificial rites express this concept. Reversals are "symbolic of a complete transfer from the secular to the sacred; normal time has stopped, sacred time is played in reverse, death is converted into birth" (1982, 129, 131–36).

Reversals have long been associated with the winter solstice. The old Roman Saturnalia and certain types of festivities that were derived from it (later including Christmas) contained such phenomena as the lord of misrule, the king of fools, the abbot of unreason, and mummers in various disguises. A "boy bishop" was placed in charge of the church, slaves and servants were waited upon by their masters, and all manner of ranks were reversed. This liminal period may relate to the divine king, for "between the removal of the old king and the installation of the new, normal life is in a state of suspension. That interval is represented in popular custom by a period of license in which the normal order of society is halted or deliberately inverted, and a slave, misshapen person, or condemned felon is allowed temporarily to exercise sovereignty. The Roman Saturnalia is evidently a relic of this institution, as is also the European Feast of Fools, with its Lord of Misrule, Abbot of Unreason, and the like" (Gaster 1964, xxiii). The change from the year's end to the year's beginning was symbolized by a reversal of social roles (Leach 1982, 129, 135). During this special period, then, there was a symbolic expression of basic kinship and unity among all classes of people that contrasted sharply with the prevailing hierarchal social system.

Lévi-Strauss discusses this period of reversal, a time of "gathering and communion" in which "distinction between class and status was temporarily abolished. Slaves and servants sat next to masters, and these became their servants. Richly stocked tables were open to everybody. There was cross-dressing." Groups of youths "indulged in outlandish behavior taking the form of abuse against the rest of the population" that "took extreme forms: blasphemy, theft, rape, and even murder." During that interval, the anthropologist asserts, "society functions according to a double rhythm of *heightened solidarity* and *exaggerated antagonism* and these two aspects act together in balanced opposition" (1993, 47). Applying this concept to the wren hunt, it explains how the usual esteem and respect for the sacred wren normally shared by society were counterbalanced by the temporary hostility and aggression toward the bird that were displayed at the time of the seasonal slaughter.

Leach asserts that the year's end also marked a transfer from secular to sacred, a time when death was converted into birth (1982, 136). Alexander Orloff reveals that this period of license, classified as "carnival time," represents "magical time outside of time in which one and all are changed, everything is reversed, . . . a period of paradox where opposites unite, where order is disorder, harmony dissonance, where profanity is sacred, where no laws and no taboos are valid. This is a time of excess . . .—a mad fleeting moment where life phrenetically embraces death." By mocking and disregarding official authority, "we have neutralized the tensions inherent in our social order." Conflicting elements are reconciled and the order rebuilt. Because life and death are locked in an elemental struggle, if we mimic acts of nature, we can manipulate natural forces. "By simulating the chaos from which life springs, we destroy our world and build it anew" (Orloff 1981, 15, 17, 91). Thus by symbolically creating chaos, the world is remade in an image closer to human desires. There is hope for the ultimate reversal—death exchanged for life. Tradition dictated that these ends could be accomplished through ritually slaughtering the ordinarily sacrosanct wren.

Exaggeration and Transformation

As previously revealed, the wren ceremony contains many burlesque elements and extreme exaggerations that are significant keys to its meaning. These are evident in "The Death of the Wren," the Breton wren song that includes penning the "wee" bird in the cowhouse to fatten, butchering it with a "carving knife," and hauling away its feathers in "four sturdy waggons" with "steel-shod wheels," still leaving enough of "his fluff" to pack "four feather-beds." Thus the tiny wren has been magically transformed into a huge creature supplying ridiculously large amounts of meat and feathers.

The same motif occurs in the versions of the wren song that are composed of a series of questions and answers following the refrain "We'll away to the woods" (see chapter 3). Here one must "hire a cart" to carry the body home, use iron bars to lift him, and find a brewery pan to boil the meat. After the king and queen have feasted, there is enough of the carcass left to feed the poor and the lame and to give the bones to the dogs. The apportionment of "eyes for the blind, the pluck for the poor, and the legs for the lame" reflects a characteristic of similar sacrifices reported from diverse cultures and regions, in which particular portions of the animal are credited with appropriate virtues. Examples are the custom of eating a brave victim's heart to obtain courage, feeding birds' tongues to young children to make them talk early, and consuming an owl's eyeballs to gain that bird's ability to see in the dark (Gill 1932, 405–6). Thus corresponding portions of the wren's magical flesh could make the lame walk and give vision to the blind.

Another closely related wren song from Oxfordshire consists of a series of cryptic questions and answers dealing first with the weaponry used to kill the bird: "bows and arrows" will not suffice; "big guns and big cannons" are necessary. Because "four men's strong shoulders" are not enough to bring her home, a "big cart and big waggons" must be used. "Knives and forks" will not do for the eating; "big hatchets and cleavers" have to be obtained. "Pots and pans" are not adequate; they must be replaced by a "bloody great brass cauldron" for the cooking. The bird's "spare ribs" will go to the poor. In a Scottish version, a "cart and horse" are needed to carry the wren, and the "door cheeks" will be "driven down" to get the bird inside the house. The weight of the huge wings and legs must be borne by separate individuals and will be eaten by designated people.

In a Gloucestershire song, three men are hired to carry the bird, six to cook it, and "all the town" are invited to partake of the meat (Armstrong 1958, 149). On the Isle of Man, not only were the brewer's cart and pan required but also "a long pitch-fork" was needed to lift out the cooked carcass of the now-ponderous wren (Killip 1975, 185). The use of that implement relates not only to the size but also to the sacredness of the wren, for often taboos dictate that parts of such revered beings should not be touched with the hands but conveyed to the mouth with something long like a sharpened stick or the point of a knife to keep distance between the person's body and the venerated food (Gill 1932, 406).

In areas of France, the slain wren was so huge as to be "tied with strong new ropes in a wagon drawn by four black oxen." In a town near Marseilles, "a numerous body of men, armed with swords and pistols" set out after the tiny songbird. When captured, the wren was "suspended on the middle of a pole" and "carried by two men on their shoulders, as if it were a heavy burden." After being paraded around the town, the bird was "weighed in a great pair of scales" (Armstrong 1958, 144, 147). In Wales, too, the ceremony involved attribution of great weight to the wren. The four men who carried it in the procession would groan under their pretended ponderous burden and look as if "they had just relieved Atlas of his shoulder-piece" (Gill 1932, 375–76). In Devonshire the villagers suspended the wren from a stout pole and carried it on their shoulders as though it were a heavy burden. As previously described, they made pretense of hoisting the monstrous creature into a wagon while repetitiously singing the lines "Hoist! Hoist!" and "always chorusing with affected labour and exertion" (Gill 1932, 397).

Thus in song and ritual following the hunt, the smallest and most beloved bird has been miraculously transformed by exaggeration into a huge creature that will constitute an infinitely bountiful sacrificial meal that all in the community may share. The wren's sparerib alone will feed the poor, even after those carrying out the ritual killing, cutting, and cooking have consumed their portions. Such a division of sparse food to satisfy a multitude or bring them salvation is a familiar religious and ceremonial phenomenon illustrated, for example, in the New Testament, when Jesus fed four thousand people with seven loaves and a few small fish (Mark 8:1–9). Gill relates the wren sacrifice to the custom of inviting friends and dependents to a feast after the slaughter of a farm animal. Poor people were supplied with broth on those occasions. That custom is reflected in a Welsh wren song: "We will boil it for broth" (see chapter 3). "The social character of the gathering," Gill notes, "together with the distribution of a part of the preparation to less favoured neighbours, suggests a kind of sacramental feast as the origin of the custom" (1932, 404).

Elements from the distant past that play a symbolic role in the wren hunt are the magic cauldron, glass, fire, lightning, and the wheel.

The Magic Cauldron

A vital key to elucidating the meaning of the wren ceremony is the cauldron in which the bird is cooked. It is mentioned in many of the songs, such as a Welsh version specifying "brass pans and cauldrons" (Gill 1932, 393). The container may also be referred to as a pan or kettle, as in the line from an Irish song, "Up with the kittle and down with the pan." The specified use of a cauldron or similar vessel is traceable to the pre-Christian Celtic magic cauldron that is regarded as the forerunner of the Holy Grail. Both cauldron and grail had power to repel the unworthy, cure the sick, and impart health to the soul (Spence 1945, 171). The Cauldron of Kerridwen, the ancient Celtic Mother Goddess, "was the source of immortality and divine wisdom, and the promise of salvation through the death of a saviour" (Stewart 1977, 19). Thus the death and rebirth of a sacrificed victim were related to the cauldron, and by cooking the wren in that vessel the bird was enabled to return to life. In this regard Stewart points out that "if we remember that the ritual death of certain individuals was a common practice of salvation and god-seeking, not by any means unique to the Christian faith," it becomes evident that the wren ceremony is related to such practices (1977, 19–20).

The cauldron represents a miraculous life-giving and life-sustaining force associated with rebirth, replenishment, and reillumination. In the cauldron, the life of the soul is renewed by immersion and metamorphosis. The vessel possesses the power to dispense youth and life, to bring about healing, to provide strength, knowledge, and wisdom, and to promote fertility. Immersion in the cauldron could change a person's consciousness from one level to another. The vessel could bestow poetic inspiration, and it had the ability to prophesy (Graves 1989, 88, 186; Jung and Von Franz 1986, 115; Mann 1985, 7; Squire 1975, 366; Bancroft 1987, 108).

In ancient times, the cauldron represented the sun, "a golden vessel which pours forth light and heat and fertility" (Rolleston 1990, 411). The cauldron can also be interpreted as the "universal womb," for belief dictated that "reincarnation and rebirth depended upon entering such a uterine vessel to be reconstituted by its magic" (Walker 1988, 125). The "earth-as-mother, or earth-as-womb and tomb" is called "vessel and cauldron of life" (Stewart 1977, 43). Miraculously, the fabulous cauldron could feed an entire army without becoming empty, but it would not boil the food of a coward or a perjurer (Graves 1989, 108). No matter how many people came to the cauldron, "they would find in it all the food each liked best and its contents were never exhausted" (Hartley 1986, 57). Everyone obtained food according to his merits, and none came away unsatisfied (Squire 1975, 54, 366).

Most significantly, "those who had been slain could be brought back to life in Bran's magic cauldron, merely forfeiting the power of speech in the process" (Jung and von Franz 1986, 114). The wren, known as "Bran's sparrow," was the totem symbol for the Celtic god Bran, "an oracular hero" who "linked the outer world with the Underworld" (Stewart 1977, 20). Bran is a patron of healing and resurrection and, according to Robert Graves, is also interchangeable with the figures of Saturn and Cronos, who are closely tied to the winter solstice rites (1989, 52, 57, 66, 118, 259, 397). Thus the pieces fit neatly together: the wren is destroyed and dismembered but will be miraculously reborn. Through immersion in the cauldron the bird is resurrected, and with it those who partake of the ceremonial feast will be themselves renewed and reborn.

Other elements link the wren with the magic cauldron. In Druid mythology, "the Day of the Cauldron" (according to the Roman calendar) is 26 December (Hartley 1986, 105), the day of the wren hunt. The cauldron is "associated with the gift of prophecy" (Spence 1945, 110), as is the wren. The cauldron imparts "the necessary aptitudes for crossing the divide to the Otherworld" (Matthews 1990, 14), and the wren, too, is a bridge to that realm because of its connection with the earth and its powers of penetration below the ground. In the North Pembrokeshire wren ceremony involving farmers, the beer with which they "wetted the plough which lay dormant under the table . . . before partaking of it themselves" was always "kept warm in small, neat brass pans in every farmhouse ready for callers" (Gill 1932, 373–74). Brass pans have a direct connection to the cauldron.

Glass Symbolism

Other richly symbolic elements of the wren ceremony shed light on the ancient roots of the associated rites. Often the wren was paraded in a "house" or container with sides or "windows" made of glass. This feature is significant, for glass is "immaterial" because "you can see through it as if it were not matter." Thus it became a "symbol of spiritual matter" (von Franz 1990, 15). Hartley, an astute interpreter of the Western mystery tradition, suggests that "the glass windowed box was a far-off representation of the glass house into which Merlin retired, and the presence of the wren within it indicated the original holiness of the symbol" (1986, 122). "The glass house is the eternal symbol for translation to the inner planes" and the traditional symbolic reference to a "transition from this material life to the inner one of the spirit" (1986, 57, 75). Significantly, the Celtic Otherworld is called "the Island of Glass" (Spence 1945, 165).

The custom of displaying a wren in a house with glass sides relates to "legends of Kings housed after death in glass castles." The Celts had a reverence for glass, which they regarded as magical. It was a symbol of separation between the living in this world and the dead in the other world (Fife 1991, 46, 48). Common belief held that King Arthur's soul was enclosed in a glass castle after his death. The glass castles of Irish, Manx, and Welsh legends were connected with "death and with the Moon-goddess" (Graves 1989, 102, 109). The wren ceremony, of course, involves death, and there is evidence that the tiny bird was indeed regarded by the ancients as associated with the moon that rules over the "wintry darkness" (De Gubernatis 1872, 2:209). Other connections with the moon are discussed in chapter 5.

Association with Fire, Lightning, and Light

In the wren ceremony, the red cloth flying from the pole on which the bird was carried is a fire symbol. This custom fits in with the idea that the wren is credited as the bringer of fire to humankind. Some legends indicate that the wren obtained the fire from above, and as she descended her wings began to burn so that she was obliged to entrust the precious burden to the robin, whose red breast plumage bears testimony to the effects of the flames (Swainson 1886, 42). As we have seen, identification of both birds as fire-bringers may help to account for the folk perception of the two as one species. Both robins and wrens were once roasted on spits to commemorate their role as fire-bearers.

There is also the notion that the wren "fetched fire from hell, and got her feathers scorched as she passed through the keyhole" (Swainson 1886, 42), an allusion to the Underworld associations of the wren and its uncanny ability to fit into tiny spaces. From the image of the wren as a culture-hero bringing fire comes the French admonition: "If a wren's nest is destroyed, the bird will set the house or barn on fire" (Armstrong 1958, 177). The Irish superstition that cautions "kill a wren but beware of fire" (O'Sullivan 1991, 35) refers to retribution for deliberately destroying the creature responsible for obtaining an element of such vast importance to humankind. The concept of the wren as a firebird includes a linkage with lightning. Among the Celts, the wren was closely associated with the sacred oak tree, being that tree's genius, indwelling spirit, or soul. The oak tree was "regarded as a storage 'tank' or reservoir of the lightning, the heavenly fire. The wren is thus the symbol or bearer of the celestial fire, precisely as is the robin, and that this fire was in some mysterious manner connected with those of the god Bel and of Will-o'-the Wisp, seems not improbable, judging from the [wren song] rhyme" (Spence 1971, 158–59).

As we have seen, the Manx lads who paraded with the bird's corpse chanted, "We hunted the wren for Robin the Bobbin," and also for "Jack of the Can" and "for everyone." In his study of the Druids, Lewis Spence points out that this is no "mere nonsense rhyme." Rather, Robin the Bobbin refers to the god Beli, and Jack of the Can is the name of a character called "Kit of the Canstick" or "Will-o'-the Wisp." These are "three deities or spirits associated with light, for Beli has a solar connection, Will-o'-the-Wisp represents the fire of the marshes, and the wren was . . . associated with the lightning and the oak" (1971, 156). Regarding this trinity, Hartley provides the insight that Beli, or Robin the Bobbin, is associated with morning light, Kit of the Canstick or Will-o'-the-Wisp is associated with the evening light, and "the wren, the light of the spirit," represents "the sun at mid-day" (1986, 122).

By stealing fire from the gods the wren would provoke their anger. At the same time the human recipients of such a beneficent gift would be pleased. Once again, this deed may place the bird in an ambiguous role. Presuming that humankind experienced guilt from the theft of fire, that feeling could represent one root of the wren hunt—a motivation to appease the supernatural forces that had once been the exclusive owners of fire by sacrificing the tiny bird that had stolen it from them. Although fire provides life-giving heat, it is also, in the form of lightning, a potentially harmful force. Fire and lightning are associated with both destruction and renewal, causing death that is followed by fertility and ultimate rebirth from the ashes. Therein lies another connection to the wren, a creature that signifies both birth and death.

"The wren's nest was said to be protected by lightning," thus anyone who attempted to steal the wren's eggs or young would "find their house struck by lightning and their hands would shrivel up" (Carr-Gomm and Carr-Gomm 1994, 128). The wren's relationship to lightning meant that its feathers were used as talismans that, through sympathetic magic, would safeguard the possessor against lightning. In the sacrifice and ritual eating of the wren, partaking of its flesh would procure immunity from lightning, because consuming the lightning-bearer fortified against lightning itself. Additionally, those who consumed the wren's body could derive "strength from the magical qualities of the celestial source whence the bird received its strange powers" (Spence 1971, 156, 158–59). The wren, as a lightning bird, was "sacred to Donar, the lightning god" (Lockley 1960, 324). The wren was also said to be sacred to the Druid thunder god, who inhabited oak trees. Thus "the oak struck by lightning is the symbol of the enlightened Druid—the sage infused with the power of the Sky Father" (Carr-Gomm and Carr-Gomm 1994, 128).

The Wheel

Like the red cloth, the wheel used in the wren ceremony is a fire symbol (Hole 1940, 74). This association may stem from the idea of a wheel producing fire by friction, or it may be a reference to the "wheel of fire" that was rolled downhill during ancient summer solstice festivals. Such wheels were designed to stimulate the sun in its activity and to ward off winter and death. Ritual wheels have been employed to mark the year's great solar days since prehistoric times and are frequently used at the winter solstice. Additionally, the concept of the sun as a spoked wheel was one of the most widespread notions of antiquity, and in many cultures the wheel remains a solar symbol (Matthews 1986, 213; Cirlot 1983, 370; Green 1991, 56, 58). This phenomenon is exemplified by the depiction of a Celtic solar divinity carrying a wheel as a symbol of the sun (MacCulloch 1992, illust. opp. 20, 21).

Wheels are associated with movement—becoming and passing away—death and rebirth. Wheels are often divided into sectors illustrating phases in the passage of time. Thus the wheel is a representation of the cyclical passage of time that is the central concern of the wren ceremony. Accordingly, in the wren procession in some areas the box containing the bird is "surmounted by a wheel from which are appended variously colored ribbands" (Swainson 1886, 40). Graves points out that "Trochilus means 'wren' and it also means 'of the wheel,' presumably because the wren is hunted when the wheel of the year has gone full circle" (1989, 186). Another explanation is that *trochilos* is the old Greek word for small ground birds, and the term was used for the very tiniest—those referred to as wrens. *Trochilos* came from the word for "wheel." It implied the possession of sturdy legs that could run over the ground as readily as a wheel could roll and originally signified "little runner" (Holmgren 1988, 177).

Another connection with the wheel as symbol is the legendary revolving wheel commonly found in front of the door of a castle. This phenomenon is exemplified by a certain magic fortress on the Isle of Man that was protected by such a structure. Belief held that "nobody could enter until the wheel was still" (Graves 1989, 103). There is a Celtic tradition in which a magical wheel at the door of a castle turns endlessly: "This turning wheel is the mill in which the gods of the Underworld reside, in which the dead are remade, and initiates reborn" (Matthews 1989, 72). And again relating to the bird's status as king, the wheel in the wren ceremony may represent the "King's Wheel," a death symbol that makes the wheel of existence for each successive ruler come full circle. For "as a reminder of his destiny, every Irish king wore a brooch in the form of a wheel, which was entailed by his successor" (Graves 1989, 194). Such a replica of the wheel would act as a reminder of the passage of time and the cyclical nature of each king's reign. The wren-song lines "His tower has been broken; / The hero has been caught" surely relate to a feature of the Celtic tradition in which the "turning tower exemplifies the Underworld" (Matthews 1989, 71).

The Crossed Hoops

The traditional arrangement of crossed hoops used to display the body of the wren on the Isle of Man (and sometimes in Ireland) remains important in the ritual as it continues today. This configuration is richly symbolic, representing both the nest of the bird and its bier—signifying the birth-to-death and return to life that are the heart of the ceremony. It is significant that tradition dictates that no metal can be used to fashion the hoops. Wood from different trees has various symbolic meanings. Willow was often used for fashioning the hoops, probably because of its suppleness, but also for its magic powers. Endless shoots can be cut from the willow, so it may symbolize regeneration. Because willow was supposed to be a "favorite dwelling place for spirits and witches" (Matthews 1986, 215), it would be the natural choice for enclosing the wren, who was believed to be the embodiment of the evil Manx fairy.

It is fitting that the crossed hoops must be made of wood, with its special powers and properties, for only the living substance from trees, representing life and growth, is appropriate to enclose the wren in its "bush." In relation to this custom, the Celtic words for "wood" and "wisdom" are very close. The Druid was "a knower of the woods," or a "wood-sage," a "seer of great knowledge" whose closeness to the natural world made possible communication with the unseen world (Stewart 1977, 35). Figures who are sacrificed—like Jesus and the Norse deity Odin—are traditionally hung from trees and ritually wounded.

The circles formed by the hoops undoubtedly represent the eternal cosmic universe, with no beginning and no end: "The Druids regarded the circle with deep reverence as being the symbol of eternity" (Hartley 1986, 93). I believe that the Manx double hoops originally symbolized the sun and moon and that this is their fundamental significance. These two celestial phenomena had prime importance in ancient religious rites, especially those pertaining to the divine kings. For it was decreed that "the Sacred King was appointed to die when the Sun and Moon were equal in the sky." This ritual sacrifice, which occurred according to the position of the two orbs in the sky, took place approximately every eight years (Stewart 1977, 26, 33–34).

Thus the many themes and symbolic elements included in the wren ceremony serve to illuminate and communicate the deep-lying meanings intrinsic to that ancient rite. It remains to determine how the little brown wren came to be featured in this strange and complex ritual. In order to fully understand the wren hunt, analysis must include consideration of how the biology and natural history of the species, in conjunction with human observations of the bird and interactions with it, resulted in the perceptions and interpretations that were ultimately woven into the web of legend, tale, and ritual that surrounds the wren.

FIVE

BIRD, SYMBOL, AND MEANING
The Convergence of Biology and Perception

The birds became a key
whereby I might unlock eternal things.
—Roger Tory Peterson

THE WREN IS A STRIKING example of the way in which a living creature becomes changed by the human mind into a multifaceted
construct mingling biology with perceptions based on preconceived
notions. The symbolic process creates a new entity that originates from
the observed characteristics of an animal but incorporates the elaborations of the nature-to-culture transformation. The manner in which one
kind of bird has been endowed with metaphoric significance and consequently regarded and treated in certain highly eccentric ways reveals
much about the symbolizing process and its effects on human interactions with that and other species.

THE CONTEXT: BIRDS IN HUMAN THOUGHT

To understand the wren as the object of the hunt ritual, one should first
consider it as an avian species. The wren must be placed in the context
of the distinctive ways in which birds have been symbolized and accorded particular roles in human life and thought. The details of the
wren's observed or perceived biology and life history and the way these
characteristics fit into or contrast with people's notions of the nature of
birds in relation to human affairs are determinative factors in the wren's
unique symbology.

Viewed as more ethereal than other creatures and possessed of
unique capacities, birds have commonly held a preeminent place in human
cognition. From earliest times, observers have been mystified by their seasonal migration and regular return to their haunts. Additionally, birds'
building capacities seemed to reveal "forethought," a "genius for work," and

"an industry" that was astounding. People thought that "such traits suggested beings that need never die; they readily conceived of souls as birds and birds as supernatural creatures." In early European lore there was a "very extensive connection of birds with gods" and "worship of the bird itself as the living representative of a god" (De Kay 1898, vii–viii, x). Thus birds' flight could carry the spirit to its union with the divine (Bancroft 1987, 116).

Mircea Eliade identified "the nostalgia for flight" as an essential element in human consciousness (1972, 480). Through their ability to fly, birds occupy the air as well as the land, and therefore they are often viewed as intermediaries between the spirit world and the human world, between gods and people. The wren's capacity for flight, as well as the tiny bird's primal existence as a forerunner of all life, its wisdom, and its power as an emissary, are reflected in Hopi Indian creation myth. According to that tradition, after the deities had formed the earth, the sun told them of a defect: "There was no living being on the face of the ground." So the gods "laid their heads together" and "resolved to make a little bird." They created a wren of clay and brought it to life. "Then they sent out the wren to fly over the world and see whether he could discover any living being on the face of the earth; but on his return he reported that no such being existed anywhere." Following that, the deities created many kinds of birds and beasts, and "last of all" molded "first a woman and afterwards a man" out of clay and brought them to life "just as the birds and beasts had been before them" (Frazer 1988, 13).

The belief that birds are forms of human souls rests on the idea that both share the ability to fly. Birds often symbolize the Otherworld, the domain of sacred power. For example, when the Druids burned the bodies of their dead on funeral pyres, "they enclosed a wren within each ark or coffin, symbolizing the continued existence of the soul freed from the body" (Hartley 1986, 120). And in the Old Testament the dove's return to Noah's Ark after it had been set free is interpreted as a message from God, indicating his willingness to make peace with humankind. Christ and the Holy Ghost have been frequently depicted as doves, exemplifying the idea that they are benevolent visitors from the supernatural realm.

Because of these numinous traits, birds can take the role of leading the dead into the next life; they may be "psychopomps. Becoming a bird oneself or being accompanied by a bird indicates the capacity, while still alive, to undertake the ecstatic journey to the sky and the beyond" (Eliade 1972, 98). In certain areas of the world and among a number of peoples, the ability to turn into a bird is the common property of shamans and medicine men. Witches, wizards, sorcerers, and fakirs also share this capacity, and Christian saints or pious persons have frequently been reported to have flown like birds (Eliade 1972, 403, 477–79, 481–82). The concept of the soul in the form of a bird leads to the phenomenon of shamans taking flight. Unlike ordinary people here on earth, shamans, whenever they wish, can experience "coming out of the body," whereas "death alone has the power to transform the rest of mankind into 'birds.'" Magical flight is the "expression both of the soul's autonomy and of ecstasy." Thus the attribution of powers of flight to the shaman has been incorporated into many different cultural complexes (Eliade 1972, 479).

Humankind's spiritual autonomy is represented by the shaman's "voluntary abandonment of the body," symbolizing "the omnipotence of intelligence, [and] the immortality of the human soul" (Eliade 1972, 480). Magical flights peculiar to shamans and sorcerers demonstrate their transcendence of the human condition. On a deeper level, by flying into the air in the form of a bird, they "proclaim the degeneration of humanity." For according to the belief of numerous societies, in primordial times all human beings could ascend to heaven by climbing or flying upward "by their own power or being carried by birds." But now, "degeneration of humanity forbids the mass of mankind to fly to heaven; only death restored men (and not all of them!) to their primordial condition; only then can they ascend to heaven, [and] fly like birds" (Eliade 1972, 480). Shamans can move between life and death, like the bird-spirits whose abilities they appropriate, and thus can manifest "the same autonomy and the same victory over death" (Eliade 1972, 481). For these reasons, shamans often wear feathers or wings to facilitate and represent their magical flights. Such flights are spiritual in nature and express "intelligence, understanding of secret things or metaphysical truths." This concept is articulated in the belief that "those who know have wings" (Eliade 1972, 479).

Not only because of their special powers of discernment but also due to their musical repertoires and ability to cover distance easily, birds are messengers. The Bible warns that statements and even thoughts cannot be kept secret, "for a bird of the air will carry your voice, or some winged creature will tell the matter" (Ecclesiastes 10: 20). Birds are seen as such adept communicators that "the language of the birds" is symbolic of special rapport between animals and humankind. Being conversant with that language implies the possession of insightful wisdom about nature and often includes the ability to predict the future. The wren, who once may have been domesticated for the purpose of giving omens, is closely associated with the belief that sounds made by birds suggest the existence of a language among them—a tradition once held "in most parts of the world, and [which] appears in many a legend and fairy tale" (Gill 1932, 427). That tradition undoubtedly inspired the writer of "Sayings to the Wise," an old Welsh verse articulating the moral maxims of birds and beasts, to ask,

> Hast thou heard the little saying of the Wren
> In the nest where she lived?
> Let every sort go where it belongs.
> (Gill 1932, 427)

According to tradition, friendships with animals and understanding their language represent past paradisal states during which people lived with animals and understood their speech. It was not until after a primordial catastrophe comparable to the Fall of Biblical teaching that human beings began to experience enmity with animals. During an ecstatic flight the shaman abolishes the present condition and recovers the paradisal situation of human-animal communication that was lost long ago. The secret language of shamans is often in the form of imitations of birdsongs: "All over the world learning the language of animals, especially of birds, is equivalent to being able to prophesy." The birds "can reveal the secrets of the future because they are thought to be receptacles for the souls of the dead or epiphanies of the gods." Many "words used during the shaman's séance have their origins in the cries of birds and other animals. . . . 'Magic' and 'song'—especially song like that of birds—are frequently expressed by the same term. The Germanic word for magic formula is *galdr,* derived from the verb *galan,* 'to sing,' a term applied especially to bird calls" (Eliade 1972, 97–99). For the Celts, the music of birds was a "truthful language in which no falsehoods [could] be tolerated." They believed in the continuity of birdsong from paradise (Matthews 1989, 71).

As inhabitants of the sky, where the weather originates, birds behave in harmony with the air and the wind. Thus from earliest times they have often been looked upon as indicators of how climatic conditions will develop and have been viewed as magically bringing rain and controlling thunder and lightning (Pennick 1989, 68; Johnson 1988, 8).

Even in the British Isles in the twentieth century, the coming of the cuckoo is a signal to start the spring planting (Johnson 1988, 8). Birds also have often been intimately linked with augury because they are "closest to heaven" (Krappe 1964, 254). Their utterances and the direction from which they sang or the way they flew were charged with vital meaning and often signified prophecies. The root of this association with prognostication, according to one theory, lies in the fact that God has always concealed himself from human beings who try to divine his cryptic intentions. Hidden from view, God was alleged to communicate his will through indications in the sky. Signs such as the flight of birds were "the first of all languages, preceding even phonetic language" (Harrison 1992, 5). Divination from these phenomena represented people's hope of obtaining an indication of a secure future in an uncertain world. For the ancient Greeks, "the word 'bird' itself was synonymous with 'omen.'" The gods gave signs to people using birds as heralds, and "the belief that birds were agents of the gods' will is fundamental in Homer," as expressed in the *Iliad* and the *Odyssey* (see Pollard 1977, 116–19). Because the Druids read omens from birds' flight, calls, and erratic behavior (Cowan 1993, 85), it is easy to understand their attitude toward the strange little wren. The song of the wren, in particular, has an "incomplete or unfinished character" (Armstrong 1992, 10) that can tantalize the listener and give the impression that there is more to come and that knowledge will be revealed.

Because of characteristics that suit it for that role, the wren has been particularly important in prognostication. The death of Caesar is said to have been predicted to happen on the Ides of March by a wren that "was torn in pieces by several other birds in the Pompeian temple, as it was carrying a laurel branch away" (De Gubernatis 1872, 2:209). An author writing in 1927 noted that "until recent days the flight of the wren used to decide the fortunes of the [French] village of Mazan, near Carpentras. A wren was captured alive by the whole village out a-hunting; after Mass it was released by the *curé* in the church. If it flew towards the high altar the happiest of auguries were drawn from this event; if it settled on the statue of a saint things would go well; but if it flew into the roof the year would be unlucky" (Johnson 1927, 142–43). Because of its abilities, "the Wren is recorded as magus avium (magus, a magician or sorcerer) in Irish hagiology" (Greenoak 1979, 241).

Dudley Young proposes that people have been drawn to birds through admiration of their defiance of gravity. Both birds and our arboreal primate ancestors, he argues, left the earth that is dominated by smells and moved upward into a world of sight and sound. Our fellow-ship with birds rests on their social and sexual activities "triggered like ours by sight and sound," which seem so familiar to us. Yet such "simi-larity only serves to highlight the crucial difference—that birds have wings to outwit the monkey's two major anxieties, snakes and the fear of falling." This defiance of "the monkey's two major problems . . . makes them seriously magical," and thus it is "not surprising that birds play such a large part in man's early religious imaginings" (1991, 45–46).

The idea that "birds are thoughts and flights of the mind" (Jung 1956, 189) is shared by D. H. Lawrence, who noted that "birds are the life of the skies, and when they fly, they reveal the thoughts of the skies" (1992, 134). Ecologist Paul Shepard likewise believes that "birds become ideas." They "are not *like* ideas— . . . They *are* ideas." The "idea is our inward occasion of the bird's presence. . . . A bird flying across the sky is an idea coming from the unseen of the pre-conscious and dis-appearing into the realm of dreams." Music is an extremely important element in human sensory perception, he asserts, and "singing and song [are] unifying for us and for our perception of birds, whose songs are the anthems of their respective races." Shepard sees birdsong as possessing "ecological purposes." Human song, he suggests, "may even have evolved from the avian example as prehuman groups moved to-ward group consciousness and cultural diversity." In much of the world "bird melody is still available during many hours of each day during the first year of life and we should not discount its importance." Bird-song may be our "first integrating experience." It is possible that "the idea of a joyous cosmos come[s] to us unbidden from a singer 'up there' unseen, an evocation of the first iridescent pleasure of sheer being." The "interplay or symbiosis between species enacts the relatedness of parts and kinds, as though the exercise of putting together the parts were it-self being demonstrated for us. Finally, we communicate this integrat-ing reality to ourselves in music and poetry, and the archetype of it is found among those harbingers of thought, the birds" (1978, 34–35, 74–75).

Richard Mabey also believes that "there are so many ways in which bird song seems to be a precursor of music that it might be more appropriate to describe music as 'bird song-like' than bird song as mu-sical." Human brains "may retain, at the deepest level, the structures and mental charts of our reptilian and bird-like ancestors," and that may be the reason "so many people feel a sense of affinity with birds.

Our admiration for their bright colours, sweet songs, and graceful flight suggests that some very large part of our brains is still up in the canopy with them" (1993, 108).

Because of their delicate beauty and upward flight, birds, more than any other creatures, appeal to the imagination, inspire the mind toward higher planes, and evoke thoughts that go beyond pragmatic concerns to become sublime similes. Emily Dickinson wrote that

> Hope is the thing with feathers
> That perches in the soul,
> And sings the tune without the words
> And never stops at all,
>
> And sweetest in the gale is heard;
> And sore must be the storm
> That could abash the little bird
> That kept so many warm.
> (Linscott 1959, 79)

Birds often take on the image of fertility, probably because of their "two-fold birth, first as an egg and then as a chick," suggesting rebirth and regeneration. Being born twice, they may obtain sacred status because of the renewal they represent, which "mirrored in the cyclical transformation of nature, consoles the living against the threat of extinction and reassures the dying and bereaved" (Johnson 1988, 8, 89). Because of the egg-laying capacity of the female, there is an "ancient mythological association of women, fertility, and birds" (Salisbury 1994, 159–60), and many cultures have worshipped bird goddesses in which the avian form is fused with the divine. The frequently occurring figure of "Bird-Goddess-Creatrix" expresses "the idea of creation taking place from the Universal Egg laid by the deity." The notion of "the bird that gave birth to the cosmos, the earth, and humankind is common to many tribal religions" (Johnson 1988, 16–17, 33).

But before birds became objects of cognition, they had to be closely observed. For much of humankind's existence, until industrialization and urbanization, birds were an essential part of life as it was known on earth. In the face of our current widespread alienation from nature, it must be remembered that not so long ago, humans and animals lived in close proximity. Consequently, the form and behavior of the creatures who shared their territory were more keenly noted and details about them were incorporated into a body of common knowledge. Information could be obtained from animals who possessed wisdom denied to human beings. Consideration of the wren's particular biological traits and the ways in which these traits have been interpreted through the lens of human belief and experience leads to a fascinating exploration into the richness of human imagination and the sense of unity and interdependence between people and other forms of life that once existed.

THE TRANSFORMATION OF THE WREN

Hidden Song, Appearance, and Habits

Throughout its range in Britain, Ireland, and Europe, the wren is one of the most abundant nesting birds. It frequently chooses to live near human habitation (though only when the area affords the required amount of wildness) and is probably second only to the robin in degree of familiarity to the general populace. With this proximity, however, there is a contradiction, for the wren often remains hidden from sight, even when loudly and repetitively indicating its location through song. Its presence is much more likely to be detected by hearing its voice than by sight. The wren seems ubiquitous, even though invisible. A special magic resides in the voice of a hidden singer, a phenomenon that has been cited to explain the unique power of Emily Dickinson's creativity: "Her swift poetic rapture was like the long glistening note of a bird one hears in the June woods at high noon, but can never see" (Farr 1992, 10).

Aristotle described the shy and secretive wren as an inhabitant of "thickets and holes" (Balme 1991, 271). "No European species of bird [is] more adept at threading its way through dense cover," notes Armstrong. The wren "has none of the abhorrence of enclosed spaces characteristic of many birds" (1955, 1, 23, 134). Even when momentarily in view, the habit of suddenly disappearing into the underbrush or a crevice makes the "den-diver" seem mysterious. This "vanishing act," as Janet Lembke calls it (1992, 50), gives the wren the character of a magician, a kind of "now-you-see-it, now-you-don't" aura that helps to explain its perceived mystical role.

The wren "doesn't care to keep company either with its own species or with other birds. It hops about in hedges, lonely" and "desires not to be noticed either by friends or strangers" (Byron n.d., 49–50). The solitary character of the wren predisposes to the idea of its role as sage, thinker, prophet, or shaman—a being in touch with spiritual and supernatural realms. As William Turner observed in 1544, it is "a bird that roves alone, and never flies in flocks" (Evans 1903, 155). Unless involved in courting, mating, or communal roosting in freezing weather, the wren is generally seen singly, a private, individualistic creature rather than a gregarious one. During mild weather wrens roost singly in suitable nooks—old nests, nest boxes, tangles of ivy, or cavities in walls and trees (Armstrong 1992, 8). The wren's plain brown plumage, in contrast to that of brightly colored birds, gives the bird a serious, contemplative aspect, like a cleric or prophet dressed in a somber robe. Observation of the wren's "piercing eye" (Hare 1952, 31) gives it an attribution of a seer. The light eyebrow lends a knowing air. Also, the wren's habit of nodding, bowing, and bobbing, its motions described as "curtsying or dipping" (Morris n.d., 137) and its constant movements, make the bird seem to be under the influence of an unseen force. Its perceived preoccupation with some inner mental state indicates its possession of hidden knowledge that could be imparted through such signals to the observer. Wordsworth alluded to this inspired quality in "The Contrast" when he described the "self-contented Wren" as "Not shunning man's abode, though shy, / Almost as thought itself, of human ken" (George 1904, 643). The poet also celebrated the wren's serene and reclusive existence in lines from "A Wren's Nest": "The hermit has no finer eye / For shadowy quietness" (George 1904, 701).

Endurance and Adaptability

Other traits of the little brown bird influence human perceptions. Braving the harshness of winter, the wren is a symbol of endurance. It remains active during snowstorms. And as mentioned earlier, even in "keen frost" the wren sings "as merrily as if it had been enjoying the sunshine of summer" (Montagu 1831, 572). Hudson noted that it has "more adaptiveness than most birds, being universal in the British Islands, and able to survive the cold and scarcity of the long northern winters, even in the most bleak and barren situations" (1898, 320). In winter, too, the bird is more frequently observed, as it ventures nearer to homes and yards. At that season wrens go to roost later in relation to sunset (Armstrong 1992, 10). They remain active, seeking food for about a half hour after the sun goes down, so their presence is more evident to people who see them in the evening and associate them with the cold dark days near the solstice. The songs and calls that serve as rallying signals for birds to roost together in the evening also make the bird more conspicuous at dusk in winter. Bewick recognized the species' "amazing powers of recovery," observing that even when many individuals die from starvation in severe winters, "within a few years, they invariably regain their former numbers" (Thomas 1982, 43).

Ornithological data reveal the extraordinary adaptiveness and tenacity of the wren, for it is one of the very few species that have successfully invaded the Old World from the New (Armstrong 1955, 7). The family of wrens first evolved in North America and spread southward, and only *Troglodytes troglodytes* managed to reach the Old World. To accomplish that feat it had to travel across the Bering Strait (Leahy 1982, 776)—an almost incredible journey for this mite of a bird appropriately called "a dynamo in feathers" (Parmelee 1959, 162). The wren's physical strength is remarkable. The species can cope with almost any type of habitat except extensive open moorland and dense urban areas (Bateman 1985, 62). The success of such a tiny and vulnerable bird is largely due to its ability to forage in areas where larger birds cannot go and to devour many kinds of creatures, mainly insects. Its small size, sharp beak, and powerful feet and legs enable it to seek its prey in cramped quarters and probe into crevices. The wren has succeeded in establishing populations throughout an enormous area of the world, occupying a wide range of habitats. This biological fact was translated into a metaphorical one by the ornithologist who drew from it the conclusion that "success is not always gained by the fierce and powerful!" (Armstrong 1955, 23; 1991, 5–6).

Paradoxes and Contradictions in Form and Behavior

Sharp contrasts generally pique the human imagination, and many conflicting dualities are embodied by the wren. Small size is one of the most striking characteristics in the complex of symbolic meanings that has grown up around this strange yet familiar bird. The intense interest attached to the wren and the great amount of lore surrounding the bird seem to exist in inverse ratio to its size. The image of the wren became axiomatic for the concept of tiny. For example, English farthings issued between 1937 and 1956 feature the "dainty little wren, one of Britain's smallest birds—a very suitable subject for the smallest British bronze coin" (Seaby 1985, 170). As one folklorist remarked, "Bobby wren now reigns supreme as king *de facto*—on our new farthings" (Hare 1952, 32). Irish folk wisdom includes axioms relating to the bird's size: "Although the wren is small it will make a noise" and "The wren spreads his feet wide in his own home" (translated as "Even the most insignificant are kings in their castles") (O'Griofa 1993, 33). The lightness of the wren is expressed in a line from an early Irish verse in which small things are enumerated: "A wren on a briar under which not even a wisp would break" (Ó Cuív 1980, 51). The bird's image as the epitome of smallness is also encapsulated in the old Irish adage "Never despair while there's meat on the shin of a wren" (O'Sullivan 1991, 35). On a deeper level, this saying refers to the minuscule carcass of the sacrificed wren being miraculously transformed into a huge feast for unlimited numbers of consumers.

An interpretation of the role of the tiny bird among the Druids is that "Drui-en [the wren] allows us to glimpse the beauty of God or Goddess in all things. He tells us that 'small is beautiful,' and that self-realization lies not in grandiosity or apparent power, but in humility, gentleness, and subtlety." The Druid, as a shaman, was known as the "cunning man," a person who "can become invisible like the wren, who can travel on the back of the noble eagle to reach his destination, saving himself energy in the process. Being small he is unobtrusive, and being small he can enter worlds that bigger people cannot—as Alice discovered in Wonderland. Being proud makes us unwieldy; being small and humble enables us to slip through the eye of a needle or down the root of a tree" (Carr-Gomm and Carr-Gomm 1994, 126, 128).

It is significant that different cultures have also found messages in the small size of the wren. The tiny bird is celebrated in one of the rituals of the Pawnee Indian Hako ceremony in which "The Song of the Wren" is set to music. The lines "Kichi ruku waku, Whe ke re re we chi" are sung over and over again, with the first three words indicating that the wren sang and the last six syllables imitating the sounds made by the bird. The leader of the ceremony explains:

> The wren is always spoken of as the laughing bird. It is a very happy little bird, and we have stories about it. Every one likes to hear the wren sing. This song is very old; I do not know how old, but many generations old. There are very few words in the song, but there is a story which has come down with it and which tells its meaning.
>
> A priest went forth in the early dawn. The sky was clear. The grass and wild flowers waved in the breeze that rose as the sun threw its first beams over the earth. Birds of all kinds vied with one another as they sang their joy on that beautiful morning. The priest stood listening. Suddenly, off at one side, he heard a trill that rose higher and clearer than all the rest. He moved toward the place whence the song

came that he might see what manner of bird it was that could send farther than all the others its happy, laughing notes. As he came near he beheld a tiny brown bird with open bill, the feathers on its throat rippling with the fervor of its song. It was the wren, the least powerful of birds, that seemed to be most glad and to pour out in ringing melody to the rising sun its delight in life.

As the priest looked he thought: "Here is a teaching for my people. Everyone can be happy; even the most insignificant can have his song of thanks."

So he made the story of the wren and sang it; and it has been handed down from that day, a day so long ago that no man can remember the time.

(Fletcher 1904, 171–72)

Thus for observers in the New World as well as the Old, the wren did not become the symbol for smallness and an embodiment of spiritual forces because of its size alone. Rather, it is the paradoxical disparity between the bird's size and the vehemence of its voice and vitality of its spirited actions that commands attention. The tenacity with which the wren sings all day long and throughout the whole year sharply differentiates it from other avian species. Singing in winter upsets the normal expectations, juxtaposing opposite seasons of warmth and cold in an unfamiliar way. The wren's sweet voice associated with summer heard against a background of the cold, barren landscape of winter unites the two solstices that represent the birth and death of life. The overall power embodied in the wren contrasted with the weight and volume of its body makes it seem as though some spiritual force is represented to explain this incongruity. One astonished listener noted that the wren's "whole body vibrates with the effort," while "pouring forth a volume of song enough almost to make the very welkin [vault of heaven] echo it" (Morris n.d., 136). The same phenomenon caused the cricket and the firefly to be revered in certain cultures due to the disproportionate amount of sound and brilliance put forth from such tiny creatures.

The wren's sudden movements are startling to the observer, who sees the "nimble little bird; how quick it will peep out of the hole of an old foggy dyke, and catch a passing butterfly" (Brand 1849, 3: 199). Its alertness and swift, adroit movements in dense cover are remarkable. The inexplicable vitality emanating from so diminutive a form suggests another order of beings—sprites, fairies, and elves—whose origins are supernatural.

The Druids believed in the manifestations of God through his creations. This meant that "whatever came to pass in Nature from the rustling of leaves to the mightiest storm or flood was the carrying out in Nature of the laws of God—that Nature was moved by the divine laws." Therefore "they gave particular attention to natural but unusual appearances and actions such as falling thunderbolts or woodland fires, to the flight of birds and their songs at unusual times or seasons." Such phenomena were among the "manifestations of the intentions of God, indications of forthcoming events, instructions or warnings that should be considered and heeded" (Hartley 1986, 106). Thus it is easy to understand that the bursting song and vehement actions of the tiny wren were associated with the unexpected in nature—a source of wonder and spiritual knowledge.

Lévi-Strauss theorizes that reality and the experience of reality are understood through the establishment of pairs of opposites. Relating to this idea, it is largely the wren's strange and contradictory embodiment of opposites that draws unusual attention to the bird. The widespread pairing of the eagle with the wren not only emphasizes contrast in size but also brings together the bird who flies highest with the one who goes deepest into the earth. According to folklorist Idris Parry, "The quest for form is expressed in magical resolution of opposites, but opposites have to be stated before they can be resolved" (1972, 39). The embodiment of opposites may signify the lost unity between all forms of life.

Parry explores the connection between the tiny wren and magical knowledge, noting that "the smallest bird is conqueror, king, the key used by Druid-man in pursuit of truth. Confidence in the wisdom of the smallest thing may represent faith in the divine detail, the finite cell as the only basis of infinity, the trivial fact which threads through all transformations" (1972, 37). A great gap separates humankind from nature, and integration needs to be restored. When human beings are given the choice of listening to animal voices, Parry argues, "either you ignore truth, sacrifice the god, dismember the wren, or you listen to the voice of the smallest thing, the irreplaceable link in creation" that comprises "a vital constituent of the whole." There is a pattern of the "friendly god who speaks only through the smallest thing, the trivial step, the finite detail, the wren" (1972, 40, 41).

In Druid tradition, "the wren symbolized wisdom and divinity." Those attributions are related to the fact that "it is difficult actually to see a wren." At the time of the New Year, an apprentice Druid would "go out by himself into the countryside in search of hidden wisdom, in the same way that a Native American would go on a vision quest. If he found a wren he would take that as a sign that he would be blessed with inner knowledge in the coming year. Finding a creature small and elusive to the point of invisibility was a metaphor for finding the elusive divinity within all life" (Carr-Gomm and Carr-Gomm 1994, 129).

The disparity between the minuscule size of the wren and the importance accorded the bird because of its particular characteristics accounts for some of the strangest of the wren ceremonies and accompanying songs. This contradiction is dramatized, for example, during the rites in which four strong men pretend to labor under the weight of the body of the wren that is so ponderous it has to be carried between two poles. The mocking words of the songs reflect the heaviness of their burden, and the assertion that the carcass of the slaughtered bird will feed such a great multitude of people adds to the irony of the situation.

Ground-dwelling Way of Life

"Cryptic coloration" is the zoologists' description of the wren's markings, a term that sheds light on aspects of the bird's symbolism. Although for scientists this means that its color helps to camouflage the wren, the term also conveys an aura of the "secret and mysterious" and even suggests association with "crypt," or underground cavern. The russet-brown wren blends with the earth, yet the bird's chthonic character is due not just to the resemblance in color but also to its habits. Engaging in only short flights, the wren rarely is observed leaving the ground, hiding when startled rather than flying away.

Belief in the Underworld was fundamental to many early religions, including that of the Celts; the "chthonic power of the Underworld" was "never far away from the Celtic Imagination." Belief held that all energy, life, power, and death came from beneath the ground. The supernatural beings who controlled "the originative and mysterious energies of death, life, and rebirth" resided in the Underworld, which was a "primal, creative place" where mortals entered into special relationship with the gods (Matthews 1989, 72; Stewart 1991, 38, 46). Descent to the Underworld once denoted the quest for wisdom. The journeys made by the heroes of Virgil and Dante, the story of Orpheus and Eurydice, and the tale of Alice in Wonderland involve entering the lower world to gain understanding.

The Underworld could be entered through a cave or a fissure in a rock or earth. As a denizen of holes and crevices with the ability to squeeze through small apertures, the wren has access to such entrances and thus became logically related to that spiritual realm below the ground. It is not surprising that the bird, having such close associations with the Underworld, should be sacrificed and ultimately buried in the ground in order to ensure the regeneration of the earth. Thus the behavioral ecology of the wren is suited to reverence within the context of the belief system that saw divinity in the lower realm. With the rise of Christianity, whose ideology looked to the sky for spiritual forces, however, the wren's status was to be greatly diminished and ultimately reversed. As one Celtic scholar points out, when Christianity spread to the Celts, the old "animal gods either found themselves the heroes of Christian legends" or, where "such adoption was hopeless, were proclaimed witches' animals and dealt with accordingly" (Squire 1975, 417).

The wren's manner of flight, typical of ground-dwelling birds, as well as its size, contributes to its image as a type of supernatural creature. The Manx legend that explains hostility to the wren, as we have seen, concerns a beautiful fairy who exerted undue influence over men by means of her sweet-singing voice, leading them into the sea, where they perished. "A knight-errant laid a clever plot for her destruction, from which she only escaped by taking the form of a Wren, when by her rapid movements she became invisible." The idea of this escape is drawn from direct observation of a biological characteristic of the bird, "for it is well known that when flying the motion of the Wren's wings is so rapid that they become invisible" (Cookson 1859, 26). And the perception that the wren's "tiny round wings beat so quickly, when it flies, that they look just like a mist around its little body" (Stokoe 1939, 24) contributes to the mysterious nature attributed to the bird. Additionally, the "strange barbarous custom" of killing the wren can be traced to the victim being "the smallest bird upon the island," making it "a proper sacrifice to the fairies (the smallest of imaginary beings) in order to appease their ill will against the poor fishermen, to whom they are such plagues in the herring season, and for the future render them propitious to them" (Townley 1791, 1: 311).

Interestingly, the wren's behavior is often likened to that of a mouse. A German name for the bird, *Mausekönig,* means "mouse king" (Armstrong 1992, 2). Ornithological field identification guides refer to the behavior of this species that scuttles along the earth instead of flying upward as "mouselike" (Peterson 1980, 214). In a tree the wren is observed "creeping like a mouse among the branches" (Morris n.d.,

136). The wren has been viewed as "too much like a mouse to lay eggs," and has been called "the mouse's brother" and "little feathered mouse" (Armstrong 1955, 23, 282) or "mouse wren" (Terres 1980, 1048). Sometimes the Manx wren boys would carry a mouse instead of a wren (Gill 1932, 369). The fact that it differs from the pattern of actions typical of birds and resembles a mammal adds to the wren's image of strangeness and highlights the bird's mysterious nature. Being perceived as somewhere between a mouse and a bird means that the wren is not easily classified. Anthropologist Mary Douglas has demonstrated that animals that do not strictly conform to their class or category, and hence are viewed as anomalous, cause uncertainty in the human mind and evoke anxiety, often becoming objects of ritual and taboo (1976). The wren's unclassifiable image is undoubtedly an important factor underlying the proscriptions regarding treatment of the bird and the ceremonies of the annual hunt. Whatever is taboo not only holds special interest but also is invested with great power. As we have seen, harming or killing the wren except in the context of the annual seasonal ritual brings severe retribution—discomfort, illness, injury, or even death.

Nesting, Roosting, Foraging, and Entering Hidden Recesses

The capacity for constructing an unusual nest is another behavioral characteristic that profoundly influences human perceptions of the wren and helps to transform it into a being that possesses magical and spiritual qualities. Aristotle admired the wren's great "knowledge of its craft" (Evans 1903, 153), and zoologists praise its "incredible power as a builder" (Nichols 1883, 328). "No bird has a stronger nesting instinct" (Woodward 1928, 29). When creating a nest, the wren "first works at the outline of the whole, and afterwards encloses the sides and top" (Morris n.d., 139), thus appearing to use cognitive foresight. British ornithologist G. Montagu marvels at the skill of the "little architect," who carries a piece of moss "almost as large as its own body" and uses its saliva for glue (1831, 573). Male wrens show an "overwhelming urge to build" (Simon 1977, 140). Ornithological observations reveal that the wren builds its intricately constructed nest with "frenzied diligence." Sometimes the nest is almost finished in one day—a feat accomplished by "few other birds which make elaborate nests" (Armstrong 1955, 148). The female wren is discriminating: if the male is careless and builds poorly constructed nests, he may not attract a mate (Simon 1977, 140).

Great skill is used to ensure that the "beautifully made" and "compact" nest blends with its surroundings, for "the wren always

Wren at nest, surrounded by ivy. Courtesy of Patrick Armstrong for the Estate of Edward A. Armstrong.

chooses its materials to match exactly, outside, the place where the nest is built" (Byron n.d., 49–50). The bird's "instinct directs it for security," determining that if built beside a hayrick, the nest is made of hay; if against the side of a tree covered with white moss, it is composed of the same; and if against a tree with green moss, it is composed of that material (Montagu 1831, 572). Feathers are commonly used as a lining. Nest-building expertise and knowledge in the use of various materials are celebrated in the Nativity legend in which "the little wren wove a blanket of feathers and green leaves and moss for the Child," earning the title "*la poulette de Dieu,* God's little chicken" (Yolen 1991, 54).

Wordsworth, with his keen eye for detail, appreciated the wren as the epitome of builders—specially endowed with unique skill:

> Among the dwellings framed by birds
> In field or forest with nice care,
> Is none that with the little Wren's
> In snugness can compare.
>
> No door the tenement requires,
> And seldom needs a laboured roof:
> Yet is it to the fiercest sun
> Impervious, and storm-proof.
>
> So warm, so beautiful withal,
> In perfect fitness for its aim,
> That to the Kind by special grace
> Their instinct surely came.
> (George 1904, 701)

Turner described the wren's nest as having "the form of an upright egg standing on one of its ends" (Evans 1903, 155)—thus associating it with fertility and metaphorically relating it to spiritual and generative power.

The nest is closely related to the sacred status of the wren in the Western mystery tradition. As Hartley explains, the tiny bird builds its nest "in the form of a ball and then conceals itself therein. This is the symbolic rendering of the manner in which the Word of God conceals itself in the human heart." Originally, before the wren hunt became "merely a cruel sport," it "had been a joyful but solemn ceremony when each man went out by himself to hunt for the hidden wisdom and he who found the actual wren believed that he had been blessed with the inner knowledge of God for the ensuing year" (1986, 120–21). The "Druid's house" was equated with the wren's nest—"a place of comfort and safety, for another important symbol in Druidry is the egg." This symbolic element articulates the idea that "in order to grow and change we need to go through periods of incubation—withdrawing from the world to allow ourselves to re-form in the womb of time" (Carr-Gomm and Carr-Gomm 1994, 128). The Druids regarded the wren as "the symbol of the Word of God." For them, the tiny bird's "round nest with central hole" represented "the vessel of the Lord, the primal egg of creation, which received and sent forth" (Rothery n.d., 59).

Once again, as with its great energy and its song that are out of proportion to its size, there is the paradox that the wren's nest is "large for [a] small bird" (Harrison 1975, 149). The bird builds a domed nest, usually with a side entrance that is well hidden. As mentioned earlier, the name *Troglodytes troglodytes* commemorates the species' nest-building capacity. From ancient times, people have likened the wren's hollow globular nest to a cavern or cave, and this comparison has greatly influenced thoughts about the spiritual role and mystical nature of such a skillful nest-constructor and cave-dweller.

Several of the wren hunt songs include the word "hall," which refers to the wren's unique nest. For example, in one version, these lines describe "the King": "He is from a cottager's stall / To a fine gilded hall." And another song indicates: "And with powder and ball / We fired at his hall" (Swainson 1886, 41). British bird folklorist Charles Swainson explains that "'hall' is used for the wren's nest, . . . and fitly so, for it is a hall or covered place. And it is from the shape of his nest that the wren gets his name, meaning *covered*" (1886, 41). It is fascinating to find that a noted scholar of early religions points to an etymological connection between "hall" and "cave" (Smith 1972, 200). Cave imagery is closely associated with the wren's symbolic roles, as will become clear.

A Pembrokeshire wren song reports:

> He was captured, the rascal
> Last night with rejoicings,
> In a snug, pretty chamber,
> And his brothers thirteen.
>
> The stronghold was broken,
> The young man was taken.
> (Gill 1932, 389)

A slightly different version says:

> The rogue has been caught
> Who last night was so proud,
> In a fair white chamber.
> With his eleven brothers.
>
> His tower has been broken;
> The hero has been caught.
> (Fisher n.d., 3)

In these verses the snug, pretty, or white chamber, the stronghold, and the tower refer to the wren's nest—the "castle" of the wren king. "Tower" may represent the Celtic turning tower or royal fortress that revolves so swiftly that its entrance cannot be found.

Montagu tells of finding "several Wrens in the hole of a wall, rolled up into a sort of ball" to keep each other warm during the night, and states that "they crowd into a cave during winter" for that purpose (1831, 571). Ornithologists have discovered that cold temperatures elicit social roosting in the species, which means that up to nine or ten of the little birds may cluster together in a "dormitory" to keep warm and conserve energy in severe weather. They often use one of the "dummy" nests or an old nest of another bird for their shelter (Skutch 1993, 152–54) (see this chapter, below). Armstrong notes that "more than forty may appropriate adjoining nests, with as many as twenty-two in a single nest" (1992, 9–10). He saw thirty-one of the "elfin creatures" squeezed into a six-inch square box, and states that "an incredible sixty" occupied a nest box (1992, 9–10; 1955, 282). Ninety-eight wrens were once found in an attic roost, all of which entered by the same small hole (Holden and Sharrock 1994, 124). A British ornithologist calling the wren the "best-known huddler" reports that "in the exceptionally severe winter of 1963, up to 50 Wrens were counted entering a tit nesting box in the Isle of Wight. Tens and twenties are commonplace. Once they are inside the box or natural cavity they arrange themselves in circles, heads to the centre, often several tiers high" (Boswall 1987, 24). Because of this habit, wrens (and sometimes other birds) are occasionally called "Juggie," which may relate to the expression "to jug," meaning to nest or collect in a covey. Long before scientists documented the phenomenon, country people knew the congregation of wrens as a "sure portent of hard weather" and predicted in verse, "When the tomtits cluster / Soon there'll be a bluster" (Armstrong 1955, 282).

It is probable that wren hunters caught their quarry when the birds were roosting during frigid weather. I have found only one reference to this practice—a mention of obtaining a roosting bird a day or two before the hunt by snatching it from its nest, "usually in the cottage eaves" (Armstrong 1958, 155). The fact that up to a dozen wrens were sometimes carried in a wren party procession suggests that the birds may have been captured as they huddled together for warmth. Armstrong says that the situation of the roosting wrens is "fraught with danger" from quadrupeds (1955, 278), but it is likely that humans who knew about this habit would have posed a threat as well.

Wrens can squeeze through small openings, hop and run, and

even move backward out of an enclosed space. The names "fence king" and "hedge king" refer to the birds' capacity for slipping in and out of fences and hedges. When snow conceals the herbage, they creep beneath it, "foraging in the dark and frosty labyrinths" (Armstrong 1955, 23, 25). A wren can fly "without seeming difficulty" through an opening "little more than the third of an inch" wide (Morris n.d., 139). These behavioral traits give the wren a mystical quality associated with the penetration of hidden recesses, for belief once held that "a particular cave, [or] a fissure in rock or earth" were entrances to the afterlife (Rutherford 1993, 42). Cave imagery is central to understanding the deep-lying meaning of the wren ceremony, shedding light on the bird's spiritual connotations and symbolic roles. "Caves are always symbolic of the receptacles of inner wisdom, that which is hidden" (Hartley 1986, 27). A cave is a place in which to ponder the nature of reality. "Grottoes and caverns of the earth" are important natural places of worship, traditionally possessing great religious significance. Caves may be "associated with the worship of chthonic deities," and sacred caverns were often regarded as "seats of divine energy" (Smith 1972, 197–98). Caves are considered to be entrances to the Underworld (Stewart 1991, 38), and thus the wren's peculiar nest connects the bird to that realm.

Esmé Wynne-Tyson notes that "the symbolic descent into the cave, and re-ascent, occurs in all the Mystery religions" (1962, 39). Christian mythology exemplifies the importance attached to caves. Jesus' birth is often depicted in a cave. After his death, his body was buried in a cave, and from there he proceeded down to Hades before rising upward to Paradise. This theme is vividly depicted in Dante's *Divine Comedy,* where the way to the heavens leads first down through the center of the earth. Without passing through hell, "the blissful experience of the journey through the Heavens would not have been experienced" (Matthews 1984, 169).

The allegory of Christ's dead body being sealed in a cave prior to his miraculous return to life embodies the "womb-tomb" theme—an archetype for the cycle of birth and death that is represented through reference to caves at both his Nativity and death. Throughout history the cave has been a symbol for creation, a place of emergence. The cave is the womb of earth, bringing forth new life, but it is also the entrance to the land of the dead. Caves have long been considered sacred, for they are at the center of the world, "places where the divine manifests itself" (Moon 1991, 244). Shamanistic ceremonies once took place in the deep recesses of caves, for descent into the dark earth was felt to be necessary for future rebirth. Darkness may have been considered holy, for caves seem "otherworldly" because the absolute blackness of such inner sanctums are "remote from ordinary life." In a cavern, "sensory perception is wiped away and only the experience of being remains. Such conditions might have been thought essential to the death and rebirth of the soul" (Bancroft 1987, 29, 31). In many traditions, initiation ceremonies took place in caves. The candidate was "left alone to meditate in solitary darkness and to combat the powers of evil which assailed him" (Hartley 1986, 111–12). Sequestration of the candidate under such conditions was necessary for progression into the next phase of life—the individual's symbolic rebirth.

As an example of the religious significance of caves, visitors to Umbria in Italy can still visit the moss-covered grotto at Monte La Verna where St. Francis of Assisi found refuge during a period when he withdrew from ordinary life to seek spiritual regeneration and communication with divine will. Isolated in that rustic cave, he found "something so profound and startling that his whole life was changed." The saint had sought out such a dark and lonely cavern in order to "burrow into the earth in search of a treasure which lies hidden from those who live only on the surface" (Nabhan 1993, 67–68).

Caves occupy an ambiguous role in human experience, being places of shelter and mystery, safety and uncertainty, of darkness and the light of revelation. Such dualities give caves a supernatural quality that is appropriate for religious rites and ceremonies. Plato's allegory of the cave, of course, centers on a search for truth. Caves are also associated with transitional states, the process of becoming, the phenomenon of being "betwixt and between." Symbolic anthropologist Victor Turner sees a cavern as "epitomizing outsiderhood and liminality" (1975, 253), and mythologist G. S. Kirk identifies the cave as a locus for the nature-to-culture transition— "for a cave belongs to nature, but is also an embryonic house" (1975, 170).

The wren, by virtue of its underground associations and its nest-as-cave image, partakes of many traits that make it a divine animal with deep significance in the most fundamental birth and death phenomena and in human visions of reawakening to the afterlife. Because the living pass into the earth at death in order to be reborn, the bird who stays close to the earth and enters it through a cave is strongly associated with the renewal of the earth and with fertility.

Sexual, Reproductive, and Social Behavior

Sexuality, as previously discussed, is a determining element of the wren's imagery and represents an ambiguous aspect of its symbolic roles. In female guise the tiny bird is the innocent and beloved Jenny Wren, the robin's lawful wife, and a nurturing mother. Conversely, she is a coquette, a lewd prostitute, or an oversexed breeder who produces an inordinate number of young. As the king, the wren is a male figure who earned royal status through cleverness and cunning but who also practices polygamy and sires an excessive number of offspring. Many of these symbolic attributions were derived from the wren's biology and reproductive behavior. Actual wrens—male as well as female—are known to be more attentive as parents than many other species (Armstrong 1992, 23–24). They are wary at the nest and will "scold most outrageously" at an intruder, even "pursu[ing] a boy or a polecat to some distance, with loud manifestations of anger" (Montagu 1831, 575).

The bird's unusual tail is a prominent oddity, one that caused Shakespeare in *A Midsummer Night's Dream* to refer to "the wren with little quill" (3.1). The fact that it is constantly "cocked" and flicked up and down, especially when the bird becomes excited, has given the wren an image of sexual prowess. The male wren's courtship displays are "numerous, varied, and lovely." They include a complex "pursuit flight" and a "pounce," as well as the rather spectacular "quill rattling," a quivering that produces sounds "similar to that of a shower of electric sparks" (Armstrong 1955, 110, 121). The idea that the wren is a fornicator is expressed by Shakespeare's King Lear, who cries,

> . . . Die for adultery? No.
> The wren goes to't and the small gilded fly
> Does lecher in my sight.
> Let copulation thrive.
> (Act IV, Scene 6)

Conversely, the wren's raising of a large brood is considered an admirable trait. Shakespeare's *Twelfth Night* contains a reference to the bird's fecundity: "Look, where the youngest wren of nine comes" (3.2). And an old country rhyme reveals

> It's as much as a pigeon can do
> To maintain two;
> But the little wren can maintain ten
> And bring them up like gentlemen.
> (Armstrong 1955, 209)

Or, according to oral tradition, when the dove and wren speak for themselves,

> The dove says, Coo, coo,
> What shall I do?
> I can scarcely maintain two.
> Pooh, pooh, says the wren,
> I have got ten,
> And keep them all like gentlemen.
>   (Munsterberg 1984, 323)

A Scottish couplet ascribes an immense clutch to the wren: "The big Cushie-doo [ring dove], only lays two, / The wee Cuddy-wran, lays twenty-wan" (Armstrong 1955, 168).

Gaelic tradition includes another comparison: "The heron feeds its single chick while by the little brown one [the wren] are fed its eleven." A Scottish version involving the same species indicates that "the heron has a single chick which is surly and unpleasant, while the wren has twelve chicks which are agreeable and pleasant" (Ó Cuív 1980, 50, 63). In Irish folklore, the wren-eagle contrast surfaces again in relation to number of offspring. Following the famous contest, after the eagle put a spell of enchantment on the wren to limit the height of its flight, the wren took revenge. Using its own power, the tiny bird told the eagle, "Though you mate once a year, as nature calls for that, you will never have more than two birds from the mating, whereas I may have a full score or more!" In Scottish tradition, because of the wren's extraordinary feat in soaring above the eagle, "the wren has twelve eggs while the eagle has two" (Ó Cuív 1980, 60–61). Mention of twelve young of the wren appears in various anecdotes that tell of a cure for *easbaidh* (evils) that is effected with the blood of the wren. The idea that it is difficult to distinguish between the old wren and his young because they are identical in appearance adds a note of confusion to determining the number of the wren's offspring (Ó Cuív 1980, 61–63).

Although it is possible that rhyming requirements determined some of the numbers of offspring mentioned in verses, still the wren is popularly known as the "small bird [who] brings up so large a family and builds such a cozy nest for them" (Parry-Jones 1988, 154). Belief that the wren produced large clutches was prevalent in England and Wales as well as in the Gaelic world (Ó Cuív 1980, 63–64). In Irish law, an unusual item that a woman might request in a dowry is "the full of a crow's nest of wren's eggs" (Ó Cuív 1980, 49). The imagery here refers to the idea of the nest of a very big bird being filled up with the eggs of a tiny bird, emphasizing the unusual egg-producing capacity of the wren. The young wrens are "assiduously attended to by the parent birds" and may "return to lodge in the nest for some time after being fledged" (Morris n.d., 136, 139). Wrens have a strong family bond, and sometimes the young of the first brood will help their parents feed the nestlings of the next generation (Simon 1977, 140). Families may stay together during the winter, with "the bond of social union" continuing "unbroken till the following spring" (Morris n.d., 135). The model parent image and the striking contrast between the tiny wren and the large size of its brood are clearly expressed in lines from Alexander Wilson's poem "The Disconsolate Wren," which draws attention to the "stupendously minute" miracle represented by

> The numerous progeny, clamant for food
> Supplied by two small bills, and feeble wings
> Of narrow range; supplied—ay, duly fed—
> Fed in the dark, and yet not one forgot.
>   (Armstrong 1955, 186)

The reputation for producing a large family is accurate, for as many as sixteen young have been found in the little bird's nest (Dyer 1883, 151). Thomas Bewick, an authority on British birds, states that the female wren "lays from ten to sixteen, and sometimes eighteen eggs" (1809, 236), although four to seven is the number given in some other ornithology texts. F. O. Morris specifies "seven to eight" eggs, "though as many as a dozen or even fourteen, have been found" (n.d., 139). As we have seen, wren-hunt songs refer to eleven or thirteen siblings, indicating people's perceptions of the bird's prolific breeding. The recurring wren-song lines "Although he is little, his family is great" and "Although she is small, her family is great" undoubtedly signify the wren's large brood. The wren's eggs, in contrast to their multiplicity, are very tiny; only two British birds—the long-tailed tit and the goldcrest—lay smaller eggs. Wordsworth saw a timeless beauty in the wren's dull white eggs with ruddy spots that "within the nest repose / Like relics in an urn" (George 1904, 701).

In P. G. Ralfe's version of the fable about the wren becoming king of all birds, qualities other than the height at which it could fly were emphasized in judging the contest. "The birds all met together once upon a time to tell of all the great things they could do." They spoke one at a time, "saying how many young they were rearing, and how good they were laboring. When the little wren came to tell what he could do, he said: 'Though I am light and my leg is small, / Eleven chicks I bring out for all'" (1905, 40). In the Manx account of the fable, "little Jinny Wren got the better of" all the larger birds, boasting: "Small though I am and slender my leg, / Twelve chicks I can bring out of the egg" (Morrison 1992, 133). "All the birds agreed that Jinny was as clever as the best of them." But when the eagle "didn't like it that a little bit of a bird like Jinny Wren should be over him," he proposed the familiar test to determine who could fly the highest. Jinny Wren hid under his wing and ultimately flew above his head to win the title of king of the birds (Morrison 1992, 133–35).

Calling the wren "an odd little bird in every way," a writer describes another well-established trait of the species: "One nest is not enough for Jenney Wren" (Byron n.d., 49–50). The male wren generally builds five or six (sometimes as many as ten or twelve) nests from which the female selects one to be used for raising offspring (Goodfellow 1977, 55). One of these multiple nests is generally more carefully constructed than the others, and the female invariably chooses that one and lines it with feathers. But "the male may seek out another female and show her the rest of his nests; if one of them is reasonably well built, he may succeed in winning another mate" (Simon 1977, 139–40). The habit of constructing an excess number of nests, called "dummy," "play," or "cock nests," gives the male wren, at least in the eyes of some observers, the reputation of being more polygynous than other birds. This idea stems partly from the belief that he might be maintaining more than one "household" at the same time and therefore is indeed a lecherous creature. In actuality, according to Armstrong, the wren is "unusual among European birds for being polygamous," but "an equal number of males may be monogamous" (1992, 19; 1955, 102).

The Wren's Faults and Evil Aspects

Thus the behavior of the wren, interpreted by observers in a variety of contradictory ways, expresses human ambivalence regarding sexuality. Perhaps the perceived wicked nature of the wren that is sometimes expressed is at least partly connected with the bird's sexual image. We have already seen in chapter 3 that the sick lady wren was less than grateful to the robin for his solicitous attention. In a traditional verse the wren wife who "lies in care's bed / In mickle dule and pyne [much dole and pain]" not only refuses the sugar sops and wine brought by her nurturing husband, the robin, by saying, "Na, ne'er a drap, Robin" but also reveals that she has been unfaithful to him as well. When the robin asks, "And where's the ring that I gied ye, / Ye little cutty quyne?" the wren answers, "I gied it till a soger [to a soldier], / A kind sweetheart o' mine, O" (Munsterberg 1984, 333). There is also an attribution of selfishness and greed to the wren in association with the robin:

> The robin and the wren,
> They fought upon the porridge pan;
> But ere the robin got a spoon,
> The wren had eat the porridge down.
>   (Munsterberg 1984, 333)

Similar traits are evident in the Irish tale in which the wren borrowed five pounds from a rich man and then failed to pay it back. The wren hoped to escape retribution because he and his young were indistinguishable in appearance. But although he hid among his offspring, he could not resist responding to his creditor's praise of his former prowess, and thus gave himself away (Ó Cuív 1980, 62). Here is the familiar pattern of duplicity in which the wren tries to gain by taking advantage of his small size, though in this case he is foiled by his own vanity. Faults like these may make the wren seem more human and possibly more endearing.

But it is clear that although generally esteemed and admired, the wren has a darker side—a sometimes hidden aspect that emerges occasionally and conflicts with the dominant image of goodness. In its commonest form, this negative image is represented by the notion that the wren has a "drop of the devil's blood" (see chapter 4). The wren's role as "an emissary of the devil" may reflect the traditional belief, dating back to the Druids, that the ancient title of "King of All Birds" was obtained "by perpetrating a fraud" (Gibson 1904, 151–52). Additionally, the vengeance meted out to people who molest or kill the wren (except during the time of the hunt) may give a malevolent connotation to the power of the wren in causing such harsh punitive retribution. This capacity is represented, for example, by the popular couplet "Malisons, malisons, mair than ten, / That harry the Ladye of Heaven's hen!" The vengeance expressed in this verse seems to indicate that "the poor little bird has met with a somewhat similar fate to that of Odin" and other gods, "and has been transformed, occasionally at least, into a spirit of evil" (Hardwick 1872, 247).

The fact that the hearer finds it difficult to tell where the wren's voice is coming from may be one cause of the bird's unfavorable image. This ventriloquial quality suggests duplicity and unreliability on the part of the clandestine singer who does not reveal its whereabouts. Interestingly, a related North American species, the canyon wren, is known to Acoma Pueblo people as a bird of war for the same reason. The bird's loud voice "echoes back and forth" among the rocks, "so it is very hard to tell exactly where the bird really is, and that, of course, is a handy trick for fooling an enemy" (Tyler 1991, 211). Thus the same trait of elusiveness can be interpreted as helpful as well as suspicious, depending on the situation.

The ancient mysterious nature of the wren's bad connotation is expressed in a curious poem entitled "A Health to the Birds," in which the author pays tribute to several avian species, such as linnets and blackbirds, emphasizing their virtues. But one bird lacks the nobility of the others and is only begrudgingly hailed:

> Here's health to the wren!
> Ay, a health to the wren, too, the devil's dear pet,
> Through thousands of years he's owed a black debt,
> And it's often we've made the vile thummikin sweat—
> But away with old scores! forgive and forget!
> Here's health to the wren!
> (MacManus 1930, 5)

During the hunt-the-wren dance on the Isle of Man, performers traditionally gesture toward the bush in the center of the circle that contains the token wren. This action may once have signified paying homage to the wren, but now dancers generally shake their fists at the bird in response to its alleged bad deeds. The evil fairy who assumed the guise of the wren on the Isle of Man reflects the malevolent attribution of the tiny bird. The phenomenon of beautiful women or fairies taking the form of birds is often encountered, and such birds may "symbolize dark, destructive fancies and ideas" (Jung and von Franz 1986, 269). The concept that the "witch is the dark side of the earth goddess" (von Franz 1990, 37) is applicable to the wren, who is associated with earth in a benevolent way except for its malicious side personified by the bad fairy. An Irish name for the wren, Briocht-èn, means bird of witchcraft (Ó Cuív 1980, 59).

Perhaps the height of ignominy is attributed to the wren by the lines of one wren song that refer to the bird and his "eleven" brothers, the number being an allegorical expression for "the disciples and the wren Judas" (Gill 1932, 390)—symbolic of the betrayal of Christ. The ability of the wren to prognosticate can be construed as evil as well as good, evoking hatred as well as esteem, and an unfavorable image of the wren is sometimes associated with this capacity. For example, St. Ceallach, while imprisoned in a hollow oak tree, was visited by various unfriendly birds. "The wren he apostrophises thus: 'O tiny wren, most scant of tail, dolefully hast thou piped prophetic lay! surely thou art come to betray me, and to curtail my gift of life!'" (Gill 1932, 426). In a slightly different version the saint, awaiting his death, addresses the bird: "O wren with the cropped tail, sadly do you prophesy in your song, if it is for this you have come to betray me and to draw my life's span" (Ó Cuív 1980, 47). A line from an ancient Celtic poem, in mentioning omens to be avoided, reflects a foreboding of bad tidings: "the voice of the wren for unrighteous profit." The gypsy name for the wren means witch, due to the belief that "when it chirps and flutters about a camping-place it is warning the party that they will soon be made to 'move on.' When there was more room in England and no police, the wren must have foretold graver afflictions" (Gill 1932, 425–26).

The story of the wren who ate St. Moling's pet fly, mentioned previously, involves a curse upon the wren. After the wren ate the fly, the fox (or cat) killed the wren and dogs killed the fox. All were restored to life, but the saint decreed that the bird who killed "the poor pet that used to be making music for me, let his dwelling be for ever in empty houses, with a wet drip therein continually. And may children and young persons be destroying him" (Ó Cuív 1980, 47–48). Thus the episode takes account of the wren's habitat, its association with damp places, and its annual hunting and destruction by young persons.

According to an etymological study, the wren "has been credited with being a sneak, and lecherous, and full of low cunning." But there is a mystery about the wren's bad connotation. In tracing the origin of wren, Stephen Potter and Laurens Sargent relate the bird to "the duality of Nature," pointing out that "by the wren our thoughts are led to the numinous—the awe-ful." They explain that "the robin and the wren, often paired in the sayings of simple countryfolk . . . illustrate the dual nature of the last form taken by Pan in England. The well-loved redbreast was equated with Robin Goodfellow, and the unpopular wren with Puck—the one being representative of the benevolence of the sprite, the other of his mild malice. *Puck* is the O.E. *puca,* one of the Little People, or a goblin. . . . It is found in the wren's by-names of Dicky

Pug and Pug or Puggy Wren, which may not refer only to the bird's diminutive size." A clue to the origin of this representation "may be found in the Scandinavian by-names which have the sense of 'hedge-sneaker' or, as we might say, 'eavesdropper.' These seem to hold the memory of the primitive belief . . . that small birds make mischief by telling tales of what they have heard or seen. For a base activity of this kind the wren seems well adapted by his small size and his habit of working his way along hedges. His triumphant, scolding song, as of one who has some scandal to relate, may further smirch his already tarnished reputation." But ultimately, the wren's evil aspect is unfathomable, and the etymologists conclude: "It is small wonder that the tiny bird chitters so angrily when his nest is approached; for he may well regard any larger living creature as a potential enemy. Yet not one of his friends or unfriends has been able to discover the secret of his name" (1974, 295–97).

The King, Jenny Wren, and Fertility

Contradictory perceptions of the wren represent an enigma as they vacillate between a male and a female personification of the bird. The confusion between Jenny Wren and the king of all birds can perhaps be reconciled by recognizing the bird as taking on the image of a female/male composite in the popular mind. In this regard, it has been pointed out that the divine child in mythology is sometimes characterized as a hermaphrodite, a figure used as a symbol for the union of opposites, including male and female. The hermaphrodite can represent the "totality of the Self," or "wholeness in its male-female aspect" (von Franz 1990, 23). This image of dual sexuality is another example of the intriguing phenomenon of pairs of opposites that are attributed to the wren. Of course, the answer may be that either gender is freely assigned to the wren according to the particular symbology people use at different times and in different contexts. It is evident that any confusion as to whether the wren is female or male—Jenny or the king—does not seem to be a problem that is addressed in most wren lore, and one cannot apply ordinary logic on this issue.

Associated with its sexuality, the little bird also symbolizes fertility. The wren's identification with the moon, and sometimes its corresponding opposition to the sun, are significant in this regard. As previously noted, one of the little bird's names is Moonie. Owing to the shape of its nest, the wren is a "moon god symbol," and "as a drinker up of sun rays is an enemy of the sun-gods." This status is related to the legendary wren-eagle contest, in which the wren "darted upwards, undoubted victor, a speck eclipsing the sun." Thus the rivalry for the title of king of birds "reveals a phase of warfare between the solar and lunar gods." Related to this concept, the traditional rhyme "The robin and the wren are God's cock and hen" can be interpreted as "a distinct allusion to the union of the sun bird, the red-breasted robin, and the moon bird, the wren of the round nest" (Rothery n.d., 53, 59–60).

In ancient lore, the wren "devours the poison of the sun." It "bewails the evils of winter, which . . . it represents." In its character of the moon, it "absorbs the solar vapors" (De Gubernatis 1872, 2:207–8, 209). This capacity adds credence to the idea that the wren was killed at the winter solstice because of its correspondence to the weakness of the sun at that time. The wren's connection to the moon—with its waxing and waning—provides another metaphoric relationship between the bird and the recurring phenomena of birth, death, and regeneration. The moon is symbolic of "both the end of life and a new beginning—there is always a new moon. The sky is dark for three nights but on the fourth night the moon is reborn. In the same way the dead were thought to find a new life" (Bancroft 1987, 42–43). Because of the cyclical nature of the moon and its association with rhythms of reproduction, the wren is also closely related to fecundity. The bird was once known as the "dwelling place of the Moon Goddess" (Walker 1988, 412). The wren, representing the moon, "was known to be the protectress of weddings," which were not to take place "while the wren was hidden in the earth." The full moon "was considered the most propitious season for weddings" (De Gubernatis 1872, 2:208–9).

In analyzing why the wren was chosen as a manifestation of the "life force," one scholar suggests that the bird "was originally revered as a manifestation of one particular aspect of that force—the mating of human beings." This association could have been acquired from "the exultant nature of its song," because the singing of birds was once "a widely accepted symbol of erotic pleasure." Additionally, the wren's "mania for nest building, the building that preceded and facilitated breeding," gave this connotation. "The wren was certainly associated with the springtime mating customs of young people" in France and England. Evidence indicates that "the bird was regarded as an erotic symbol in the sixteenth and seventeenth centuries." In Medieval and Renaissance literary traditions, the little bird signified a successful lover and stood as a symbol of eros. This attribution "supports the theory that the wren-hunts and wren-songs of West European folklore derive from ancient fertility ceremonies." Accordingly, interpretation of the Manx legend of the beautiful fairy who escaped in the form of a wren may be that "the wren was hunted and killed annually in token exorcism of erotic desire" (Wentersdorf 1977, 193–94, 197–98).

The wren's close connection to human fruitfulness is evident in many of the wren-hunt traditions. These include wren parties singing under the bedroom windows of newly married couples and the tug-of-war between occupants of the wagon carrying the wren, in which the long-married and newly married compete. There is also the French custom that dictates it is the duty of the newly married to carry the wren to the Lord of the Manor. In Scottish lore the wren was understood to cause fertility. It was considered lucky to have a wren around one's dwelling, and a Scotch maxim declares, "No house ever dies out that the wren frequents" (Gill 1932, 377–78). The fact that the wren is "a charm for fertility" and the "spirit of fertility must be feminine" may account for the change from the image of king of all birds to the role of "queen of birds" (Macmillan 1926, 77).

The Wild Wood and the Garden: Nature and Culture

The wren exemplifies many oppositions in addition to the male/female or king/queen personifications. It is admired for cleverness and simultaneously hated for deceit due to the ruse by which it gained victory over the eagle. The wren is familiar yet elusive; friendly yet aloof; tiny but great in voice, spirit, and reproductive powers; winged yet terrestrial; both bird and mouse. It is slight and frail and strong and hardy, endearing and cunning, polygamous and yet a diligent mate and an ideal parent. It is sacred and profane, associated with life and death, envisioned as god and devil, identified as solar and lunar, and is protected yet hunted. Most significantly, the wren bridges the domains of the wild and the tame. It is noteworthy for converting the wild plants from its habitat into an intricately constructed chamber nest or "home." The wren will frequent areas near houses and in gardens, but avoids populous areas and lives "only where bricks and mortar do not predominate over greenery" (Armstrong 1955, 15). Wrens are "fond of seclusion, and are of solitary habits, being never seen in flocks, and seldom but in spring in pairs, and choosing sombre, quiet, and lonely places for their tenantship" (Morris n.d., 136). Paradoxically, a superimposed explanation for the prohibition on killing wrens is that this act would be "a breach of hospitality" because of the birds "taking refuge" near homes (Brand 1949, 3: 193), yet such behavior is not consistent. At times the wren shows unusual interest in the human realm, but it can also be wary, remote, and unapproachable. The species is characterized as "half-sociable, half shy" (Parmelee 1959, 162). Wrens travel freely between the domesticated sphere and the untamed world beyond. The tiny birds seldom seek sustenance from humankind and do not generally go to bird feeders.

Hudson's intimate knowledge of birds caused him to comment that the wren, though "one of the few general favourites," is not quite so popular as the swallow, house-martin, and the robin. The reason for this is that the wren is "less domestic, never so familiar with man or tolerant of close observation. The wren is never tame nor unsuspicious; he is less dependent on us than other small birds that attach themselves to human habitations, never a 'pensioner' in the same degree as the blue tit, dunnock, blackbird, and sparrow." The "creeping things to be found in obscure holes and corners in wood-piles, ivy-covered walls, and outhouses, are more to his taste than the 'sweepings of the threshold.'" The wren is distinguished from other small birds by its ability to "find everywhere in nature a neglected corner to occupy" (1921, 102). Wordsworth, too, elaborates on this nondomesticated aspect of the little bird. In his poem "The Contrast," the mysterious wren, as "Nature's Darkling" (George 1904, 643), has an image as wild and free in contrast to the tame, captive parrot that is under the care and domination of people.

In human perceptions the wren exists on the border between nature and culture. Numerous wren songs attribute special importance to the woodland setting where the hunters go to find the wren. That wild, somewhat mysterious, outlying area, contrasting with the domesticated, familiar, inner realm, receives emphasis in lyrics exemplified by: "We'll away to the woods," "Will ye go to the woods?" "I went hunting in the wood," "We're off to the wildwood," and "Jenny Wren is shot in the woods" (see chapter 3). Such forested areas mark the edge of the human world. The wren hunters deliberately set forth to those symbolic wild places to seek and catch their quarry and "bring it in"—that is, back to their domestic sphere. Once captured and killed, the wren's corpse is almost always displayed with some type of greenery whose symbolism, often initially derived from the bird's own habits, is of prime importance in the messages communicated by the ensuing ritual. For example, the wren commonly nests and roosts in ivy—a plant associated with mortality and the grave, but also with summer and the renewal of life (Flaherty 1992, 49; Crippen 1923, 15). Thus the frequent use of ivy to adorn the wren or its bier for the ritual procession is especially appropriate. Wren lore often involves ivy, as when the robin, spirit of the New Year, sets out to kill his predecessor the Gold Crest Wren, spirit of the Old Year, whom he finds hiding in an ivy bush. The Gold Crest does actually frequent ivy bushes at Christmas time. Additionally, "ivy and holly were both associated with Saturnalia, holly being Saturn's club, ivy being the nest of the Gold Crest Wren, his bird" (Graves 1989, 184, 186).

An Irish wren song includes the lines "Up with the holly and ivy tree / Where all the birds will sing to me" (Armstrong 1958, 156). Today, as in the past, the wren or its substitute in the ceremony is surrounded by ivy, holly, or mistletoe—all species that bear fruit in winter. Holly was sometimes viewed as sacred in Britain and was hated by witches. Mistletoe, worshipped by the Druids and the object of Celtic ritual, has been an object of veneration in Europe from time immemorial. It was believed to be "the universal healer" and a remedy against all poison. A potion made from it could cause barren animals to be fruitful and when carried about by women it assisted them to conceive a child (Miles 1976, 275; MacCulloch 1991, 205; Frazer 1963, 763–64). In the French wren ceremonies involving newlyweds, the bird was carried in a bunch of mistletoe because of its erotic symbolism (Armstrong 1958, 151).

Wrens are often observed in association with oak trees and, correspondingly, sometimes a garland of oak was used to enclose the dead wren—a tree revered by the Druids as a fire-giver and for its association with the sun. The wren's role as the soul of the oak has already been mentioned. The Druids believed that everything that grows on the oak, including mistletoe, was sent from heaven. Mistletoe could spring directly from seeds deposited by birds on trees. When found on the oak, the Druids ascribed its growth to the gods, who chose the tree. The bird was the gods' messenger or a god in disguise. Mistletoe could protect a homestead from fire and other disasters. The life of the oak was perceived to be in the mistletoe because it was still alive in winter when the tree itself appeared to be dead. A divine king's life might be bound up with a particular tree and both may have perished together. The sacred kings are also linked to the oak through their role as promoters of fertility and well-being (Hardwick 1872, 62; Spence 1945, 124–25; MacCulloch 1991, 162, 270).

The wild bush called furze plays a role in the most commonly cited wren song: "The wren, the wren, the king of all birds, / On St. Stephen's Day was caught in the furze." Furze is a spiny evergreen shrub common in the British Isles and Europe and is often inhabited by the wren. Its tangled foliage would undoubtedly serve to entrap the hidden bird for capture by its assailants. Especially in Ireland, wrens were chased and caught in areas where that bush flourished. Interestingly, when the wren song was transplanted from Ireland to Newfoundland, it was adapted to its new surroundings by the substitution of "firs" for "furze" (Armstrong 1958, 142). In some areas of England the wren was carried in the ritual procession in a furze bush.

In winter, when everything in the landscape is brown and dead, the evergreens are "manifestations of the abiding life within the plant-world, and they may well have been used as sacramental means of contact with the spirit of growth and fertility, threatened by the powers of blight" (Miles 1976, 272). Thus various types of evergreen boughs, as symbols of eternal life, are used in many areas to adorn the bird's container or "wren bush."

According to Walter Burkert's studies of ancient ritual, the plant or portion of a tree brought from the woods to the city, village, or town— its transference from outside to inside the human realm—represents "a mediation between nature and culture." Civilized life is "invigorated by fresh input from the surrounding wilderness." The opposition between the tree or bush versus the city may represent "the sequence of hunting and agriculture." The hunting and killing of the wren and bearing it on structures surrounded by plants seems to be related to an early sacrificial tradition in which animal victims were tied to trees and "brought into the sanctuary, finally to be burned together with them" (1979, 136–37).

Another use of plants is relevant to the wren ceremony. Almost universally, a branch is "ceremoniously carried by somebody pleading for peace or pardon" (Burkert 1979, 43–44). It is fascinating that birds, too, have appeasement rituals consisting of handing over twigs or other plant materials that they use in nest construction. The herbage displayed in the wren ceremony may well represent a tribute to the sacrificed wren, a presentation made to foster reconciliation between people and the slaughtered bird and, more broadly, to facilitate harmony between humankind and nature.

SYMBOL AND METAPHOR: WREN AND HUMANKIND

Legends and ceremonies such as those revolving around the wren express the deeply rooted connections that may exist between the human psyche and the natural world. Lévi-Strauss argues that in order to discover the nature of man we must understand how man is related to nature (Leach 1974, 36). Seeking to find its identity, humankind must first clarify its relations with other living beings. This concept is articulated by the poet Siegfried Sassoon, in "Wren and Man":

> What does it mean to call oneself a man,
> As though to no one else the name applied?
> I tried to think. Before my thoughts began
> Some voice quite unexpectedly replied—
>   'This afternoon, as you remember, came
> And flew around your room a Jennie Wren . . .
> Not till that nimble creature knows its name
> Will you have learnt your meaning among men.'
>   (1957, 25)

Although birds are different from humans, their many resemblances cause people to identify with them and see their world as a reflection of our own. Both birds and people are two-legged, and both are perceived to have vocal expressions capable of articulating and evoking emotions. Wrens have a very beautiful courtship that is accompanied by the male's "subsong" rendered with slower and more subdued notes than its usual utterance,—"a meditative song [that] is audible only a few metres from the singer." Delight in hearing this outpouring caused an ornithologist to remark: "We must be wary of attributing to birds emotions like our own, but this courtship song has been compared to the soft endearments of lovers" (Armstrong 1992, 11, 14). In the devoted parenting of birds, people see human parallels, and with their skill in building, avian creatures demonstrate artistic ability that resembles human creativity.

No other British or European bird seems to have been granted the same degree of familiarity in being called by a human name as the one so commonly referred to as Jenny Wren. Lévi-Strauss has much to say about societal conventions concerning the names given to animals that sheds light on attitudes toward the wren. For example, he points out that dogs, being part of human society but not quite human, usually have names that are like human names but slightly different, such as stage names or mythological names. In contrast, when birds are given nicknames like Jenny Wren or Tom Tit, they are normal human names. The difference is that the nonhuman names of pet dogs are names of individuals, whereas the human names of birds are applied indiscriminately to any member of a whole species. He argues that

> birds are given human Christian names in accordance with the species to which they belong more easily than are other zoological classes, because they can be permitted to resemble men for the very reason that they are so different. They are feathered, winged, oviparous and they are also physiologically separated from human society by the element in which it is their privilege to move. As a result of this fact, they form a community which is independent of our own but, precisely because of this independence, appears to us like another society, homologous to that in which we live: birds love freedom; they build themselves homes in which they live a family life and nurture their young; they often engage in social relations with other members of their species; and they communicate with them by acoustic means recalling articulated language.
>
> Consequently everything objective conspires to make us think of the bird world as a metaphorical human society.
>
> (1966, 204–5)

To an extraordinary degree the wren's role in human life depends upon metaphor. Unlike animals that became important for food, fiber, transportation, traction, or other service, sport, recreation, companionship, or aesthetic uses, the focus placed upon the wren is cognitive. The bird has been utilized for its profound symbolic power. It has attracted attention not by means of noble or grandiose qualities, nor by fearsomeness, but rather because of many striking and idiosyncratic traits and certain characteristics that seem contradictory or incongruous. Lévi-Strauss has remarked that "species possessing some remarkable characteristics, say of shape, colour or smell" cause the observer to postulate that "these visible characteristics are the sign of equally singular, but concealed, properties" (1966, 16). One of the wren's most salient characteristics, minuscule size, has many deep and far-reaching implications that have become clear throughout this study. The concept that Lévi-Strauss postulated for works of art may be also true of natural creatures such as birds—that all small-scale models or miniatures "seem to have intrinsic aesthetic quality" deriving "from the dimensions themselves." In the case of miniatures, he asserts, in contrast to objects or living creatures of ordinary dimensions, "knowledge of the whole precedes knowledge of the parts" (1966, 23–24).

The wren embodies the universal enigma of the great contained within the small—*multum in parvo.* The diminutive creature represents the classic sacrifice of something small given in exchange for something great and illustrates the concept frequently found in religious thought that events of cosmic proportions and influence arise from minuscule origins. Christianity exemplifies this principle in the centrality of its traditional worship of a helpless newborn infant—the tiny babe in the manger who even at birth reigned as the mighty king of glory. Knowledge of Christ's world-shaking Nativity was first imparted to simple shepherds and to animals possessing no status other than their use to humans. Humble circumstances paradoxically gave rise to the Savior of humanity. In a reversal of everyday secular order, unseen power radiates from small but sanctified sources. The wren's holy status is encapsulated in the couplet "Birds look up and behold your king, / Great of soul, though a tiny thing" (Woodward 1928, 29).

The diminutive wren with its mysterious incarnated energy appears strange, and strangeness kindles thought. I believe there is a close correlation between the wren's propensity for stimulating thought and the reverence with which the bird has been generally regarded. Ideational responses, according to their richness, seem to result in worship. The wren's sacredness derives partly from the intensity with which it has been viewed as an object of thought. The rich complex of symbolism that clings to the wren has made it a spiritual rather than a material being. The peculiar bird's extraordinary outward, observable traits became indicative of even more extraordinary invisible inner qualities.

The wren, as we have seen, demonstrates characteristics that defy ordinary classification—being winged yet earthbound, tiny yet huge in forcefulness and voice, female yet male, and sacred yet profane. The bird embodies a "metaphoric confusion of categories" and is thus an anomalous creature. Barbara Babcock-Abrahams, drawing on the work of Claude Lévi-Strauss, Mary Douglas, and Victor Turner, points out that myth and ritual, by using "symbols of anomaly, can incorporate evil and death along with goodness and life into a single, grand, unifying pattern" (1975, 168, 174). This concept applies to the wren ceremony that so clearly combines the polarities of birth and death. Many wren traditions and songs express ambiguity, being capable of several interpretations, and these ambiguous symbols are used in ritual "for the same ends as in poetry and mythology, to enrich the meaning or call attention to other levels of existence." Religious rites often include ambiguous symbols that serve to "implement communication" between "man and the supernatural." Through use of terms usually kept separated, such "combined opposed attributes" acquire a character "be-twixt-and-between Spirit and Creation," and "such ritual . . . estab-lishes contact between [the] two spheres" (Babcock-Abrahams 1975, 174–75). Through these means the tiny brown wren attains cosmic sig-nificance by expressing universal and transcendent messages and as-sumes the role of mediator between nature and culture and between humankind and the divine.

Out of metaphor was created the king of all birds, who must die to retain the fertility of the land. And in the same manner was fashioned little Jenny Wren—the symbol for rebirth, the regeneration of life—an image, ultimately, that must be female, for the bearing and raising of young is itself a sacrificial and redeeming act. Both Jenny and the king were once worshipped and ritually killed to cause the sun to return, to make green the living universe, to find a kernel of wisdom, discern the will of the gods, to unlock eternal things, and achieve everlasting life. The images of the king of all birds and Jenny Wren represent the trans-formed biological bird—a small thing made magnificent—a being that is part living creature and part imaginary figure and whose numerous and varied meanings represent a unique and vividly expressive aspect of the cosmic dialogue between people and the animal world.

THE WREN HUNT IN PERSPECTIVE: PROVOCATIVE QUESTIONS

There is no other case quite like the wren hunt, and its richness and complexity evoke consideration of many issues encapsulated within its lore that have contemporary importance regarding the human relation-ship with nature. The wren hunt, like other rituals that once connected humankind with the earth and its inhabitants, represents much that we in the modern industrialized world have lost. Because of its great an-tiquity, the ceremony relating to the wren reflects to a marked degree the wide ideological chasm that separates us from our ancestors, who waited so intensely for the sun to reverse its direction at the solstice, trusting that their actions could accelerate that life-renewing process and avert disaster. Reciprocal relationships between humankind and nature formerly ruled people's behavior and were believed to influence the course of events for all forms of life. As set forth in common admo-nitions about the wren, punishments for those who hurt the bird or damaged its nest or eggs ranged from ostracism by neighbors, bad luck, unproductiveness of livestock, and loss of prosperity, to stunted growth of children, disfigurement, injury, illness, and death, to the ultimate penalty of exclusion from heaven and being deprived of seeing the face of God. Natural forces orchestrated retribution for killing the wren except during the annual hunt—lightning would strike the perpetrator or his home would be struck and burn down.

As mentioned in chapter 2, in the preindustrialized world, this concept of reciprocity with nature generally guided human actions. Judging from what is known through ethnographic analogy from study of tribal peoples of historic times, a common pattern existed according to which animals could be killed and used, but at the same time they were respected as worthy fellow beings. Ceremonies dedicated to their spirits or their kind could appease the dead individuals and their species, so that no animosity would exist and future hunters might still obtain their quarry. A guiding principle dictated that recompense must be given to the living earth in return for good things derived from it. This tradition persists among some native peoples. During fieldwork among the Crow Indians of Montana, for instance, I found that because of the extraordinary benefits once bestowed upon them by acquisition of the horse, there is a tribal injunction against injuring or killing horses. Misfortune follows those who break this taboo (Lawrence 1985, 51–52).

Numerous examples of reciprocity could be cited, all of which highlight the absence of such attitudes in modern Western culture. Sacrifice of a highly regarded animal facilitated communication with the divine and was carried out with the aim of obtaining blessings or expressing thanks for gifts already received. In our present society, the culturally sanctioned killing of animals commonly takes place in a segregated area, a slaughterhouse, where, with some exceptions, causing death is a secular matter. Phenomena like the original sacrificial wren hunt, and the associated conditions from which they sprang, are undoubtedly lost forever by the dominant society.

Today, even country dwellers within the wren's range probably do not know much about the habits of any kind of wildlife living in their territory. People are not likely to be very familiar with the type of nest or eggs characteristic of a certain regional bird (unless they have a special interest in ornithology). So, unlike some of their forebears, they are not going to set out on a dark wintry day to find a seed of enlightenment, a divine insight, in the guise of a tiny brown wren. From fleeting observations of animals in their back yards, modern people will probably find few metaphors to provide insights that can be woven into complex rituals to mediate between their imagination and the natural environment.

Lacking the old ideologies that once inextricably bound humanity to all forms of life, today we must seek harmony with nature in new ways that are more difficult to establish than they were for the wren hunters of old. Concerned environmentalists in the past few decades have been urging people to abandon selfish materialism and overconsumption and to replace them with sacrifice of immediate gratifications for the sake of the future health and survival of the planet and preservation of all of its inhabitants. Human beings, they assert, instead of being arrogant masters and controllers of nature, should become part of the whole community of earth, existing more humbly within nature rather than setting themselves apart from it and perceiving themselves above it. Surely if we are to reverse the destruction of nature that characterizes our era of ecological crisis, such measures are necessary. But without some basis in a widespread, strongly felt, and firmly rooted belief system to motivate actions, the question remains whether adoption of those altruistic precepts and values is possible, and if so, whether they can be put into operation in time to save the earth's rapidly disappearing species and halt the escalating damage to the biosphere.

Pointing to the bonds of symbiotic interdependence between all species on the planet that have been discovered by the science of ecology, philosopher and "deep ecologist" Arne Naess asserts that there now exists "a cognitive basis for a sense of belonging," a kinship between all forms of life on earth (1989, 168). It appears certain that in order to establish harmony we must view the human relationship to other life forms in those terms and learn to appreciate the intrinsic value of each living creature and the role it plays in the totality of nature. It is equally certain that we must understand the human propensity for transforming animals into symbols and take this tendency into account in our dealings with nature. Rather than choosing which species shall live and which shall die on the basis of usefulness to humans or on whims concerning their perceived qualities that we find pleasing or repugnant, we must adopt an ecological view embracing the whole, valuing biodiversity. But at the same time, we should devote attention to the individual as a being with its own interests—and these dual concerns involve difficult dilemmas. By considering the wren both sacred and protected and yet still hunting and killing it, the issue of the conflict between the individual and the group is embodied in the ancient ceremony. No attempt was made to annihilate the species on 26 December, since individual wrens had to survive for people to cherish the rest of the year and to hunt again on the following St. Stephen's Day. Cyclical rebirth out of death was the ritual's major theme. "Wrenness"—the essence of the species with all of its multiple meanings—was always sacrosanct, even with the deaths of Jenny and the king.

French scholar Georges Bataille posits a connection between this issue of individuality/group identity and the phenomenon of animal sacrifice. "Death," he observes, "does not affect the continuity of existence, since in existence itself all separate existences originate; continuity of existence is independent of death and is *even proved by death.*" Bataille reasons that the sacrificial "victim dies and the spectators share in what his death reveals. This is what religious historians call the sacramental element. This sacramental element is the revelation of continuity through the death of a discontinuous being [a distinct individual] to those who watch it as a solemn rite. A violent death disrupts the creature's discontinuity; what remains, what the tense onlookers experience in the succeeding silence, is the continuity of all existence with which the victim is now one. Only a spectacular killing, carried out as the solemn and collective nature of religion dictates, has the power to reveal what normally escapes notice." The sacrificial killing that "deprives the creature of its limited peculiarity" bestows on it the limitless, infinite nature of sacred things." Religious sacrifice involves a "divine transfiguration" of the victim; "it is the common business of sacrifice to bring life and death into harmony" (1986, 21–22, 82, 90, 91, 92).

The sacrifice of the wren reflects a fundamental dilemma in human-animal relationships: the utilization of animals in ways that require them to suffer and die while simultaneously professing high regard and fellow-feeling for them. One suggested explanation for this prevalent and persistent "existential dualism" is that from the very beginning of their observation of the living world around them, people saw that animals were "both like and unlike man." Additionally, animals were apprehended to be both "mortal and immortal" because, although killing an animal meant death of that individual, its "species was undying" because "each lion was Lion, each ox was Ox" (just as each wren was Wren). This dualism involving animals' "similar/dissimilar lives" then became reflected in the treatment of nonhumans—they could be both revered and persecuted (Berger 1985, 277). Vestiges of this phenomenon, which were much more evident before the time of large-scale factory farming, are exemplified by stock-raisers who are fond of the animals they raise for slaughter. Rural children who are 4-H Club members routinely meet this paradox head-on when they lavish intense solicitous care upon a young food animal they undertake to raise knowing it is destined to be killed. This same paradox is general and widespread, for presently, although we are often regarded as a society of animal lovers, we not only make use of nonhumans on a huge scale for meat and research but also carry out the yearly execution of literally millions of dogs and cats as superfluous unwanted "pets" and homeless strays.

There are no easy answers to modern-day controversies about human interactions with domesticated or wild animals. The humane, or animal protection, movement and the animal rights philosophy, which tend to favor the individual, may be often at odds with the ecological view that endorses preservation of populations or species when the interests of individuals and populations are opposed. If, for example, certain local woodlands must be periodically burned to provide Michigan's tiny population of endangered Kirtland's warblers with the habitat they need to survive and this procedure destroys individual animals of other (nonendangered) species, is this action justified? Should feral horses be allowed to continue to run free on western rangelands? Advocates of the wild horses as individuals say the animals have the right to remain in their domain, and they argue that the horses possess aesthetic value and are important symbols of American freedom, representing the vital contribution that horses made to the winning and settling of the continent. Those who want the horses removed assert that, as a domesticated species, the feral horses are interlopers who threaten the survival of native wildlife populations and indigenous plants and destroy the region's natural balance. Understanding the issues at stake and the compromises that may be necessary is the first step in facing such problems as these, which did not have to be addressed in the time of the ancient wren hunters.

It is the wren's peculiar and salient characteristics that evoke such intense human responses, leading to profound and extensive lore, legend, and ritual. Today, we still live in a world in which our perceptions of animals often determine their fate. Studies show that Americans generally wish to expend effort and money to preserve only those animals that are aesthetically appealing, such as butterflies, colorful birds, gentle creatures such as deer, and, sometimes, symbolic species such as the bald eagle. But few citizens will make material sacrifices to save endangered species that are unattractive, inconspicuous, or threatening to humans, and fewer still will take an interest in conservation of perceptually repugnant animals such as beetles and spiders (Kellert 1993, 849).

Attribution of historic, aesthetic, or religious value to a species does not automatically guarantee protection. Our national symbol, the American bald eagle, was brought to the verge of extinction and then rescued only by emergency last-ditch measures, motivated in large part by its status as an icon, implemented in the nick of time. The resplendent quetzal, a Guatemalan bird traditionally regarded as the representative of gods and royalty, and whose image appears on stamps, coins, and various official emblems of that country, nevertheless has been persecuted there to the point of virtual extirpation. The extraordinary beauty and conspicuousness of that bird have not ensured its preservation but have acted as liabilities to its very existence. Hudson lamented the human propensity for destruction of birds that is evident throughout many areas of the world, and specifically described the paradox involving immigrants to his native Argentina:

> How amazing it seems that the chief destroyers should be the South Europeans, the Latins, who are supposed to be lovers of the beautiful and who are undoubtedly the most religious of all people! They have no symbol for the heavenly beings they worship but a bird. Their religious canvases, illuminations, and temples, inside and out, are covered with representations of ibises, cranes, pigeons, gulls, modified so as to resemble human figures, and these stand for angels and saints and the third person of the Trinity. Yet all these people, from popes, cardinals, princes, and nobles down to the meanest peasant on the land, are eager to slay and devour every winged creature, from noble crane and bustard even to the swallow that builds in God's house and the minute cutty wren and fairy-like firecrest—the originals of those sacred emblematic figures before which they bow in adoration.
>
> (1920, 37)

There are many cases in which symbolism associated with some of an animal's peculiar characteristics, in conjunction with cultural and societal views, may directly affect its destiny. For example, the aye-aye of Madagascar is now scarce not only because of its diminished habitat but also because of the attribution of evil to this curious primate. An elongated middle digit on its hands causes people to fear the animal's unusual appendage as the finger of doom. Consequently, as "harbingers of grave misfortune," regional belief dictates that aye-ayes should be killed on sight (Tattersall 1982, 112). The way in which animals are classified can also arbitrarily cause their death or help to save them. In some areas of the United States, for example, the mourning dove is categorized as a song bird and thus is granted protected status, whereas in other regions it is known as a game bird to be hunted. A wildlife official once explained to me that "biologically, there is no reason not to hunt" doves, but "people hear the dove cooing and so they put it in the same light as a robin, rather than as a game bird." He attributed the vote against hunting this species in his area to the idea that "if a dove were as ugly as a vulture and did not sit in the back yard and coo, people wouldn't care" (Lawrence 1982, 259). Thus, reminiscent of the wren, the dove is characterized by certain observed salient traits that influence human interaction with its species.

Religious symbolism rooted in these traits still clings to the dove. The case of the "prodove" faction, opponents of dove hunting, "rests heavily on the Bible. The mourning dove, its protectors contend, ought not to be hunted because it symbolizes peace." A spokesperson for one such group explains, "As a universal symbol of peace, the dove has held and does hold a place of reverence—even awe. Its religious significance in our Christian society, used in art to signify the presence of the Holy Spirit, is known to us all." Another argument stems from doves' legendary devotion to one another: "Hunters are likely to bag two at a time because the mourning dove almost always comes to the rescue of his or her mate." But prohunting groups maintain that doves are delicious food and represent "tons of protein now going to waste." Mourning doves, they assert, "ought to be hunted because lots and lots of people enjoy hunting them, because there is nothing wrong with hunting them, and because hunting does not affect dove numbers" (Williams 1985, 42, 44).

Some western cattle ranchers hate magpies, and I have seen dead bodies of these birds nailed to barn doors "as a warning to keep the others away." Many stockmen believe that these birds they classify as vermin will attack healthy animals and cause great harm, even pecking out their eyes. Thus cattlemen often perceive the conspicuous black and white birds as "just plain bad," whereas ecologists say the magpies, as carrion eaters, consume only necrotic tissue and maggots from animals' wounds, not healthy flesh, and actually benefit injured cattle by their feeding habits. But the birds, conservationists argue, often take on symbolic roles as the ranchers' scapegoats when raising cattle becomes difficult (Lawrence 1982, 257–58, 259). As described in chapter 1, bats are commonly hated and destroyed because of the ghoulish symbolism people attribute to them, and until recently these anomalous creatures—seemingly part bird and part mouse—have not been appreciated for their important role in nature's balance.

Wolves have been victims of human hatred and extreme persecution. According to one wolf researcher, "Never has one species so completely waged war on a fellow species" (McIntyre 1993, 12). The campaign of annihilation was motivated in large measure by human fear of symbolic concepts of malice that were projected upon that species, transforming it to the incarnation of evil—a creature quite unlike its true biological self. Ironically, studies of wolf ethology reveal that the animals possess many traits and social behaviors that are admired by humans—altruism, group loyalty, close kinship ties, and solicitous parenting. But the biology of the wolf is still overshadowed by its image in human perceptions. The 1995 program to reestablish the "mythic gray wolf" in certain areas of the western United States, in spite of opponents who view it as "the Saddam Hussein of the animal world," is described as an event with "potent symbolism." This "reintroduction is not about increasing tourist revenues, any more than it is about 'saving' wolves." Rather, returning wolves to Yellowstone National Park and to Idaho is "a symbolic act, just as exterminating them in the West was a symbolic act," according to the director of the Wolf Fund. The animal "has come to stand for the overwhelming changes buffeting the West—suburban sprawl, attacks on federally subsidized grazing on public lands, a shift from a Marlboro Man culture to one of cappuccino bars and ranchettes. Powerless against these forces, ranchers seized on the wolf as one change they could, perhaps, prevent. The wolf became a vehicle for grappling with the profound value shifts occurring in the West" (Begley and Glick 1995, 53).

Beliefs about animals, such as those involving the wren, often begin with empirical observations, but take liberties with or disregard that data in favor of convictions that spring from strong religious or cultural traditions. One avian legend recorded among American settlers is the "miracle of the gulls," which "appeared from nowhere to save the crops in the new Mormon settlement in Utah." When hordes of crickets descended on their fields and were devouring "every green thing, and every day destroying their sole means of subsistence," suddenly "myriads of snow-white gulls" came and consumed the insects (Bancroft 1987, 302–3). The Mormons assumed that the "sea gulls" flew hundreds of miles from the ocean specifically to help them. Thus they construed an ordinary natural event as idiosyncratic, attributable to an act of God designed to preserve their lives. In actuality, the bird involved is a species that commonly feeds on insects, a native of that region of Utah still residing there.

Few wild species have been endowed with as many human traits as the king of all birds and Jenny Wren. This extreme anthropomorphism raises the question of the existence of similarities and differences between animals and people. Babcock-Abrahams, drawing from Edmund Leach, suggests that in distinguishing ourselves from animals, in order to bridge the gap between us and them without confusing our categories, we use a third category that is unlike either of the others to mediate between the two. Animals in such a category "are regarded as dangerous and powerful and are typically the focus of taboo and ritual observance" (1975, 169). Because it possesses many odd pairs of oppositional traits that make it difficult to classify, and is perceived as having human as well as animal characteristics, the wren fits closely the criteria for mediation between the human and animal worlds.

Vestiges of this role linger in popular culture. One of country singer Anne Murray's hit songs, entitled "A Love Song," features the wren as a helper who communicates with a lovelorn person and provides inspiration based on a sense of identity between bird and human:

> There's a wren in the willow wood
> Flies so high and sings so good;
> And he brings to you
> What he sings to you.
>
> Like my brother the wren and I,
> Well, he told me if I try
> I could fly for you.
> And I want to try for you,
> 'Cause I want to sing you a love song.
>   (George and Loggins 1980)

A 1995 book on present-day superstitions refers to "winsome wrens" who have a reciprocally beneficial relationship with people. Extending hospitality to a wren nesting in a person's back yard still brings good luck as well as ensuring the enjoyment of hearing its frequently repeated song. Moreover, as of old, the direction from which the wren sings can reveal important information about future events and the well-being of loved ones. Thus the reader is cautioned: "Don't forget to fill the bird feeder for the wrens" (Spencer 1995, 123–24). The idea of the wren as mediator between people and nature—in this case between the human and avian realms—is also exemplified by an illustration from a cookbook entitled *Yankee's Christmas Sweet Treats,* which was included with the December 1993 issue of *Yankee* Magazine. Reminding readers that "by no means should we forget our feathered friends," the little bird with the stumpy tail perching on the branch of a British species of oak (a tree not native to the United States) is the familiar Old World wren figure that has somehow found its way into Yankee country. Various recipes for seasonal treats to be prepared and offered to wild birds are provided (Thibault 1993, 42).

Currently, the issue of differences between animals and humankind assumes vital importance in determining attitudes toward and treatment of various species. Animal rights advocates in general view animals as very similar to people and see continuity between the human and animal realms. On the other hand, their opponents believe that there is a deep gulf between human beings and animals. In any analysis of human interactions with animals, this issue of perceived differences appears to be the most influential factor (Lawrence 1994, 177; 1995). If nonhumans are qualitatively different, any type of exploitation of animals can be much more easily rationalized, but belief in similarity makes the use of animals strictly for the benefit of human welfare less easily justified.

The recent expansion of scientific data from the field of animal behavior—especially advances in cognitive ethology—that clearly demonstrate animals' possession of qualities and capacities previously considered to be unique to humankind, continues to narrow the gap between the two. Through the media, especially television, today there is widespread dissemination of information about animals, even as many of the animals themselves are swiftly disappearing. The more we learn about animals, the more we come to realize and appreciate their similarities to people. Much of the momentum of the current animal rights movement traces to this increase in knowledge. But large numbers of people evidently continue to deny evolutionary continuity between species, embracing the creationist doctrine of absolute qualitative differences separating animals and humans. According to a 1993 Gallup poll, 47 percent of Americans believe that human beings were specially created about ten thousand years ago (Buikstra 1993, 1).

Far back in the time of the origin of the wren hunt, animals and people lived in a perceptually continuous world that did not feature the strict demarcations between the two that generally characterize views held in the modern Western world. As demonstrated in the case of the wren, animals possessed wisdom and could inform people on matters about which no other source could teach them. But with the rise of industrialization, the acquisition of human control over nature, and the influence of the Judeo-Christian tradition that sharply divides humans from nature, excludes nonhumans from sacredness, and denies them salvation, animals were no longer seen as powerful or sentient. Today, we do not seek animals' advice but, rather, require them to conform to our standards. We may "love" them, but domination is the strongest imperative in many of our interactions with them. Domestic animals are bred and used to suit human purposes, and the remaining wild species are increasingly being brought under supervision. In experiments that attempt to teach apes and dolphins to "talk" to us, we force our language upon them, rather than seeking to understand theirs. Held hostage by anthropocentricism and indoctrinated with skepticism, we cannot easily go to the wild wood to hear a cosmic message from a tiny, hidden brown bird.

Deprivation of direct personal experiences with nondomesticated animals is likely to become more complete if human alienation from nature and extirpation of the wild continue at the present rate. Physical damage to the planet will then be accompanied by mental impoverishment. For various forms of wildlife, particularly birds, have played a vital part in enriching the aesthetic and spiritual spheres of human life—a role whose power and value may not be generally appreciated as it should be. Loss of species considered from this aspect alone may have a devastating effect on the human psyche. Birds are frequently featured in literature, for both their intrinsic characteristics and their metaphoric associations, and are prominent in poetry, whose rhythm and form are particularly well suited to reflect their unique characteristics, especially their flight and lyrical voices. Birds are well represented in art, where accurate depiction of detail is combined with creative expressions of the awe they inspire. Music bears a close relation to birdsong, and throughout history human aesthetic responses to avian sounds have often been profound. Beginning in prehistoric times, reaction to the beauty and power of animals seems to have been as much aesthetic and spiritual as utilitarian. Scholars point out that cave paintings, for example, often depict animal species that were not generally hunted with the same delicate artistry that prey animals' likenesses were created. John Berger speculates that before they were perceived as sources of meat and other commodities, "animals first entered the imagination as messengers and promises." Magical, oracular, or sacrificial functions, he believes, took precedence over practical uses of certain species. Animals were humankind's "first symbols" and initial metaphors for "charting the experience of the world," because "the essential relation between man and animal was metaphoric." Animals "lent their name or character" as explanations for qualities or circumstances of daily life that seemed mysterious (1985, 275, 278, 279).

Because of our disconnection from the natural world, it is doubtful that any animal symbols and metaphors as complex and profound as those involving the wren will be constructed in the future. Yet psychological totemism and animism still exist, and if indeed humankind possesses the trait I have called cognitive biophilia (Lawrence 1993, 301–2), we will continue to employ animals as vehicles of thought. Even if we persist in following our present policy of destructiveness toward nature, we will undoubtedly still use animals symbolically, for all other types of referents are sterile in comparison. As the domesticated sphere that we have created inexorably expands at the expense of the wild, people may increasingly draw linguistic imagery from those animals that are controlled or near at hand. But probably the human mind will nostalgically persist in imaging the faraway wild realm, using that newly cherished but forever lost kingdom as a measure of the diminished and artificial universe.

The elaborations of symbolism and ritual stemming from human observations about and perceptions of the wren demonstrate the complexity of the human relationship with nature and the ways in which that relationship is influenced by traditions and beliefs about the world and about the human condition. We have seen how the original sacrificial nature of the wren hunt was changed when religious doctrines and cultural forces deprived animals of their sacred status. As a result, new legends making the wren an object of hatred and scorn were superimposed upon the ancient rites to give logic to and justify the killing that once was a sacred act. Vengeance for the bird's alleged betrayal, evil deeds, or pagan associations was introduced into wren lore as a fresh motive to explain a ritual that was no longer understood because time and changing ideologies had obliterated both the meaning of the sacrifice and the general population's intimate knowledge and insight about the bird upon which its old status had depended. To revere an animal and yet kill it as a sacred being seems incongruous in the Western world today. Sacrifice involves placing great value on an animal yet giving it up for the cause of some higher principle or a supernatural force that is perceived to demand or to be pleased or appeased by that action. Such motivation, rooted in strong conviction, induces the believer to carry out actions that on a pragmatic level would be against that person's best interests. That is, the animal sacrificed may be the best and most perfect specimen of its kind or an individual that is especially prized, loved, or needed by the one who kills it out of devotion to some superhuman being or allegiance to an ideal that overrides all practical considerations.

In a comparable way, some concerned environmentalists argue that preservation of nature might be accomplished or facilitated even today if spiritual factors were involved in ecological concerns. Thus various contemporary religious movements and spiritually focused environmental organizations seek to incorporate into mainstream religion a mandate for fellowship with other species and regard for the natural environment; or they create new age religions or revitalized nature religions whose adherents regard all life as sacred and advocate solicitous care of the earth. Such organizations are formed in the hope that nature-oriented belief systems will provide the strength and urgency to motivate individuals to make the requisite personal sacrifices of pleasure, comfort, ease, and financial gain at the present time on behalf of the altruistic purpose of preserving and protecting the living environment for the future. It is relevant that some animal rights activists say they have a spiritual tie to animals and they credit the empathy generated by that bond with impelling them to continue campaigning on behalf of animals in spite of the many obstacles, inconveniences, and hardships that they encounter in working for their cause.

People who identify with animals and view them as distinct individuals may grant personhood to their fellow creatures. In discussing the question of human-animal differences, anthropologist Tim Ingold points out that according to the Western tradition of thinking in parallel dichotomies, "the opposition between animality and humanity is aligned with those between nature and culture, body and mind, emotion and reason, instinct and art, and so on." These oppositions, he argues, are represented in the academic division between the natural sciences, with their concern about the composition of structures of the material world, and the humanities, whose realm is the study of language, history, and civilization. If personhood is denied to nonhumans, then the assumption follows that approaches using the humanities are appropriate only to understanding human behavior and that the worlds of animals can be comprehended only within a natural science paradigm. The consequence of that decision has been to interpret human actions as motivated by intentional design and the actions of nonhumans—even when these appear similar in nature and consequences— as automatic and governed only by instinct (1994, 24). Thus the choice of discipline employed to understand the dynamics of nonhuman lives can sharply limit knowledge about animals and their capabilities, emphasizing their otherness and further removing them from human aesthetic and spiritual spheres.

The appropriateness of a broader multidisciplinary approach to gaining knowledge about wildlife is well articulated by Edward Garnett in his description of the inclusive methodology used by field naturalist W. H. Hudson in his superbly detailed analyses of bird life. If "artistic and poetic shades of feeling" were eliminated, and reliance were placed on scientific explanation alone, Garnett argues, "the bald facts recounted would remain as a groundwork, but the very spirit of life in the thing seen would be altered, [and] our insight and comprehension would be indefinitely lessened. So the 'impassive' scientists themselves are in a dilemma. We cannot actually comprehend nature's life without being emotionally affected by it." Therefore, when studying wildlife, "'scientific observation' must be supplemented and inspired by artistic and poetic methods" of understanding. "To comprehend sentient life we must employ . . . all those shades of aesthetic sensibility and of human imagination by which the great artists and poets seize and apprehend the character of life." Scientists "are in their element in investigating the working of physical laws, in determining the properties or the functions of living organisms, but a knowledge of these laws no more qualifies them to apprehend the character, nature, or spirit of the life of nature's wild creatures under the open sky than a perfect knowledge of anatomy can make a man a Praxiteles" [a celebrated Greek sculptor] (1917, 85–86).

Views of animals have fluctuated greatly through the ages, running the gamut from the anthropomorphism that formerly included belief in animal societies that closely resemble human ones—finding expression in personifications such as King Wren and Jenny—to the scientific detachment that sees birds as virtual automatons. Where once avian creatures could talk, marry, boast about their children, hold contests, and elect kings, later mechanistic viewpoints endowed them with nothing but inflexible instinctual responses to stimuli. Perhaps such contrasting concepts soon will be replaced by new acknowledgment of

and appreciation for the actual capacities of animals that current studies reveal—both intrinsic differences from humankind that would come
to be respected and proven likenesses that cement the bond of animal-
human kinship. The field of cognitive ethology, though still in its in-
fancy, has already made significant strides toward demonstrating that
some animals, including certain birds, indeed possess mental characteristics qualitatively similar to those of humankind, enabling them to
think and even to feel emotions.

"Sciencespeak" is the term anthropologist Elizabeth Marshall
Thomas uses to denote the limited way scientists generally define and
describe animals, "sanitizing" their language by avoiding all traces of
sentiment and eliminating any implication that animals share the emotional and cognitive world of humankind. She points out that individual animals are customarily given numbers rather than names in
order to depersonalize them. To differentiate them from people, animals
are described as "using food resources" rather than eating, for example.
Rather than kill animals, scientists say they "harvest" or "cull" them.
Thomas, whose data result from her field studies in animal behavior,
argues that condemning the use of empathy as misleading, rather than
using it to understand animals, results in erroneous conclusions. She
asserts that the capacities of animals for experiencing feelings such as
love and their possession of certain cognitive abilities confer evolutionary advantage on nonhuman species, just as they do in human beings.
She deplores the tendency of "some arrogant, narrow-minded hard scientists" to insist that their view of animals as automatons is the only
correct one, and that all other views are merely sentimental and anthro-
pomorphic. Thomas believes that evidence of evolutionary continuity
between animals and people dictates that the same terms may be used
accurately in behavioral studies of animals and people (1995).

Feelings of awe and affection are traditionally disparaged in the
context of science. The prevalent belief that there is antipathy between
love and science and an unbridgeable gap between the two reflects the
Cartesianism that is ingrained in Western culture. Affective bonds with
animals are often considered incompatible with science. For example,
when the formation of an association of veterinarians devoted to wildlife medicine was proposed in the early 1980s, the initial announcement
of the organization called for prospective members of the new group to
be limited to those professionals whose interest in wild animals was
"not sentimental." Interestingly, in one scholar's search for a connection between love and the science of life, he examined a large number

of biology texts currently used in schools without finding the word love mentioned (Orr 1992). Yet the barriers to accepting the importance of affective ties as they pertain to the preservation of nature may be weakening. Biologist Stephen Jay Gould argues that "we cannot win this battle to save species and environments without forging an emotional bond between ourselves and nature as well—for we will not fight to save what we do not love (but only appreciate in some abstract sense). . . . We must really make room for nature in our hearts" (1991, 14). If the biophilia hypothesis proves to be valid—and there is considerable evidence for the existence of this innate propensity to affiliate with other forms of life (Kellert and Wilson 1993)—then love for nature is more than a frivolous emotion possessed by certain groups of people. Rather it is a natural manifestation of what it means to be human—a quality that not only enhances our species' well-being but may be vital to the health and preservation of the planet with all its inhabitants.

Today's citizens of the urbanized world typically have little or no direct interaction with wild nature. In contrast, preindustrial people acquired intimate knowledge about the animals in their vicinity from daily experience. The original wren hunters knew a great deal about the habits of the mysterious bird they pursued and about its relatedness to the environment in which it lived. Detailed understanding of its life history caused people to empathize with the bird's day-to-day struggle to survive and cope with that environment, and made them draw comparisons with their own lives. But those keen observers also identified in the wren certain capacities and skills that surpassed their own and endowed the tiny creature with spiritual status. In the minds of people who were secure in their conviction about the interconnectedness between all forms of life, and who held an unshakable belief in the cyclical continuation of rebirth after death, the act of killing the wren had profoundly different meanings than those we would attribute to such an event today. By examining those old meanings, we do not find definitive answers, but we identify vital questions that bring relevant contemporary issues into sharp focus. From the resulting vantage point, reflecting on the enormity of the evocative qualities embodied by the tiny wren, we can begin to redefine what humankind's relationship is, or should be, with the rest of nature and to pursue a more enlightened and humane path to harmonious coexistence with our fellow creatures.

References

Aarne, Antti, and Stith Thompson
  1928   *The Types of the Folktale: A Classification and Bibliography.* Folk-lore Fellows Communications, no. 74. Helsinki: Suomalainen Tiedeakatemia.
Abercrombie, John
  1884   "Irish Bird-Lore." *Folk-Lore Journal* 2:65–67.
Abrahams, Roger D., and Richard Bauman
  1978   "Ranges of Festival Behavior." In *The Reversible World,* ed. Barbara A. Babcock. Ithaca, N.Y.: Cornell Univ. Press.
Allen, Francis H., ed.
  1993   *Thoreau on Birds: Notes on New England Birds by Henry David Thoreau.* Boston: Beacon Press.
"Ancient Game Revived as Hunt the Wren Continues."
  1991   *Isle of Man Examiner,* 1 Jan., p. 11.
Archbold, Rick
  1990   *Robert Bateman: An Artist in Nature.* Toronto: Madison Press Books.
Armstrong, Edward A.
  1955   *The Wren.* London: Collins.
  1958   *The Folklore of Birds.* London: Collins.
  1992   *The Wren.* Haverfordwest, England: C. I. Thomas and Sons.
Babcock, Barbara A.
  1978   Introduction to *The Reversible World,* ed. Barbara A. Babcock. Ithaca, N.Y.: Cornell Univ. Press.
Babcock-Abrahams, Barbara
  1975   "Why Frogs Are Good to Think and Dirt Is Good to Reflect On." *Soundings* 58 (Summer): 167–81.
Balme, D. M., ed.
  1991   *Aristotle: History of Animals.* Books 7–10. Cambridge: Harvard Univ. Press.

Bancroft, Anne
    1987   *Origins of the Sacred*. New York: Arkana.
Bancroft, Hubert Howe
    1987   "The 'Miracle of the Gulls.'" In *Treasury of North American Bird
            Lore*, ed. Paul S. Eriksson and Alan Pistorius. Middlebury, Vt.: Paul
            S. Eriksson.
Bataille, Georges
    1986   *Eroticism: Death and Sensuality*. San Francisco: City Lights Books.
Bateman, Graham, ed.
    1985   *All the World's Animals: Songbirds*. New York: Torster Books.
Beaton, Katherine
    1986   *The Real Santa Claus*. Richmond, Surrey: H and B Publications.
Begley, Sharon, with Daniel Glick
    1995   "The Return of the Native." *Newsweek,* 23 Jan., 53.
Bell, David N.
    1992   *Wholly Animals: A Book of Beastly Tales*. Kalamazoo, Mich.:
            Cistercian Publications.
Berger, John
    1985   "Why Look at Animals?" In *The Language of the Birds,* ed. David
            M. Guss. San Francisco: North Point Press.
Bewick, T.
    1809   *A History of British Birds*. London: Longman.
Boissière, Robert
    1990   *The Return of Pahana*. Santa Fe: Bear.
Bolte, Johannes, and Georg Polívka
    1918   *Ammerkungen zu den Kinder und Hausmärchen der Brüder Grimm*
            3. Leipzig: Dieterich'sche Verlagsbuchhandlung.
Bonwick, James
    1986   *Irish Druids and Old Irish Religions*. N.p.: Dorset Press.
Bord, Janet, and Colin Bord
    1982   *Earth Rites*. London: Granada.
Boswall, Jeffery
    1987   "Roosting Riddles." *Aviculture Magazine* 93 (1): 23–27.
Brand, John
    1849   *Observations on the Popular Antiquities of Great Britain*. 3 vols.
            Ed. Sir Henry Ellis. London: Henry G. Bohn.
Brightman, Robert A.
    1993   *Grateful Prey: Rock Cree Human-Animal Relationships*. Berkeley
            and Los Angeles: Univ. of California Press.
Brockway, Robert
    1993   *Myth from the Ice Age to Mickey Mouse*. Albany: State Univ. of
            New York Press.
Brown, Joseph Epes
    1967   *The Sacred Pipe*. Norman: Univ. of Oklahoma Press.

Brown, W. J.
    1936   *The Gods Had Wings*. London: Constable.
Bruun, Bertel
    1967   *Birds of Europe*. New York: Golden Press.
Buday, George
    1964   *The Christmas Card*. London: Spring Books.
Buikstra, Jane, ed.
    1993   *Newsletter of the National Center for Science Education, Inc.* Sept.
Burkert, Walter
    1979   *Structure and History in Greek Mythology and Ritual*. Berkeley
            and Los Angeles: Univ. of California Press.
Burkert, Walter, Rene Girard, and Jonathan Z. Smith
    1987   *Violent Origins: Ritual Killing and Cultural Formation*. Stanford,
            Calif.: Stanford Univ. Press.
Byron, May
    N.d.   *The Bird Book*. New York: Hodder and Stoughton.
Caine, J. B.
    1987   "A Manx Christmas." *Manx Life* 16, no. 10 (Dec.): 15–16.
Campbell, Joseph
    1990   *The Hero with a Thousand Faces*. Vol. 2, *The Cosmogenic Cycle*. Au-
            diotape. Read by Ralph Blum. Los Angeles: Audio Renaissance Tapes.
Carr-Gomm, Philip, and Stephanie Carr-Gomm
    1994   *The Druid Animal Oracle*. New York: Simon and Schuster.
Cartmill, Matt
    1993   *A View to Death in the Morning: Hunting and Nature Through His-
            tory*. Cambridge: Harvard Univ. Press.
Chamberlain, Montague, ed.
    1896   *A Popular Handbook of the Ornithology of Eastern North America
            by Thomas Nuttall*. Vol. 1, *The Land Birds*. Boston: Little, Brown.
Chapman, Frank M.
    1899   *Bird-Life*. New York: D. Appleton.
Choate, Ernest A.
    1973   *The Dictionary of American Bird Names*. Boston: Gambit.
Cirlot, J. E.
    1983   *A Dictionary of Symbols*. New York: Philosophical Library.
Clague, John
    1911   *Manx Reminiscences*. Castletown: M. J. Blackwell.
Clausen, Lucy W.
    1962   *Insect Fact and Folklore*. New York: Collier Books.
Coffin, Tristam P.
    1973   *The Illustrated Book of Christmas Folklore*. New York: Seabury Press.
Collins, Henry Hill, Jr., ed.
    1960   *Bent's Life Histories of North American Birds*. Vol. 2, *Land Birds*.
            New York: Harper and Brothers.

Colum, Padraic
    1918   *The Boy Who Knew What the Birds Said.* New York: Macmillan.
Cookson, Elizabeth
    1859   *Mylecharane: The Popular and Most Ancient Manx National Song.*
    Douglas, Isle of Man: M. A. Quiggan.
Cooper, J. C.
    1992   *Symbolic and Mythological Animals.* London: Aquarian Press.
Coues, Elliott
    1962   "The House Wren's Notion of Architecture." In *A Treasury of Bird Lore,* ed. Joseph Wood Krutch and Paul S. Eriksson. New York: Paul Eriksson.
Cowan, Tom
    1993   *Fire in the Head: Shamanism and the Celtic Spirit.* San Francisco: HarperSanFrancisco.
Crippen, T. G.
    1923   *Christmas and Christmas Lore.* London: Blackie and Son.
Davies, Jonathan Ceredig
    1911   *Folk-Lore of West and Mid-Wales.* Aberystwyth, Wales: Welsh Gazette.
Davies, W. H.
    1992   "Jenny Wren." In *100 Favorite Animal Poems,* ed. Laurence Cotterell. London: Piatkus.
Deane, Tony, and Tony Shaw
    1975   *The Folklore of Cornwall.* Totawa, N.J.: Rowman and Littlefield.
De Gubernatis, Angelo
    1872   *Zoological Mythology.* 2 vols. New York: Macmillan.
De Kay, Charles
    1898   *Bird Gods.* New York: A. S. Barnes.
Descartes, René
    1979   *Discourse on Method and Meditations.* New York: Penguin.
Dixon, Charles
    1895   *Rural Bird Life of England.* New York: Werner.
Douglas, Mary
    1976   *Purity and Danger.* London: Routledge and Kegan Paul.
Douglas, Mona
    1963   "It's Just an Old Manx Custom." *Isle of Man Weekly Times,* 27 Dec., p. 2.
Drummond, William H.
    1838   *The Rights of Animals, and Man's Obligation to Treat Them with Humanity.* London: John Marden.
Dunbar, Nan, ed.
    1995   *Aristophanes Birds.* Oxford: Oxford Univ. Press.
Dundes, Alan
    1980   *Interpreting Folklore.* Bloomington: Indiana Univ. Press.

1991a "The Apple Shot: Interpreting the Legend of William Tell." *Western Folklore* 50, no. 4 (Oct.): 327–360.

1991b "The Psychological Study of Folklore in the United States, 1880–1980." *Southern Folklore* 48 (2): 97–120.

Dyer, T. F. Thiselton
  1880 *English Folk-Lore*. London: David Bogue.
  1883 *Folk Lore of Shakespeare*. London: Griffith and Farran.

Dyer's British Popular Customs
  1876 *Saturday Review* (London) 41 (4 Mar.): 313–14.

Edwards, Carolyn McVickar
  1995 *Sun Stories*. New York: HarperSanFrancisco.

Ehrlich, Paul, David S. Dobkin, and Darryl Wheye
  1988 *The Birder's Handbook*. New York: Simon and Schuster.

Eliade, Mircea
  1972 *Shamanism: Archaic Techniques of Ecstasy*. Princeton, N.J.: Princeton Univ. Press.
  1975 *Myth and Reality*. New York: Harper and Row.

Eliot, T. S.
  1963 *Murder in the Cathedral*. New York: Harcourt Brace Jovanovich.

Evans, A. H., ed.
  1903 *Turner on Birds: A Short and Succinct History of the Principal Birds Noticed by Pliny and Aristotle*. 1544. Reprint, Cambridge: Cambridge Univ. Press.

Evans, E. Estyn
  1967 *Irish Folkways*. London: Routledge and Kegan Paul.

Fargher's Sixpenny Edition of the Master Mariner's Pocket Book
  1853 Douglas, Isle of Man: Robert Fargher.

Farmer, David Hugh
  1987 *The Irish Dictionary of Saints*. New York: Oxford Univ. Press.

Farr, Judith
  1992 *The Passion of Emily Dickinson*. Cambridge: Harvard Univ. Press.

Field, John Edward
  1913 *The Myth of the Pent Cuckoo*. London: Elliot Stock.

Fife, Graeme
  1991 *Arthur the King*. New York: Sterling Publishing.

Fine, Gary Alan, and Lazaros Christoforides
  1991 "Dirty Birds, Filthy Immigrants, and the English Sparrow War: Metaphorical Linkage in Constructing Social Problems." *Symbolic Interaction* 14 (4): 375–93.

Fisher, Chancellor
  N.d. "The Hunting of the Wren: Folk-Life and Folk-Lore." Typescript in *Two Welsh-Manx Customs*. Douglas, Isle of Man: Manx Museum.

Flaherty, Robert Pearson
    1992   "Todaustragen: The Ritual Expulsion of Death at Mid-Lent—
    History and Scholarship." *Folklore* 103 (1): 40–55.
Fletcher, Alice C.
    1904   *The Hako: A Pawnee Ceremony.* Twenty-Second Annual Report
    of the Bureau of American Ethnology to the Smithsonian Institution
    1900–1901. Washington, D.C.: Government Printing Office.
Foley, Daniel J.
    1963   *Christmas the World Over.* New York: Chilton Books.
Ford, Alice, ed.
    1957   *The Bird Biographies of John James Audubon.* New York: Mac-
    millan.
Forman, H. Buxton, ed.
    1896   *The Poetical Works of John Keats.* London: Reeves and Turner.
Frazer, James George
    1963   *The Golden Bough: A Study in Magic and Religion.* New York:
    Collier Books.
    1988   *Folklore in the Old Testament.* New York: Avenel Books.
"Fur, Fins and Fasts."
    1992   *Economist* 322, no. 7748 (29 Feb.): 93.
Garai, Jana
    1973   *The Book of Symbols.* New York: Simon and Schuster.
Garnett, Edward
    1917   "W. H. Hudson." *Dial* 57, no. 735 (8 Feb.): 83–87.
Gaster, M.
    1915   *Rumanian Bird and Beast Stories.* London: Sidgwick and Jackson.
Gaster, Theodore H., ed.
    1964   *The New Golden Bough.* New York: New American Library.
Geertz, Clifford
    1973   *The Interpretation of Cultures.* New York: Basic Books.
George, Andrew J., ed.
    1904   *The Complete Poetical Works of William Wordsworth.* Boston:
    Houghton Mifflin.
George, D., and K. Loggins
    1980   "A Love Song." Gnossis Music/Portofino Music/ASCAP.
Gibson, Frank
    1904   *Superstitions about Animals.* New York: Walter Scott Publishing.
Gilchrist, A. G.
    1926   "The Wren." *Word-Lore* 1, no. 2 (Mar.–Apr.): 78.
Gill, W. Walter
    1932   *A Second Manx Scrapbook.* London: Arrowsmith.
Gillespie, Angus K., and Jay Mechling, eds.
    1987   *American Wildlife in Symbol and Story.* Knoxville: Univ. of Ten-
    nessee Press.

Girard, René
    1977   *Violence and the Sacred.* Baltimore: Johns Hopkins Univ. Press.
Glassie, Henry
    1983   *All Silver and No Brass.* Philadelphia: Univ. of Pennsylvania Press.
Gomon, Harriet
    1993   "New-Lease-on-Life Party." *Woman's Day,* 18 May, 14.
Goodfellow, Peter
    1977   *Birds as Builders.* New York: Arco.
Gordon, Edmund I.
    1958   "Sumerian Animal Proverbs and Fables: Collection Five." *Journal of Cuneiform Studies* 12:1–21.
Gould, Stephen Jay
    1991   "Unenchanted Evening." *Natural History* 100, no. 9 (Sept.): 4–15.
Graf, William
    1991   *Book Catalogue Number 165.* Iowa City: William Graf.
Graves, Robert
    1989   *The White Goddess.* New York: Farrar, Straus and Giroux.
Green, Miranda
    1989   *Symbol and Image in Celtic Religious Art.* New York: Routledge.
    1991   *The Sun-Gods of Ancient Europe.* London: Hippocrene Books.
Greenoak, Francesca
    1979   *All the Birds of the Air.* London: Andre Deutsch.
Gruson, Edward S.
    1972   *Words for Birds.* New York: Quadrangle Books.
Guénon, René
    1993   "Symbolism of the Cross." *Parabola* 18 (3): 80–81.
Hadas, Moses, ed.
    1988   *Birds.* In *The Complete Plays of Aristophanes.* New York: Bantam.
Handoo, Jawaharlal
    1994   "Cultural Attitudes to Birds and Animals in Folklore." In *Signifying Animals: Human Meaning in the Natural World,* ed. Roy Willis. New York: Routledge.
Hardwick, Charles
    1872   *Traditions, Superstitions, and Folk-Lore.* London: Simpkin, Marshall.
Hardy, Thomas
    1984   *Tess of the d'Urbervilles.* New York: Macmillan.
Hare, C. E.
    1952   *Bird Lore.* London: Country Life.
Harris, Mary Corbett
    1980   *Crafts, Customs and Legends of Wales.* London: David and Charles.
Harrison, Hal H.
    1975   *Eastern Birds' Nests.* Norwalk, Conn.: Easton Press.
Harrison, Robert Pogue
    1992   *Forests: The Shadow of Civilization.* Chicago: Univ. of Chicago Press.

Hart, Cynthia, John Grossman, and Priscilla Dunhill
    1990   *A Victorian Christmas: Joy to the World.* New York: Workman Publishing.
Hartley, Christine
    1986   *The Western Mystery Tradition.* Wellingborough, Northamptonshire: Aquarian Press.
Hartshorne, Charles
    1992   *Born to Sing.* Bloomington: Indiana Univ. Press.
Hazlitt, W. Carew
    1905   *Faiths and Folklore of the British Isles.* 2 vols. London: Reeves and Turner.
Heinberg, Richard
    1995   *Memories and Visions of Paradise: Exploring the Universal Myth of a Lost Golden Age.* Wheaton, Ill.: Quest Books.
Henderson, George
    1911   *Survivals in Belief Among the Celts.* Glasgow: James Maclehose and Sons.
Henderson, William
    1879   *Notes on the Folk-Lore of the Northern Counties of England and the Borders.* London: W. Satchell, Peyton.
Hervey, Thomas
    1848   *The Book of Christmas.* New York: George P. Putnam.
Holden, Peter, and J. T. R. Sharrock
    1994   *The Royal Society for the Protection of Birds Book of British Birds.* London: Macmillan.
Hole, Christina
    1940   *English Folklore.* London: B. T. Batsford.
    1975   *English Traditional Customs.* London: B. T. Batsford.
    1984   *A Dictionary of British Folk Customs.* London: Paladin Books.
Holmgren, Virginia C.
    1988   *Bird Walk Through the Bible.* New York: Dover Publications.
Hopes, David
    1990   "The Pavarotti of Birds." In *The Joy of Songbirds.* Washington, D.C.: National Wildlife Federation.
"How to Hunt the Wren."
    1965   *Isle of Man Daily Times,* 31 Dec., p. 11.
Howard, Michael
    1995   *Sacred Ring: Pagan Origins of British Folk Festivals and Customs.* Chievely, Berkshire, England: Capall Ban.
Howells, William
    1986   *The Heathens: Primitive Man and His Religions.* Salem, Wisc.: Sheffield Publishing.
Hubbell, Sue
    1993   "'Hopping John' Gets the Year Off to A Flying Start." *Smithsonian* 24, no. 9 (Dec.): 83–88.

Hubert, Henri, and Marcel Mauss
  1964   *Sacrifice: Its Nature and Functions.* Chicago: Univ. of Chicago Press.
Hudson, W. H.
  1898   *Birds in London.* New York: Longmans, Green.
  1919   *Birds in Town and Village.* New York: E. P. Dutton.
  1920   *Adventures Among Birds.* New York: E. P. Dutton.
  1921   *British Birds.* New York: Longmans, Green.
  1989   *Green Mansions.* New York: Dover Publications.
Hunt, Cecil
  1954   *British Customs and Ceremonies.* London: Ernest Benn.
"Hunting the Wren."
  1914–16   *Journal of the Welsh Folk-Song Society* 5 (18): 77–79.
"Hunting the Wren."
  1982   *Manx Star,* 17 Dec., p. 10.
"Hunt the Wren."
  1972   *Manx Star,* 8 Jan., p. 6.
"Hunt the Wren Contest Success."
  1973   *Isle of Man Examiner,* 28 Dec., p. 11.
"Hunt the Wren Event."
  1972   *Isle of Man Examiner,* 29 Dec., p. 2.
"Hunt the Wren Must Be Preserved."
  1988   *Isle of Man Examiner,* 5 Jan., p. 10.
"Hunt the Wren on Boxing Day."
  1987   *Isle of Man Examiner,* 12 Dec., p. 19.
"Hunt the Wren Organized."
  1972   *Mona's Herald,* 4 Jan., p. 5.
Iles, Norman
  1986   *Who Really Killed Cock Robin?* London: Robert Hale.
  1989   *The Restoration of Cock Robin.* London: Robert Hale.
Ingersoll, Ernest
  1923   *Birds in Legend, Fable and Folklore.* New York: Longmans, Green.
Ingold, Tim
  1994   "Humanity and Animality." In *Companion Encyclopedia of Anthropology.* ed. Tim Ingold. New York: Routledge.
James, E. O.
  1962   *Sacrifice and Sacrament.* London: Thames and Hudson.
Jobling, James A.
  1991   *A Dictionary of Scientific Bird Names.* New York: Oxford Univ. Press.
Johnson, Buffie
  1988   *Lady of the Beasts.* San Francisco: Harper and Row.
Johnson, William Branch
  1927   *Folktales of Provence.* N.p.: Chapman and Hall.

Jones, Charles W.
  1978   *Saint Nicholas of Myra, Bari, and Manhattan: Biography of a Legend*. Chicago: Univ. of Chicago Press.
Jones, Gwyn, and Thomas Jones, trans.
  1991   *The Mabinogion*. Rutland, Vt.: Everyman's Library.
Jonsson, Lars
  1993   *Birds of Europe with North Africa and the Middle East*. Princeton, N.J.: Princeton Univ. Press.
Jung, Carl G.
  1956   *The Integration of the Personality*. London: Routledge and Kegan Paul.
Jung, Emma, and Marie-Louise von Franz
  1986   *The Grail Legend*. Boston: Sigo Press.
Kanze, Edward
  1995   *Wild Life: The Remarkable Lives of Ordinary Animals*. New York: Crown.
Kellert, Stephen R.
  1993   "Values and Perceptions of Invertebrates." *Conservation Biology* 7, no. 4 (Dec.): 845–55.
Kellert, Stephen R., and Edward O. Wilson, eds.
  1993   *The Biophilia Hypothesis*. Washington, D.C.: Island Press.
Kelly, Fanny
  1973   *My Captivity Among the Sioux Indians*. Secaucus, N.J.: Citadel Press.
Kennelly, Brendan
  1989   "The Wren-Boy." In *Christmas in Ireland*, ed. Colin Morrison. Dublin: Mercier Press.
Kermode, E.
  1885   *Celtic Customs*. Leeds: Moxon Press.
Kermode, P. M. C., ed.
  1902   "Wren Hunting on St. Stephen's Day (26th December)." In *The Isle of Man Natural History and Antiquarian Society*, vol. 3. Douglas, Isle of Man: Brown and Sons.
Kheel, Marti
  1995   "License to Kill: An Ecofeminist Critique of Hunters' Discourse." In *Animals and Women*, ed. Carol J. Adams and Josephine Donovan. Durham, N.C.: Duke Univ. Press.
Killip, Margaret
  1975   *The Folklore of the Isle of Man*. London: B. T. Batsford.
Kirk, G. S.
  1975   *Myth: Its Meaning and Functions in Ancient and Other Cultures*. Berkeley and Los Angeles: Univ. of California Press.
Klingender, Francis
  1971   *Animals in Art and Thought to the End of the Middle Ages*. Cambridge, Mass.: MIT Press.

Krappe, Alexander Haggerty
1964   *The Science of Folklore*. New York: W. W. Norton.
Kroodsma, Donald E.
1980   "Winter Wren Singing Behavior: A Pinnacle of Song Complexity." *Condor* 82, no. 4 (Nov.): 357–65.
Langstaff, Nancy, and John Langstaff
1985   *The Christmas Revels Songbook*. Boston: David R. Godine.
Lawrence, D. H.
1992   *Birds, Beasts and Flowers! Poems by D. H. Lawrence*. Santa Rosa, Calif.: Black Sparrow Press.
Lawrence, Elizabeth Atwood
1982   *Rodeo: An Anthropologist Looks at the Wild and the Tame*. Chicago: Univ. of Chicago Press.
1985   *Hoofbeats and Society: Studies of Human-Horse Interactions*. Bloomington: Indiana Univ. Press.
1993   "The Sacred Bee, the Filthy Pig, and the Bat Out of Hell: Animal Symbolism as Cognitive Biophilia." In *The Biophilia Hypothesis,* ed. Stephen R. Kellert and Edward O. Wilson. Washington, D.C.: Island Press.
1994   "Conflicting Ideologies: Views of Animal Rights Advocates and Their Opponents." *Society and Animals* 2 (2): 175–90.
1995   "Cultural Perceptions of Differences Between People and Animals: A Key to Understanding Human-Animal Relationships." *Journal of American Culture* 18, no. 3 (Fall): 75–82.
Leach, Edmund
1976   *Culture and Communication*. New York: Cambridge Univ. Press.
Leach, E. R.
1974   *Claude Lévi-Strauss*. New York: Viking Press.
1982   *Rethinking Anthropology*. New York: Athlone Press.
Leahy, Christopher
1982   *The Birdwatcher's Companion*. New York: Hill and Wang.
Lembke, Janet
1992   *Dangerous Birds*. New York: Lyons and Burford.
Lévi-Strauss, Claude
1963   *Totemism*. Boston: Beacon Press.
1966   *The Savage Mind*. Chicago: Univ. of Chicago Press.
1993   "Father Christmas Executed." In *Unwrapping Christmas,* ed. Daniel Miller. Oxford: Oxford Univ. Press.
Lewis, H. Durbin
1926   "The Wren." *Word-Lore* 1, no. 2 (Mar.–Apr.): 76–78.
Linscott, Robert N., ed.
1959   *Selected Poems and Letters of Emily Dickinson*. New York: Anchor Books.
Llewelyn, Nesta
1926   "The Hen-Headed Horses of Taliesen." *Word-Lore* 1, no. 5 (Oct.): 214–16.

Llewelyn, Nesta, cont.
    1927   "The Wren in Welsh Folk-Lore." *Word-Lore* 2, no.5 (Oct.): 158–59.
Lockley, R. M., ed.
    1960   *The Bird-Lover's Bedside Book*. London: Country Book Club.
Lockwood, W. B.
    1989   "The Marriage of the Robin and the Wren." *Folklore* 100 (2): 237–39.
    1993   *Oxford Dictionary of British Birds*. New York: Oxford Univ. Press.
Luce, William
    1991   *The Belle of Amherst*. New York: Samuel French.
Lurker, Manfred
    1991   *The Gods and Symbols of Ancient Egypt*. London: Thames and Hudson.
Lynd, Robert
    1938   "Wren." In *A Book of Birds,* ed. Mary Priestly. New York: Macmillan.
Mabey, Richard
    1993   *Whistling in the Dark*. London: Sinclair Stevenson.
MacCulloch, J. A.
    1991   *The Religion of the Ancient Celts*. London: Constable.
    1992   *Celtic Mythology*. New York: Dorset Press.
Macdonald, Hugh
    1901   "The Birds of Scotland." In *Songs of Nature,* ed. John Burroughs. New York: McClure Phillips.
MacManus, Seumas
    1930   "A Health to the Birds." In *The Bird-Lover's Anthology,* ed. Clinton Scollard and Jessie B. Rittenhouse. Boston: Houghton Mifflin.
Macmillan, Douglas, ed.
    1926   "The Wren." *Word-Lore* 1. London: Folk Press.
    1928   "The Wren Song." *Word-Lore* 3. London: Folk Press.
McIntyre, Rick
    1993   *A Society of Wolves: National Parks and the Battle over the Wolf*. Stillwater, Minn.: Voyageur Press.
Mann, Nick
    1985   *The Cauldron and the Grail*. Glastonbury, England: Annenterprise.
"Manx Museum Folk Life Survey."
    1950   Typescript. Douglas, Isle of Man: Manx Museum.
"Manx Museum Folk Life Survey."
    1959   Typescript. Sept. Douglas, Isle of Man: Manx Museum.
"Manx Museum Folk Life Survey."
    1970   Typescript. Sept. Douglas, Isle of Man: Manx Museum.
Martin, Ernest Whitney
    1914   *The Birds of the Latin Poets*. Palo Alto, Calif.: Stanford Univ. Press.

Mason, Michael, ed.
1988   *William Blake*. New York: Oxford Univ. Press.
Mathews, F. Schuyler
1936   *Field Book of Wild Birds and Their Music*. New York: G. P. Putnam's Sons.
Matthews, Boris, trans.
1986   *The Herder Symbol Dictionary*. Wilmette, Ill.: Chiron Publications.
Matthews, Caitlin
1989   *The Celtic Tradition*. Longmead, Dorset: Element Books.
Matthews, John
1990   *The Grail Tradition*. Longmead, Dorset: Element Books.
Matthews, John, ed.
1984   *At the Table of the Grail*. London: Arkana.
Matthews, John, and Caitlin Matthews
1988   *British and Irish Mythology: An Encyclopedia of Myth and Legend*. London: Aquarian Press.
Mauss, Marcel
1967   *The Gift*. New York: W. W. Norton.
Mead, Chris
1984   *Robins*. London: Whittet Books.
Miles, Clement A.
1976   *Christmas Customs and Traditions: Their History and Significance*. New York: Dover Publications.
Montagu, Colonel G.
1831   *Ornithological Dictionary of British Birds*. London: Hurst, Chance.
Moon, Beverly, ed.
1991   *An Encyclopedia of Archetypal Symbolism*. Boston: Shambhala.
Mooney, James
1982   *Myths of the Cherokee and Sacred Formulas of the Cherokees*. Nashville: Charles and Randy Elder.
Moore, A. W.
1971   *The Folk-Lore of the Isle of Man*. East Ardsley, Yorkshire: S. R. Publications.
Morris, F. O.
N.d.   *British Birds*. London: Groomsbridge and Sons.
Morrison, Sophia
1992   *Manx Fairy Tales*. Peel, Isle of Man: L. Morrison.
Munsterberg, Peggy, ed.
1984   *The Penguin Book of Bird Poetry*. New York: Penguin Books.
Murray, Margaret A.
1970   *The God of the Witches*. Oxford: Oxford Univ. Press.
Myerhoff, Barbara
1978   "Return to Wirikuta: Ritual Reversal and Symbolic Continuity

on the Peyote Hunt of the Huichol Indians." In *The Reversible World*, ed. Barbara A. Babcock. Ithaca, N.Y.: Cornell Univ. Press.

Nabhan, Gary Paul
    1993   *Songbirds, Truffles, and Wolves: An American Naturalist in Italy.* New York: Penguin Books.

Naess, Arne
    1989   *Ecology, Community and Lifestyle.* Cambridge: Cambridge Univ. Press.

Nichols, Arthur
    1883   *Zoological Notes.* London: L. Upcott Gill.

Ó Cuív, Brian
    1980   "Some Gaelic Traditions About the Wren." *Éigse* 18:43–66.

O'Curry, Eugene
    1991   "Druids and Druidism in Ancient Ireland." In *A Celtic Reader*, ed. John Matthews. Wellingborough, Northamptonshire: Aquarian Press.

O'Griofa, Mairtin
    1993   *Irish Folk Wisdom.* New York: Sterling Publishing.

O'Leary, Sean C.
    1988   *Christmas Wonder.* Dublin: O'Brien Press.

Opie, Iona, and Peter Opie
    1961   *The Lore and Language of School Children.* Oxford: Clarendon Press.
    1988   *The Oxford Dictionary of Nursery Rhymes.* Oxford: Oxford Univ. Press.

Opie, Iona, and Moira Tatem
    1989   *A Dictionary of Superstitions.* New York: Oxford Univ. Press.

Orloff, Alexander
    1981   *Carnival: Myth and Cult.* Worgl, Austria: Perlinger.

Orr, David W.
    1992   "Love It or Lose It: The Coming Biophilia Revolution." Paper presented at the symposium, "The Biophilia Hypothesis: Empirical and Theoretical Investigations," Wood's Hole, Mass., 26 Aug.

O'Sullivan, Patrick V.
    1991   *Irish Superstitions and Legends of Animals and Birds.* Dublin: Mercier Press.

Ovid
    1983   *Metamorphoses.* Translated by Rolfe Humphries. Bloomington: Indiana Univ. Press.

Owen, Trefor M.
    1959   *Welsh Folk Customs.* Cardiff: National Museum of Wales.

Palmer, Roy
    1991   *Britain's Living Folklore.* London: David and Charles.

Parmelee, Alice
    1959   *All the Birds of the Bible.* New York: Harper and Brothers.

Parry, Idris
 1972   *Animals of Silence*. London: Oxford Univ. Press.
Parry-Jones, D.
 1988   *Welsh Legends and Fairy Lore*. London: B. T. Batsford.
Paton, C. I.
 1942   *Manx Calendar Customs*. London: Folk-Lore Society.
Peate, Iorwerth
 1936   "The Wren in Welsh Folklore." *Man* 36, no. 1 (Jan.): 1–3.
"Peel Keeps 'Hunt the Wren' Tradition."
 1973   *Manx Star,* 31 Dec., p. 1.
Pennick, Nigel
 1989   *Practical Magic in the Northern Tradition*. London: Aquarian Press.
Peterson, Roger Tory
 1961   *A Field Guide to Western Birds*. Boston: Houghton Mifflin.
 1980   *A Field Guide to the Birds East of the Rockies*. Boston: Houghton Mifflin.
Peterson, Roger Tory, Guy Mountfort, and P. A. D. Hollom
 1993   *A Field Guide to Birds of Britain and Europe*. Boston: Houghton Mifflin.
Philip, Neil, ed.
 1990   "Robin Redbreast's Testament." In *A New Treasury of Poetry.* New York: Stewart, Tabori and Chang.
Pollard, John
 1977   *Birds in Greek Life and Myth*. New York: Thames and Hudson.
Ponder, Sarah, ed.
 1992   *The Press-Out Victorian Christmas Book*. New York: Dorling Kindersley.
Potter, Stephen, and Laurens Sargent
 1974   *Pedigree: The Origin of Words from Nature*. New York: Taplinger.
Pulver, Max
 1978   "Jesus' Round Dance and Crucifixion According to the Acts of John." In *The Mysteries: Papers from the Eranos Yearbooks,* ed. Joseph Campbell. Princeton, N.J.: Princeton Univ. Press.
Ralfe, P. G.
 1905   *The Birds of the Isle of Man*. Edinburgh: David Douglas.
Read, D. H. Moutray
 1916   "Some Characteristics of Irish Folklore." *Folk-Lore* 27, no. 3 (Sept.): 250–78.
Reade, Winwood, and Eric Hosking
 1967   *Nesting Birds*. London: Blandford Press.
Roberts, Morley
 1924   *W. H. Hudson: A Portrait*. New York: E. P. Dutton.
Roeder, C., ed.
 1904   *Manx Notes and Queries*. Douglas, Isle of Man: Broadbent.

Roheim, Géza
    1930   *Animism, Magic, and the Divine King.* London: Kegan Paul, Trench, Trubner and Company.
    1992   *Fire in the Dragon and Other Psychoanalytic Essays on Folklore.* Princeton, N.J.: Princeton Univ. Press.
Rolleston, T. W.
    1990   *Celtic Myths and Legends.* New York: Dover.
Rothery, Guy Cadogan
    N.d.   *Armorial Insignia of the Princes of Wales.* London: Newberry and Pickering.
Rowland, Beryl
    1978   *Birds with Human Souls.* Knoxville: Univ. of Tennessee Press.
Rutherford, Ward
    1993   *Celtic Lore.* London: Aquarian/Thorsons.
Salisbury, Joyce E.
    1994   *The Beast Within: Animals in the Middle Ages.* New York: Routledge.
Sassoon, Siegfried
    1957   *Sequences.* New York: Viking Press.
Saunders, Aretas A.
    1951   *A Guide to Bird Songs.* Garden City, N.Y.: Doubleday.
Seaby, Peter
    1985   *The Story of British Coinage.* London: Seaby.
Shepard, Paul
    1978   *Thinking Animals.* New York: Viking Press.
Simon, Hilda
    1977   *The Courtships of Birds.* New York: Dodd, Mead.
Skutch, Alexander F.
    1987   *Helpers at Birds' Nests: A Worldwide Survey of Cooperative Breeding and Related Behavior.* Iowa City: Univ. of Iowa Press.
    1993   *Birds Asleep.* Austin: Univ. of Texas Press.
Smith, Jonathan Z.
    1987   "The Domestication of Sacrifice." In *Violent Origins: Walter Burkert, Rene Girard, and Jonathan Z. Smith on Ritual Killing and Cultural Formation,* ed. Robert G. Hamerton-Kelly. Stanford, Calif.: Stanford Univ. Press.
Smith, Martha
    1995   "How to Tell if Wrens Are Nesting in the Pitcher's Other Sleeve." *Providence Journal,* 22 Oct., p. E10.
Smith, W. Robertson
    1972   *The Religion of the Semites.* New York: Schocken Books.
Sorabji, Richard
    1993   *Animal Minds and Human Morals.* Ithaca, N.Y.: Cornell Univ. Press.

Spence, Lewis
    1945   *The Magic Arts in Celtic Britain.* London: Rider.
    1947   *Myth and Ritual in Dance, Game, and Rhyme.* London: Watts.
    1971   *The History and Origin of Druidism.* London: Aquarian Press.
Spencer, Linda
    1995   *Knock on Wood.* Nashville, Tenn.: Rutledge Hill Press.
Squire, Charles
    1975   *Celtic Myth and Legend.* Van Nuys, Calif.: Newcastle Publishing.
Stenning, Canon E. H.
    1950   *Isle of Man.* London: Robert Hale.
Stewart, Bob
    1977   *Where Is Saint George?: Pagan Imagery in English Folklore.* Bradford-on-Avon, Wiltshire: Moonraker Press.
Stewart, R. J.
    1991   *Celtic Gods, Celtic Goddesses.* London: Blandford.
Stewart, Susan
    1989   *Nonsense: Aspects of Intertextuality in Folklore and Literature.* Baltimore: Johns Hopkins Univ. Press.
Stokoe, W. J.
    1939   *Mother Nature's Birds.* New York: Frederick Warne.
Swainson, Charles
    1886   *The Folk Lore and Provincial Names of British Birds.* London: Elliot Stock.
Swann, H. Kirke
    1968   *A Dictionary of English and Folk-Names of British Birds.* Detroit: Gale Research.
Tattersall, Ian
    1982   *The Primates of Madagascar.* New York: Columbia Univ. Press.
Taylor, Alice
    1994   *An Irish Country Christmas.* New York: St. Martin's Press.
Tegid, Llew
    1911   "Hunting the Wren." *Journal of the Welsh Folk-Song Society* 1:99–113.
Terres, John K.
    1980   *The Audubon Society Encyclopedia of North American Birds.* New York: Alfred A. Knopf.
Thibault, Rose, ed.
    1993   *Yankee's Christmas Sweet Treats.* N.p.: Yankee Magazine.
Thie, Sleih Gyn
    N.d.   *Dances of Man.* Douglas, Isle of Man: Norris Modern Press.
Thomas Bewick's Birds
    1982   Cambridge, Mass.: MIT Press.
Thomas, Elizabeth Marshall
    1995   "Sciencespeak." Paper presented at Center for Animals and Pub-

lic Policy Seminar. Tufts Univ. School of Veterinary Medicine, Grafton, Mass., 22 Sept. 1995.

Thomas, N. W.
    1906   "The Scapegoat in European Folklore." *Folk-Lore* 17 (3): 258–87.

Thompson, C. K. S.
    1989   *The Hand of Destiny: Folklore and Superstition for Everyday Life.* New York: Bell Publishing.

Thompson, E. P.
    1992   "Rough Music Reconsidered." *Folklore* 103 (1): 3–26.

Toulson, Shirley
    1981   *The Winter Solstice.* London: Jill Norman and Hobhouse.

Townley, Richard
    1791   *A Journal of the Isle of Man.* 2 vols. Whitehaven, Cumbria, England: J. Ware and Son.

Train, Joseph
    1845   *An Historical and Statistical Account of the Isle of Man.* 2 vols. Douglas, Isle of Man: Mary A. Quiggin.

Travers, P. L.
    1989   *What the Bee Knows.* Wellingborough, Northamptonshire: Aquarian Press.

Trevelyan, Marie
    1909   *Folk-Lore and Folk-Stories of Wales.* London: Elliot Stock.

Turnbull, A. L.
    1943   *Bird Music.* London: Faber and Faber.

Turner, Victor
    1975   *Dramas, Fields, and Metaphors.* Ithaca, N.Y.: Cornell Univ. Press.

Tyler, Hamilton A.
    1991   *Pueblo Birds and Myths.* Flagstaff, Ariz.: Northland Publishing.

Von Franz, Marie-Louise
    1990   *Individuation in Fairy Tales.* Boston: Shambhala.

Waddell, Helen
    1934   *Beasts and Saints.* London: Burns Oats and Washbourne.

Waldron, George
    1731   *A Description of the Isle of Man.* Douglas, Isle of Man: Manx Society.

Walens, Stanley
    1986   "Animals." In *The Encyclopedia of Religion,* vol. 1. Ed. Mircea Eliade. New York: Macmillan.

Walker, Barbara G.
    1988   *The Woman's Dictionary of Symbols and Sacred Objects.* San Francisco: Harper and Row.

Walsh, Michael, ed.
    1991   *Butler's Lives of the Saints.* San Francisco: HarperSanFrancisco.

Ward, John
1902   *The Sacred Beetle.* London: John Murray.
Wentersdorf, Karl P.
1977   "The Folkloristic Significance of the Wren." *Journal of American Folklore* 90, no. 356 (Apr.–June): 192–98.
Wernecke, Herbert
N.d.   *Christmas Customs Around the World.* Louisville: Westminster Press.
Whitlock, Ralph
1979   *In Search of Lost Gods: A Guide to British Folklore.* London: Phaidon Press.
Wilde, Lady
1899   *Ancient Legends, Mystic Charms & Superstitions of Ireland.* London: Chatto and Windus.
Williams, Ted
1985   "The Quick Metamorphosis of Indiana's Doves." *Audubon* 87 (2): 38–45.
Willis, Roy
1974   *Man and Beast.* New York: Basic Books.
1994   "Preface to the Paperback Edition." In *Signifying Animals: Human Meaning in the Natural World,* ed. Roy Willis. New York: Routledge.
Wilson, E. O.
1984   *Biophilia.* Cambridge: Harvard Univ. Press.
Woodward, Marcus
1928   *How to Enjoy Birds.* London: Hodder and Stoughton.
Wright, A. R.
1940   *British Calendar Customs.* 3 vols. London: William Glaisher.
Wynne-Tyson, Esmé
1962   *The Philosophy of Compassion.* London: Vincent Stuart.
Yolen, Jane
1991   *Hark! A Christmas Sampler.* New York: G. P. Putnam.
Young, Dudley
1991   *Origins of the Sacred.* New York: St. Martin's Press.
Zeleny, Robert O., ed.
1985   *Christmas in Ireland.* Chicago: World Book Encyclopedia.
Zipes, Jack, ed.
1987   *The Complete Fairy Tales of the Brothers Grimm.* New York: Bantam Books.

Index

146–47, 148, 151, 153, 168, 173–74,
179, 182–83, 185–86, 187, 188, 192;
beat and tempo of, 91, 93; music
of, 81, 112; percussion in, 91
souls, 9, 10, 40, 69, 70, 82, 84, 106,
113, 117, 148, 150, 151, 155, 156,
157, 158, 161, 176, 188, 192
sparrow, 7, 39, 55, 57, 63, 130, 149,
187
spit, 57; turning of, 57, 83–84; robins
and wrens roasted on, 83–84, 151
St. Calasius, 35
St. Ceallach, 183
St. Dol, 35
St. Francis of Assisi, 176
St. Malo, 35–36
St. Moling, 101, 183
St. Paul, 101
St. Stephen, 48, 52, 85, 99–101,
125–26; identification of wren
with, 125–26
St. Stephen's Day, 14, 48, 52, 55, 59,
64, 67, 72, 73, 74, 75, 76, 78, 80,
81, 85, 99, 100, 108, 120, 125–26,
195–96
stag, 138
streamers. See ribbons
sun, 5, 12, 18, 26, 29, 32, 34, 69, 91,
123, 127, 135, 139–43, 149, 150,
151, 152, 154, 156, 163, 165, 166,
172, 184–85, 186, 188, 189, 193
swallows, 12, 187, 198

tail of wren, 9, 14, 20, 21, 22, 28,
29, 42, 58, 73, 122, 134, 137, 177,
183, 202
Taliesin, 29, 107
terms for wren hunt, 47, 56, 64
tiger, 8
totemism, 4, 109–11, 120, 138, 149,
204
toucan, 110

Underworld, 70, 149, 151, 153,
168–69, 175

wheel in wren ceremony, 111, 148,
152–53
willow, 49, 153–54, 201
winter wren, 11, 14–15
witches, 49, 154, 157; animals associated with, 169; holly associated
with, 188; wrens as, 85, 101, 105,
106, 108, 154, 169, 182, 183
wolverines, 5–6
wolves, 5–6, 7, 200
woodcock, 48, 58
woods (wood, wildwood, forest),
18, 53, 57, 85, 86, 87, 88–89, 90,
105, 143, 146, 153, 154, 172, 186–
89, 203
wren-eagle contest. See eagle-wren
contest
wren house in ceremony, 53, 59, 79,
150; illustration of, 54